Advance Praise for
Battle Tested!

"*Battle Tested!* uses one of the greatest crises in the history of the nation—the Battle of Gettysburg—to illustrate leadership concepts and principles that are enduring. The lessons from this book are as applicable to modern leaders as they were in 1863. Every leader will find it not only an engrossing read but an invaluable contribution to their professional library."

—ADMIRAL JIM STAVRIDIS, US Navy, Supreme Allied Commander at NATO (2009–2013) and Dean, The Fletcher School of Law and Diplomacy at Tufts University (2013–2018)

"*Battle Tested!* provides an exceptional leadership education in a contextualized format, the Battle of Gettysburg, making the lessons learned both powerful and relevant for every reader. This is the exact style of leadership book that needs to be shared with teams, colleagues, even family members. Not only does it offer a refreshed definition of leadership, but one that can be applied in both everyday business environments and leading in crisis scenarios."

—ANGIE MORGAN, Captain, USMC and author of *Leading from the Front* and *New York Times* Bestselling *Spark: How to Lead Yourself and Others to Greater Success*

"Many books have been written on leadership, even more on military history, and a few have combined the two. But rare are those that have so successfully mined the historical record to extract valuable leadership lessons as *Battle Tested!*. Jeff McCausland has combined his experience as a scholar, his own battle-tested career as a military officer and his years of studying America's most consequential battle to provide us with contemporary business lessons. Not only a riveting civil war history of the Battle of Gettysburg, but also a present-day primer on how to lead in uncertain times, Battle Tested! rewards careful reading and demands a very wide audience."

—AMBASSADOR MITCHELL REISS, former President and CEO of the Colonial Williamsburg Foundation

"McCausland and Vossler have extracted from the courage and chaos of Gettysburg yet another set of lessons useful for 21st century leaders. Their creative linkages translate hard choices of battle into guidelines useful today and tomorrow. The essence of leadership—optimizing human potential—survives the passing of time and place."

—WALTER F. ULMER, JR. Lieutenant General, U. S. Army (Retired), Former President and CEO, Center for Creative Leadership

"Jeff McCausland and Tom Vossler masterfully combine the historical analysis of the Battle of Gettysburg with the leadership lessons learned for modern day leaders. *Battle Tested!* captures hundreds of leadership moments and messages from the Battle of Gettysburg and describes them in such a way that they become relevant and as powerful today as they were during that time in our history. Once you read this book you will understand that leadership is everyone's job, but it begins with you."

—Kent Bechler, Executive Leadership Coach

"A timely, practical, historical and most importantly, wonderful opportunity for real thinking, discussing and learning. Jeff and Tom use their years of both hands-on leadership and academic rigor to gift us with this leadership learning journey. Their unique writing style of using the past (the Battle of Gettysburg) and the present (Enron, Walmart, and so on), skillfully and effectively walks the reader through a leadership journey that is second to none. Their keen insights and questions provide the reader with real leadership learning points and skills that can (and should) be used in any organizational setting. A must read for those interested in either Gettysburg, leadership development, or better yet...both! Well done!"

—Joe Doty, Executive Director, Feagin Leadership Program, Duke University

"Using the crucible of crisis that was Gettysburg as their classroom, the authors have woven a compelling and impactful analysis of leadership. Examining the challenges and decisions made by leaders who fought the battle, he translates their actions over one hundred and fifty years ago into lessons that are relevant to business and corporate leaders today. Their analysis of how leaders lead, how subordinates follow and how both interact is sharply defined in his keen analysis of the battle and the step by step decisions each made throughout the three-day struggle. Uniquely valuable is his tie-in to modern leadership examples from sports teams to Fortune 50 companies. For the history buff or the corporate leader, *Battle Tested!* is a worthy addition to your must-read list."

—Jack Tomarchio, former Principal Deputy Under Secretary of Homeland Security for Intelligence

"I have walked the Gettysburg Battlefield in the company of the authors as they guided business and military students, educators, and company executives through the history and strategy of the battle. The lessons drawn by McCausland and Vossler during these visits have inspired each of us to reflect deeply not only on the character, actions, and decisions of the officers who led their troops into battle, but also on what future generations of leaders in business, nonprofit organizations, and government can learn and apply. What you will learn from reading this book will illuminate your own path forward."

—DR. CHRIS MAXWELL, Senior Fellow, Center for Leadership and Change Management, The Wharton School of the University of Pennsylvania, author of *Lead Like a Guide*

"Following this dramatic and imaginative reexamination of the three days of intense conflict between the Union and Confederate armies at Gettysburg in July of 1863, McCausland and Vossler proceed skillfully to elicit contemporary leadership lessons from several of the individual encounters and campaigns of those rival armies. The authors invite us to focus on visionary strategic success and tragic failure, as well as on grave tactical errors and extraordinary innovative achievements. Based on the US Army's learning concept of battlefield 'Staff Rides,' these lessons in human courage, innovation, and failure under fire take full advantage of the imaginative hold this historic battle has upon the American consciousness in order to teach essential aspects of successful leadership applicable then, now, and for future generations. Readers will not be able to put down this remarkable, insightful, and instructive book!"

—GEORGE LUCAS, PhD, Distinguished Professor of Ethics *Emeritus*, US Naval Academy

BATTLE TESTED!

GETTYSBURG LEADERSHIP LESSONS
FOR 21ST CENTURY LEADERS

JEFFREY D. McCAUSLAND
TOM VOSSLER

Post Hill
PRESS

A POST HILL PRESS BOOK

Battle Tested!:
Gettysburg Leadership Lessons for 21st Century Leaders
© 2020 by Jeffrey D. McCausland and Tom Vossler
All Rights Reserved

ISBN: 978-1-64293-453-3
ISBN (eBook): 978-1-64293-454-0

Cover art by Cody Corcoran
Interior design and composition by Greg Johnson, Textbook Perfect

Post Hill Press
New York • Nashville
posthillpress.com

Published in the United States of America

DEDICATION

This book is dedicated to Barbara and Marianne.
Their love and support not only for this project, but also throughout
our careers have been fundamental to any success we have achieved.
We would also like to dedicate Battle Tested! *to the soldiers we have*
had the honor to command and lead in peace time and in war.

Contents

Introduction

Leadership is the indispensable quality that separates the great organizations from the bad. Modern effective leaders know that leadership involves vision, motivation, and trust. They must move both the individual and the collective organization into the future while simultaneously dealing with the dynamic requirements of change. All leaders should seek to convince their teams that together they can accomplish more than they may individually believe is possible.

But how do we define this critically important concept? There are many definitions for "leadership," but the one ascribed to General Dwight Eisenhower captures its essence. Ike observed that *leadership is the ability to decide what has to be done and get people to want to do it.*[1] We will use this definition throughout this book for three reasons.

First, it is provided by a wise and famous leader of the modern age known for his ability to skillfully influence and steer men and women successfully. Eisenhower was a five-star general who led Allied forces across the Normandy beaches to eventual victory in Europe during World War II. After leaving active military service he became an educator, serving nearly five years as president of Columbia University in New York City. Not to mention, Ike also served two terms as president of the United States at the onset of the Cold War, a particularly challenging period in our history.

Second, this definition is concise and can be easily remembered. It contains fewer than twenty words. Anyone can memorize it and share it with the members of their organization. This allows it to be a reference point for the organization as the leader discusses associated concepts and principles with his or her team.

Photo courtesy of the Eisenhower National Historic Site

Dwight D. Eisenhower, 34th President of the United States

Third, the most important part of this definition may be the second part—"get people to want to do it." We might imagine that Eisenhower, as a former five-star general, college chief executive, and president of the United States, was used to having his orders obeyed quickly and without question. But, the second portion of his definition shows his true wisdom. Ike realized that subordinates, or employees, may follow orders, but the leader can only get maximum performance from the team if the members have bought into the organization's goals and objectives.

Still, that doesn't mean it's a perfect characterization. Eisenhower's definition ignores an essential concept—ethics, or integrity. James Hackett, CEO of Ford Motor Company, once said, "If I were to rank the most important qualities of effective leadership, I would put trustworthiness at the top…and you cannot have their trust without integrity." If ethics was not an essential part of our definition, then we would have to accept that Joseph Stalin, Adolf Hitler, Pol Pot, and Osama bin Laden were all great leaders. They all defined a vision for their organization and sadly convinced a large group of people to follow them enthusiastically. It's a distinction integral to the foundations of our democracy. John Adams, our nation's second president, underscored this point in a letter to his wife, Abigail, shortly after moving into the White House in 1800. Adams declared his hope that "may none but honest and wise men ever rule under this roof." This quotation is now inscribed on a mantle in the executive mansion.

The definition does, however, describe a necessary drive that can be absent in some supervisory roles. Frequently, the terms "leadership" and "management" are used interchangeably, but this is imprecise. There is no doubt that these two concepts overlap, and both are critical if an organization is going to survive and flourish. But there is an important difference.

The modern study of "management" began in the early part of the twentieth century with the advent of complex organizations and corporations. Harvard University established the nation's first Graduate School of Business Administration in 1908 with fifteen faculty members and thirty-three students. "Management" focuses on such things as work standards, resource allocation, and organizational design. As one of the first female admirals in the US Navy, Grace Hopper once observed, "You manage things, you lead people."

No doubt the success, if not survival, of any organization depends on solid management, but management often focuses on the near term for the organization, as opposed to the more distant future. Every leader must make effective management decisions to deal with day-to-day issues. But the wise leader knows that they must also spend some time each day considering the following questions: Where will my organization be in a year or more? What must we begin doing now that we may not see fully implemented for a long time, in order to deal with the emerging environment?

The study of "leadership" is as old as time. Some have argued that it began with Plato, Sun Tzu, or Machiavelli, but it has only been a focal point in contemporary academic programs for roughly the last two or three decades. Leadership studies concentrate on creating a vision for organizations, motivating groups to maximum performance, and developing trust. The essence of leadership is devoted to the continuous development, of both people and organizations, to deal with change. General Eric Shinseki, former chief of staff of the US Army and Secretary of Veterans Affairs once remarked, "If you don't like change, you are going to like irrelevance even less."

Effective leaders in the past have sought to learn as much as possible from history—disasters as well as triumphs. The Greek historian Polybius, who wrote about the Roman Republic, expressed this point well. "There are two roads to the reformation for mankind," he observed. "One through misfortunes of their own, the other through the misfortunes of others; the former is the most unmistakable, the latter the less painful...the knowledge gained from the study of true history is the best of all educations for practical life."

Centuries later Otto von Bismarck, chancellor of Germany's Second Reich during the late nineteenth century, agreed on the practical value of history for leaders. "Fools, say they learn by experience," said Bismarck. "I prefer to profit by other people's experience."

Those who desire to be among the best contemporary leaders must draw on historical examples if they want to avoid the mistakes of the past. That's why this book focuses on, what is arguably, the most important battle in American history. In these pages, we hope to examine critical leadership challenges faced by both commanders and soldiers at the Battle of Gettysburg. The concepts and principles they applied during those traumatic three days remain invaluable and applicable to contemporary leaders because they illustrate the dynamics of people leading people.

A battle is a crisis and a deadly competition between two rival organizations with conflicting missions. As one of the largest battles ever fought on the North American continent, the Battle of Gettysburg demanded that the leaders of the competing armies make critical leadership decisions under enormous pressure of time and circumstances. The fate of the nation hung on the outcome. Approximately 163,000 Union and Confederate soldiers were decisively engaged during three days of fighting—July 1–3, 1863. On July 2 alone, more than 15,000 soldiers were killed or wounded in approximately six hours. (This is nearly three times the number of killed and wounded the United States would suffer during the D-Day landings at Normandy on June 6, 1944.) By the morning of July 4, 1863 (Independence Day), roughly 25 percent of the soldiers in the Union Army of the Potomac, and one of every three soldiers in the Confederate Army of Northern Virginia, had been killed, wounded, or captured.

Gettysburg provides not only a superb opportunity to examine organizations under enormous stress but also the decision-making and leadership skills of several well-known military officers—Robert E. Lee, James Ewell Brown "Jeb" Stuart, James Longstreet, George Gordon Meade, Daniel Sickles, and John F. Reynolds—as well as less famous leaders who played crucial roles at Gettysburg, such as Union Colonel Strong Vincent and Confederate General Richard Ewell.

There are over one million visitors annually to the Gettysburg Battlefield due to its importance to the American Civil War and the history of the United States. The victory at Gettysburg was, unquestionably, of enormous significance in Union efforts to end the rebellion, preserve the nation, and set a course for the nation's future. As a result, many historians refer to the battle as "the high watermark of the Confederacy." If Robert E. Lee and his troops had been victorious at Gettysburg, Abraham Lincoln may well have lost his reelection bid in 1864, and the Confederacy might have been successful in securing its independence as a sovereign state. Confederate General Josiah Gorgas reflected on this in his diary a few days after the battle, *"Yesterday we rode on the pinnacle of success—today absolute ruin seems to be our portion. The Confederacy totters to its destruction."* Everything would be different after Gettysburg.

But the "Gettysburg story" is not complete without considering the importance of the Gettysburg Address. Lincoln's legendary speech is integral to understanding the course on which the now legendary president set the country. On November 19, 1863, President Abraham Lincoln delivered brief remarks at the dedication of the cemetery for the Union dead. Today, these 272 words are remembered as one of the most important speeches in the history of the nation, if not the world. But this is not just a speech; the Gettysburg Address also exhibits the essence of strategic leadership for any organization. Lincoln sought to communicate a revised vision to the American people in the aftermath of a major crisis.

Battle Tested! consists of individual chapters focused on each of the three days of the battle, as well as the Gettysburg Address. Each chapter will begin with a brief description of fighting at a critical moment as the battle progresses. This vignette will be followed by one or more leadership questions for the reader to ponder, as if they had been in a leadership role at that critical juncture. This is not meant to be a history test, as there are frequently many options, and several can be equally justified. It is rather an effort to reinforce the learning experience for readers as they consider difficult choices today that are not dissimilar to those faced by leaders in combat. Each chapter will conclude with a description of what the leader did, further analysis of the question by the authors, and a review of other leadership principles illustrated by this example. This will frequently include contemporary examples of how modern, nonmilitary leaders have used these principles in making difficult decisions for their organizations. As a result, the leadership lessons discussed will resonate with both those currently in leadership positions and those seeking to develop their leadership skills in their chosen career fields.

T. S. Eliot once reflected on "not only of the pastness of the past, but its presence." In sum, *Battle Tested!* will use historical analysis of the iconic Battle of Gettysburg to examine enduring leadership principles and concepts that are as applicable in the twenty-first century as they were in 1863. It will consider lessons that are at the forefront of contemporary thinking on the study of leadership, to include such topics as emotional intelligence, the impact of technology on organizations, succession crises, effective communications, dealing with risk, strategic vision, and more. The reader will discover that these lessons apply in their professional lives today just as they did on the fields of Gettysburg. Whether they are students or professionals (in business, government, or nonprofits), readers will be both inspired by the history of Gettysburg and benefit from the leadership analysis. They may never visit the battlefield, but what they will learn from *Battle Tested!* will have a profound influence on their lives, organizations, and careers.

Colonel Joshua Chamberlain, whose men would successfully defend Little Round Top from repeated Confederate assaults on July 2, 1863, predicted that future generations would ponder the lessons of Gettysburg. In 1889 Chamberlain remarked during a dedication ceremony for a monument at Gettysburg to the men of his regiment, the 20th Maine, *"In great deeds something abides. On great fields something stays. Forms change and pass, bodies disappear, but spirits linger, to consecrate ground for the vision of place of souls. And reverent men and women from afar, and generations that we know not of, heart-drawn to see where and by whom great things were suffered and done for them, shall come to this deathless field, to ponder and dream....."* Perhaps he even had a book like this in mind.

The Leaders, the Led, and Their Organizations

On March 4, 1861, the Regular Army of the United States consisted of 1,108 commissioned officers and 15,259 enlisted men, organized into ten regiments of infantry, four regiments of artillery, and five regiments of mounted troops—cavalry and dragoons. Of the 198 companies which composed these regiments, 183—92 percent—were widely scattered across the broad American frontier west of the Mississippi River in company-sized outposts mostly relegated to constabulary duty against the Native American tribes and white revolutionaries.[2]

With the firing on Fort Sumter, South Carolina, by Confederate forces on April 12, 1861, it quickly became obvious that this small army of full-time, professional soldiers would not be sufficient to put-down the rebellion and restore the Union. A military mobilization would be required. The challenge became even more acute when, almost overnight, 313—28 percent—of the commissioned officers of the Regular Army resigned or accepted dismissal to enter Confederate service.

THE LEADERS

On April 15, 1861, President Abraham Lincoln, under authority of the Militia Act of 1792, issued a mobilization call to the eighteen loyal Union states for 75,000 soldier volunteers. Among that number to be called were positions for five major generals and seventeen brigadier generals to be appointed by the state governors. Quotas to fill the ranks of the enlisted men were immediately issued to the states based on the national census of 1860. A second call for additional volunteers issued on May 3, 1861, also gave authority to state governors to appoint company and regimental officers within those regiments raised in their state. By the end of 1861 the US Army had expanded from just over 16,000 men to 660,000 men.[3] It is one thing to call for an immediate expansion of the army. The greater challenge perhaps is finding the leaders for these untrained masses of soldiers.

These facts illustrate another key aspect of this book. The new leaders will be found for the most part within the civilian population itself. Our readers will be interested to read of the leadership experiences not only of the professional soldier but of the judge-turned-soldier, the businessman-turned-soldier, the educator-turned-soldier, and so on. How did they make the transition from civilian to military life? How did they continue to be effective in a new role? After the war, if they survived, what did they do with the experience they gained? As the accompanying chart illustrates, of the 583 men commissioned as general officers or senior leaders in the Union army during the four years of the war, only 194—33 percent—were professional soldiers; that is, they were educated, trained, and experienced in the military profession. The remainder were lawyers and judges (22 percent), businessmen (20 percent), and so on. Proportions for the 425 Confederate general officers are similar, with 125—29 percent—coming from the ranks of the professional soldier and as many from the law courts. Other civilian occupations make up the balance of prewar experience of the senior leaders.

THE LED

Perhaps one of the greatest myths we confront on the field at Gettysburg, in the modern era, is the misunderstanding that the American Civil War was fought by a bunch of teenagers drafted by the government to fight the war. Nothing could be further from the truth. Beginning with President Lincoln's call for 75,000 troops in April 1861, there were a dozen calls for volunteers during the war. In the end, 2.6 million men served enlistments during the war, the majority being volunteers from the eighteen loyal states and several loyal territories.

PRE - WAR OCCUPATIONS OF
AMERICAN CIVIL WAR GENERALS

U.S.A.			C.S.A.	
33%	194	PROFESSIONAL SOLDIERS	125	30%
22%	126	LAWYERS & JUDGES	129	30%
20%	116	BUSINESSMEN	55	13%
	23	FARMERS & PLANTERS	42	
	47	POLITICIANS	24	
	16	EDUCATORS	15	
25%	26	CIVIL ENGINEERS	13	27%
	8	STUDENTS	6	
	11	DOCTORS	4	
	16	OTHERS	6	

Ezra J. Warner, *Generals in Blue -Lives of the Union Commanders* and *Generals in Gray - Lives of the Confederate Commanders,* (Baton Rouge: Louisiana State University Press, 1964 and 2006)

It was not until the summer of 1863 that the conscription act, approved the previous March, was first implemented. The draft was a failure due to its numerous loopholes in favor of the wealthy who, if their number was called, could legally buy their way out of obligated service through payment for substitution or commutation. Only 6 percent of those who ultimately served in the ranks of the army arrived there by means of the draft.[4]

In spite of all of the romanticism on television and in fictional novels, if the average Billy Yank stood before you, you would find him standing at five foot eight inches tall and weighing just under 150 pounds. There was a better than average chance that his eyes were blue and his hair light colored. Again, on the average, he was two months short of twenty-six years of age, about the same as the average American soldier in World War II. In the ranks with him were perhaps a few soldiers as young as seventeen or as old as their early forties, but not many. Less than 1.5 percent of the 2.6 million men who enlisted in the Northern army were outside the standard service range of eighteen to forty-six years of age.[5]

If you speak to Billy Yank in English, he might not understand you, as he might be among the one in four of over 2.6 million serving Union soldiers who were not born in the USA. This should not be surprising considering the immigration pattern from Western Europe into North America and the USA in the decade prior to the war. As a recent immigrant or first-generation naturalized citizen, he, and his family, sees the Southern rebellion as a threat to their adopted country. This he will defend. You should not be surprised when he tells you that he, and half the soldiers like him, grew up on a farm back home and his time in the army, and this battle in Pennsylvania, is his first time away from home.

What of Johnny Reb? Man for man, he would not be much different from Billy Yank. In comparative factors, he might be a little younger on the average but of the same physical confirmation. However, with an estimated available "military population" at the beginning of the war of just over 1 million men, compared to the North's 4.5 million, there would not be as many of him compared to his adversary. The term "military population" is defined to encompass all white males in the age cohort of eighteen to forty-five years.[6] There would also not be as many immigrant soldiers in the ranks. A higher proportion of Johnny Rebs would have agricultural occupations, but only one in five would have a black slave on the farm or plantation back home. While their superior officers might have the family fortune invested in the slave-based agricultural economy, the primary motivation of the rank and file would be to defend their homes from what they believe to be Northern aggression and an oppressive national government.

THE SOLDIER'S ORGANIZATIONS—THEIR UNITS

For those of us who spent the better part of our adult lives in the profession of arms, military organization and titles easily come to mind. For readers not as familiar with military matters, we offer the following brief introductions of terms used in the following chapters.

Apart from the command structures and the staff departments of subsistence and commissary (food and forage), quartermaster (supplies), ordnance (ammunition), medical, and signal communications, the vast majority of the soldiers were in the combat arms organizations that did the fighting—infantry (marching troops with rifles), the cavalry (mounted units with carbines and sabers) and artillery (cannons).

The basic organizational entity for the infantry and cavalry was the regiment. Each state, having received an assigned mobilization quota for volunteer soldiers from the federal government, recruited throughout the state regionally by city, by county, or by multiples of them. Each regiment was numbered sequentially by state as it was formed and entered into federal service, carrying with it a state designation, e.g., 64th New York Volunteer Infantry Regiment. By army regulation, each infantry regiment was to contain 1,000 men and be commanded by a colonel with a lieutenant colonel and a major as his deputies, and a command sergeant major—the senior enlisted man in the regiment. A small staff of lieutenants and sergeants took care of feeding and supplying the troops, while a surgeon, an assistant surgeon, and a chaplain were to oversee the well-being of the soldiers. Each regiment was authorized to have ten companies of one hundred men each. Each company carried an alphabetical designation of a letter A through K (the letter J was not used). A captain commanded each company with two lieutenants to assist in command and control. The noncommissioned officer component of each company consisted of a first sergeant and four other sergeants to provide direct leadership in the ranks assisted by eight corporals. The remaining sixty-four to eighty-two soldiers held the rank of privates.[7]

So much for regulations and theory. What actually happened was that authorized and assigned strengths of the regiments varied widely as they were subjected to successive combat engagements with increasing numbers of men becoming casualties or succumbing to disease. While both armies utilized a loosely formed system of replacements to existing regiments, most often any additional available manpower was organized into newly formed regiments rather than reinforcing existing units. There never were enough surgeons trained and chaplains ordained, even with the reduced ranks of the companies and regiments. By the time the infantry regiments of both armies reached the field at Gettysburg, most had decreased significantly in strength. The Union's 247 infantry regiments and 33 cavalry regiments each averaged 304 men who actually engaged in the fighting. The 172 infantry regiments

AMERICAN CIVIL WAR COMMAND AND ORGANIZATIONAL HIERARCHY

FIELD ARMY ← **GENERAL**
MULTIPLE CORPS OF INFANTRY AND/OR CAVALRY AND SUPPORTING ARTILLERY AND LOGISTICS UNITS.

STRATEGIC LEADERS NATIONAL / GLOBAL VIEW

INFANTRY CORPS ← **LIEUTENANT GENERAL**
2 TO 3 DIVISIONS

DIVISION ← **MAJOR GENERAL**
2 TO 5 BRIGADES **BRIGADIER GENERAL**

OPERATIONAL LEADERS REGIONAL VIEW

BRIGADE ← **COLONEL**
3 TO 5 REGIMENTS **LIEUTENANT COLONEL**

REGIMENT **MAJOR**

CAPTAIN
FIRST LIEUTENANT
SECOND LIEUTENANT

TACTICAL LEADERS MIDDLE MANAGEMENT VIEW

10 INFANTRY COMPANIES OF 100 MEN EACH

and 26 cavalry regiments in the Confederate Army of Northern Virginia each averaged 328 men engaged.[8]

Two to five regiments were formed into a brigade. At Gettysburg the 58 Union infantry and cavalry brigades averaged 1,433 men engaged. The 42 Confederate infantry and cavalry brigades averaged 1,518 men.[9] In theory, brigades were to be commanded by brigadier generals, but at the midpoint of the war, it was not at all unusual for colonels to be the ranking officer in a brigade. Divisions were then made up from brigades, the norm being three brigades in each Union division and four brigades in each Confederate division. The divisions were formed into army corps. At the top of the hierarchy was the field army. At Gettysburg it was the Union's Army of the Potomac versus the Confederacy's Army of Northern Virginia.

Organization of the infantry, cavalry, and artillery was similar, but titles were different. Within the infantry regimental organization, we had the subunit, called a company. In the cavalry the unit of the same size and organization was known as a troop. In the artillery the equivalent was known as a battery. At Gettysburg, 358 Union cannons were organized into 65 batteries. Across the line, 273 Confederate cannons were organized into 68 batteries.

CHAPTER 1

The Day Before

The Leaders and the Context...

Leaders must deal with change within their organization and the environment in which they live. If we are to fully understand change as a phenomenon for an organization or a society, then we must first consider the context in which that change is occurring. There can be little doubt that the American Civil War was a *tipping point* for the United States, as the very future of the nation hung in the balance. But within that massive shift, the Battle of Gettysburg served as a pivotal moment. So, what was going on in America in the decades prior to the beginning of this horrific conflict? The United States experienced enormous change in three areas—technology, society, and government—that changed the very fabric of American identity.

People in the twenty-first century often marvel that they live in a period of rapidly accelerating technological change, which is undoubtedly true. But Americans living in the decades prior to the Civil War thought so as well, and rightfully so. It was during this period that railroads and steamships dramatically expanded the ability of Americans to travel and move goods inside the United States and around the world. The arrival of the telegraph would allow the average American to send a message almost instantaneously from New York to Chicago. Prior to this innovation it would have taken weeks to deliver the same message. This was occurring as the Industrial Revolution was rapidly transforming the American North with dramatic growth in manufacturing. But civilian industries weren't the only ones affected; scientists and the military in the United States and Europe were experimenting with new technologies such as observation balloons, repeating rifles, rifled artillery, and other weaponry that would have a dramatic impact on the nature of future warfare.

At the time, two issues had a huge influence on American society—immigration and slavery. In early 1848, revolution broke out initially in Italy and quickly spread across Europe. These upheavals would ultimately affect fifty countries due to widespread dissatisfaction with political leadership, as well as demands for more participation in government and democracy. Revolutions were most significant in France, the Netherlands, the states of the German confederation, Italy, and the Austrian Empire. Eventually, revolution would also break out in what is now Colombia and Brazil. Tens of thousands would be killed. This was the most widespread revolutionary challenge to authoritarianism in European history, but by early 1849 reactionary forces were able to regain control and the oppressive regimes returned.

Many failed revolutionaries quickly concluded that their prospects were now much better in the New World than in the Old. Other events encouraged an ever-increasing flow of refugees to America. In Ireland a massive "potato famine" in the mid-1840s resulted in large-scale immigration to America. The discovery of gold in California further encouraged an initial wave of immigrants to the shores of America. The vast majority settled in the Northeast and Midwest states where the slogan *Free Soil, Free Men, Free Labor* was a common theme. Some were attracted by the opportunity to own their own farmland, others by work available in the growing factories that dotted the New England and Mid-Atlantic landscape. All this was industrial progress and opportunity that the agrarian South with its slave-based economy could never match. Consequently, as war broke out in 1861, nearly 25 percent of the Union army were first-generation immigrants not born in the United States. The Union army had entire regiments of German- and Irish-speaking soldiers, with smaller numbers of other European immigrants thrown in for good measure. At night, many different languages could be heard around Union army campfires.

Slavery was an issue for American society from its very creation. The Continental Army led by George Washington was in many ways integrated, as free black Americans fought for the fledgling nation's independence. During the Revolution, the British army offered freedom to slaves if they deserted their American masters and joined the king's army. And while some supported freedom for the slaves, the signers of the Constitution in 1787 realized there was no way that slavery could be ended in the new nation if they wanted to secure the support of the Southern states.

This led to a historic compromise, which is why the Constitution actually affirms the legality of slavery in several ways, though the words "slave" or "slavery" never appear. Article I, Section 2 refers to "three fifths of all other Persons" for voting purposes, a politically calculated reference to slaves. Section nine allowed the "immigration of such Persons as any of the States now existing shall think proper to admit" until 1808. This a direct reference to the ending of the slave trade, and it further allowed Congress to impose a tax or duty on "such Importation, not exceeding ten dollars for each Person." Finally, Article IV, Section 2 affirmed that a "Person held to Service or Labor in one State" will be "delivered upon Claim of the Party to whom such Service may be due" if they escape to another state. In essence, this served as the basis for what would become the Fugitive Slave Act of 1850.

Many of the Founding Fathers believed slavery, or the so-called "peculiar institution," would die out over time, but industrialization coupled with a dramatic growth in demand for Southern cotton, particularly from British and French clothing manufacturers, proved this to be untrue. Still, from the ratification of the Constitution in 1789 until the inauguration of Abraham Lincoln in 1861, American leaders formulated a number of compromises to avoid catastrophe. These included the Missouri Compromise of 1820, the Wilmot Proviso, the Compromise of 1850, and the Kansas-Nebraska Act of 1854. But these compromises were insufficient to find a lasting solution for the challenge that slavery presented to the nation.

Photos: US Army Military History Institute

General Winfield Scott, USA

US President James Buchanan

The rapid change that had occurred in America during its first eighty years was epitomized by the lives of two American leaders in 1861—President James Buchanan and General Winfield Scott. In March 1861, President Buchanan would leave office as the only American ever elected to the presidency from the state of Pennsylvania. Buchanan was born when George Washington was president. General Winfield Scott was general in chief of the United States Army in 1861 and had held this position for twenty years. He was commissioned as an officer in the American Army during the presidency of Thomas Jefferson. One can only imagine the change they had witnessed in their lifetimes.

In November 1860, former US Congressman Abraham Lincoln of the newly-formed Republican Party won the national election for president. Of key concern to southerners was the Republican Party promise to prohibit the expansion of the institution of slavery into the western territories of the country which had not yet been granted statehood. Before President-elect Lincoln could assume the office as President in March, 1861, seven southern states withdrew from the Union, formed their own central government (the Confederate States of America), elected their own President (former US Senator and Secretary of War Jefferson Davis), began the formation of their own army and navy, and a week after Lincoln's inauguration, adopted their own constitution. After the opening engagement of the war, four additional southern states seceded from the union and joined the southern Confederacy.

US Army Military History Institute

US President Abraham Lincoln

On March 4, 1861, Abraham Lincoln was inaugurated as the sixteenth president of United States. Seven states had already seceded from the Union. The new president used this opportunity to urge Southern states to reconsider and pledged to support both the Constitution and existing laws. He concluded his remarks with these words:

> *In your hands, my dissatisfied fellow-countrymen, and not in mine, is the momentous issue of civil war. The Government will not assail you. You can have no conflict without being yourselves the aggressors. You have no oath registered in heaven to destroy the Government, while I shall have the most solemn one to "preserve, protect, and defend it."*

Sadly, it was to no avail. At 4:30 a.m. on April 12, 1861, Confederate artillery batteries began their bombardment of Fort Sumter, the federal fort in the port of Charleston, South Carolina. The American Civil War had begun.

At the onset of the conflict in 1861 a Confederate congressman remarked that "all of the blood that will be spilled in this conflict will be able to be wiped up by one lady's handkerchief." That assertion would soon prove to be both false and irresponsible, as more than 600,000 soldiers, and an untold number of civilians, perished over the next four years.

As the fighting commenced, the Union and the Confederate leadership was forced to formulate distinct strategies for the war. Strategy for any organization—large or small—is the formulation of *ends,* or the objectives that are trying to be accomplished. What is the future the leader or leaders are attempting to shape? They must then consider *ways,* or the policies, plans, and procedures that will be put into effect to move toward the end state. Finally, the *means,* or resources, must be galvanized to execute these efforts. Obviously, this includes people, money, and material resources; but this also includes a calculation of how much time is available and potential risks.

The South's strategy envisioned a "perimeter defense" of its territory with the goal of exhausting the North and convincing Union leadership to sue for peace. Southern military leaders did, however, conduct limited strategic offensive operations throughout the war. In the fall of 1862, for example, Robert E. Lee led his Army of Northern Virginia into Maryland only to fight a bloody battle along Antietam Creek at Sharpsburg and ultimately retreat back into Virginia. Lee would try that stratagem once more—in southern Pennsylvania during the summer of 1863.

Prior to his retirement from the army in the fall of 1861 Union General Winfield Scott devised the Northern strategy that the nation would broadly pursue throughout the war to end the rebellion and preserve the Union. Newspaper editors of the time caricatured Scott's plan as a giant snake enveloping and then slowly crushing its prey—thus the nickname, the Anaconda Plan.

Scott's plan had three parts. First, the Union would rapidly expand its navy and use it to blockade Confederate ports in order to deprive the South of the ability to export cotton and other agricultural products in return for military supplies from foreign powers. Second, the Union army would be dramatically increased in strength, and state militias mobilized. In the West, federal forces would seek to secure the Mississippi River and the port of New Orleans—effectively dividing the Confederacy in half. Finally, the Union army in the east would capture the Confederate capital at Richmond and complete the defeat of the South by force of arms.

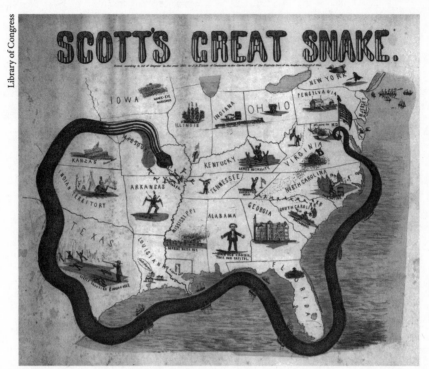

Newspaper caricature of Winfield Scott's Anaconda Plan circa 1861

As 1863 and the third year of the war arrived, enthusiasm for the conflict had waned on both sides. Citizens of both the Union and Confederacy were appalled as they watched the casualty numbers grow exponentially. The South had been successful with a string of victories in the east that resulted in growing confidence. In December 1862, the Army of Northern Virginia had decisively defeated the Union Army of the Potomac at the Battle of Fredericksburg. This was followed in May 1863 with a stunning Southern victory at the Battle of Chancellorsville. However, Confederate forces had suffered significant setbacks in the west. The Union army had secured all the Mississippi River except for the last Southern stronghold at Vicksburg, Mississippi. By late spring 1863, Union General Ulysses S. Grant had encircled the city and was preparing to lay siege to the remaining Confederate soldiers and citizens trapped inside.

Abraham Lincoln had weathered more than two years of war and made decisions that in retrospect might seem amazing to modern politicians. Lincoln had dramatically expanded his powers as president during wartime to a level never seen before or since. He suspended writ of habeas corpus in 1861 for thousands of Americans, including the mayor of Baltimore, and federal agents arrested several pro-Confederate members of the Maryland state legislature and imprisoned them to ensure the so-called "border states" of Delaware, Maryland, Kentucky, and Missouri did not secede from the Union. Lincoln also supported the arrest of former Ohio congressman Clement Vallandigham for treason, as the congressman had publicly denounced the president and the war. Under pressure from the press and his cabinet, Lincoln relented, commuting Vallandigham's sentence and banishing him to the Confederacy for the remainder of the war.

A considerable part of the Democratic Party in the North opposed the war from the very onset and wished to negotiate a two-state peace. So-called "Copperhead Democrats" were particularly powerful in the Midwest. Their candidates were largely successful in the election of 1862, and the Republican Party lost several seats in Congress as well as several key governorships in Northeastern states such as New York and New Jersey. Abraham Lincoln and his supporters knew the president faced a difficult reelection challenge in November 1864. By the spring of 1863, most Americans believed he had little chance of success. Many in his own party thought he might not even receive the party's nomination in 1864.

In the aftermath of the Confederate victory at Chancellorsville in early May 1863, General Lee took steps to recondition and strengthen his dwindling army. Even before the Chancellorsville battle took place, Lee and selected members of his staff had been putting together a summer campaign plan with the goal of taking the fighting north of the Potomac River, for several good reasons. First, he did not wish to, again, fight General Joseph "Fighting Joe" Hooker's Union Army of the Potomac on the defensive line of the Rappahannock River. Having done so at Fredericksburg in December 1862, Lee found he could not attack the enemy with advantage nor have the ability to exploit any victory that might follow. Second, he wished to move the fighting out of Northern Virginia

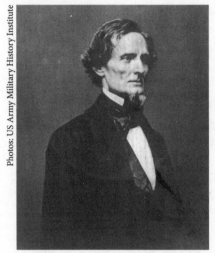

*General Robert E. Lee, CSA,
Commander, Confederate Army of
Northern Virginia*

Confederate President Jefferson Davis

and into enemy territory.[1] Third, he predicted that transfer of any of his forces to General Bragg in Tennessee, and/or to Generals Johnston and Pemberton in Mississippi, would force what was left of his army back into the defenses of the Confederate capital at Richmond, Virginia. It was Lee's view that the best defense for Richmond was at a distance from it rather than his falling back to it and allowing the Army of the Potomac to place the Confederate capital under siege.[2]

On May 14, 1863, Lee was called to Richmond for what turned out to be a four-day conference attended by Confederate political and military leaders to discuss present and future strategic concerns, alternatives, and choices.[3] While detailed official record of the conference did not survive the war, we do know that apart from Lee, there were two chief concerns of those attending the conference.

First, what to do about the enemy army, then commanded by General Rosecrans, in middle Tennessee. Following the Union victory in December 1862 at the Battle of Stones River, also known as Murfreesboro, Rosecrans's Army of the Cumberland was positioned to advance toward the Confederate railroad center at Chattanooga. Only the presence of the Confederate Army of Tennessee, commanded by General Braxton Bragg, opposed them. If suitably reinforced—Longstreet had previously volunteered two of his divisions—Bragg could drive Rose-crans's Army of the Cumberland back north to the Ohio River, and threaten northern cities like Cincinnati. Such action might further inflame and encourage Copperhead Democrats in their opposition to the war.

Second, and perhaps more importantly, what to do about the large enemy force in Mississippi commanded by General Ulysses Grant. As of April 30, Grant had successfully transferred his troops from the west bank of the Mississippi River to the east bank, from which they could attack throughout central Mississippi, while also threatening the Confederate stronghold at Vicksburg—the last major Confederate stronghold on the Mississippi River.

Lee, his partially developed summer campaign plan in hand, offered a third consideration to the assembled group of decision makers— President Davis, his cabinet members, and Secretary of War Seddon. In summary, our research gives voice to Lee's plan and recommendation as reported in his after-action reports of the Gettysburg campaign on July 31, 1863, and January 1864:

> *Break contact with the enemy army along our mutual Rappahannock River defensive line. Move our army north-west over the Blue Ridge mountains into the Shenandoah Valley of Virginia, while accepting risk that current forces in defense of Richmond will be sufficient. Advance down the valley while clearing away all enemy garrisons. Cross the Potomac River into Maryland and then into Pennsyl-vania. Provision our army on enemy soil over the summer. Defeat the enemy army on their soil when they arrive with their attempts to force us back across the Potomac River as they would be obligated to do by public opinion, political demands, and military necessity.*[4]

LEADERSHIP MOMENT   You are Confederate President Jefferson Davis. Assembled in the Confederate capitol are the leaders of your fledgling nation. You realize that the fate of the Confederacy may be determined by the decision that you will ultimately have to make. You do not have all the information you would like to have, and the country's leadership is clearly divided in their opinions. You ponder the possible options.

- Send part of the Army of Northern Virginia to central Tennessee and expand the army of General Braxton Bragg. Order Bragg to advance into the Midwestern states of Indiana or Ohio. This would encourage Northern Copperhead Democrats to increase their opposition to the war and force Lincoln to negotiate.
- Reinforce General Johnston's army with troops from Lee's army and defeat enemy forces in central Mississippi. This will prevent the Yankees from splitting the Confederacy.
- Allow General Lee to lead his army north into Maryland and Pennsylvania and seek a decisive battle against the Army of the Potomac on northern soil.

What do you decide and why?

WHAT CAN WE LEARN FROM THIS VIGNETTE ABOUT LEADERSHIP?

Strategic planning. It is clear that the Confederate leadership was holding a strategic planning conference as it attempted to decide what action to take in a rapidly changing environment. All organizations find this necessary, and many leaders schedule such meetings routinely. For any institution, "strategy" relates to the identification of long-term or overall aims and interests. It further considers the means to achieving them, which involves planning and is often done on an annual basis.

Organizations conduct strategic planning for a number of reasons. First, it helps to organize the institution in a coherent and integrated manner in order to achieve its goals or objectives. Second, it helps to understand its current situation more clearly and prepare for major, often complex, problems or opportunities. Third, such efforts serve to shape the entire organization. It facilitates the effort to create the best capabilities and modify the organization as required. Fourth, planning often can identify and lead to better understanding of the inherent risks associated with various options, organizational shortfalls, or the lack of particular capabilities. Finally, it forces an organization to examine the environment in which it is operating and consider ongoing changes, as well as the potential actions of competitors.

As previously stated, the planning process includes the careful consideration of three variables: "ends, ways, and means." "Ends" are the long-term goals and objectives of the organization. This requires a careful consideration of the organization's purpose, mission, vision, and values. For the Confederacy, this included winning the war in order to assert its independence as a nation, and the preservation of the "peculiar institution" that underpinned its economy and social structure—slavery. "Ways" refers to actions plans, policies for subordinate organizations, and often the leader's strategic initiatives. The Southern leadership had carefully discussed three plans or options that they believed in the summer of 1863 might move them toward their long-term goals. "Means" includes material resources such as people, money, and equipment. It should also include a careful consideration of time and the prioritization of resources for maximum effect.

Robert E. Lee clearly preferred the third option, or "way." By the end of the conference he had successfully convinced the Confederate leadership to accept it. Lee's success over the preceding months and recent victory at Chancellorsville obviously strengthened his arguments. Renowned American Civil War historian James M. McPherson writes, "Lee's opinion carried so much weight that Davis felt compelled to concur...the Virginian dazzled Davis and Seddon with a proposal to invade Pennsylvania with a reinforced army and inflict a crushing defeat on the Yankees in their own backyard. This would remove the enemy threat on the Rappahannock, take the armies out of war-ravaged Virginia, and enable Lee to feed his troops in the enemy's country. It would also strengthen Peace Democrats, discredit Republicans, reopen the question of foreign recognition, and perhaps even conquer peace and recognition from the Union Government itself."[5]

Furthermore, this option—if successfully accomplished—seemed to offer the clearest path to victory. Confederate leaders, especially in Virginia, vividly remembered that it was foreign intervention with the arrival of the French fleet off Yorktown that had secured victory during the Revolutionary War. Most likely believed that a major victory in the east might tip the scales in favor of the Confederacy in the eyes of European leaders, and encourage them to recognize the Confederacy as an independent state, and intervene.

Lee and his staff then began the final planning for the campaign that would take the Army of Northern Virginia over the Blue Ridge Mountains into the Shenandoah Valley and then north down the valley into Maryland and eventually Pennsylvania. Like any good leader Robert E. Lee formulated goals at the strategic, organizational, and direct levels of planning. Nonmilitary leaders might refer to this as strategic, organizational, and direct leadership requirements. Lee's goal or "end" at the strategic level was a decisive victory on Northern soil, and an end to the war.

As early as February 1863, Jedediah Hotchkiss, then chief engineer for the General Thomas Jonathan "Stonewall" Jackson, had been instructed by Lee to prepare detailed maps for just such a campaign into Pennsylvania stretching as far north up the Cumberland Valley as the state capital at Harrisburg.[6]

At the operational or organizational level, Lee's goals were to sever the Union lines of communication that crossed the Susquehanna River near Harrisburg. These were critical to the North for the movement of military supplies to support the Union armies in the West. Lee believed that a disruption of supply lines might serve to slow Union offensive operations against Vicksburg as well as other Confederate forces operating in Tennessee and Mississippi. The capture of Harrisburg, the capital of a large Union state, would be a major success for the South. This would strengthen opposition to the war in the North and encourage support for the Confederacy from the European powers.

Finally, Lee had to carefully consider the "means" available to him. At the tactical, or direct, level of leadership Lee wished to accept battle at both a time and place of his choosing, and under conditions favorable to the Army of Northern Virginia. This he could not do if he remained on the defensive on the south bank of the Rappahannock River where he forfeited the initiative to the Union army. Instead he preferred to take the initiative by maneuvering his army into open country where he could, in his words, "attack the enemy with advantage." Also, Lee knew he had to feed and provide water daily for his army of 75,000 soldiers and over 30,000 horses and mules. Second, he wanted to seize the initiative and force his opponent to react to his actions—rather than the reverse.

All leaders must consider "risk" in making any decision, and Lee was no exception. He knew the Confederate army would be outnumbered but banked on the quality of his soldiers, subordinate leaders, morale, and offensive maneuver in order to achieve success. All leaders carefully weigh potential gains versus the potential impact of failure in making any risk assessment. The wise leader will not risk the very existence of the organization for something trivial. Lee would be leading his army into enemy country, but he also knew that success might mean victory and an end to the war.

Lee carefully considered the forces available to him for the campaign as well as his immediate subordinate commanders. By the summer of 1863, the Army of Northern Virginia numbered roughly 75,000 troops and 277 pieces of artillery. This was the largest number of soldiers the army achieved throughout the war. During the preceding Battle of Chancellorsville, Lee's army in the east had been organized in two corps plus a division of cavalry. Lieutenant General James Longstreet and Lieutenant General Stonewall Jackson each commanded a corps, and both were very experienced commanders who had been in these positions since Lee assumed command of the army in June 1862. Major General "Jeb" Stuart ably led the cavalry division. But Lee decided to reorganize the army prior to heading north due to its overall size and the tragic death of Jackson at Chancellorsville.

Lee decided the new organizational structure for the Army of Northern Virginia would consist of three infantry corps with approximately 21,000 soldiers each, a cavalry division of 7,550 troopers, and sixteen artillery battalions averaging seventeen cannon each.[7] Longstreet and Stuart remained as two of Lee's immediate subordinates and provided a strong base of experience. On May 30, 1863, Lee announced his appointment of Major General Richard Ewell and Major General Ambrose Powell (A. P.) Hill as new corps commanders. Ewell and Hill, both former commanders of infantry divisions, had been very successful at the tactical and operational/organizational level of command, but clearly corps level would prove to be a challenging transition for both. They would only be in their new positions roughly a month when the battle began. Corps command required the leader to think and operate strategically. The large number of troops assigned to a corps, as well as the geographic frontage upon

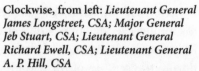

Clockwise, from left: *Lieutenant General James Longstreet, CSA; Major General Jeb Stuart, CSA; Lieutenant General Richard Ewell, CSA; Lieutenant General A. P. Hill, CSA*

which it operated, meant that a corps commander had to "think in time," anticipate, and "lead through others."

Each of Lee's principal subordinate commanders had unique background and experience. James Longstreet was born in South Carolina, in 1821. Spending his youth in Georgia, he graduated in 1842 from West

Point, where his family nickname of "Peter" was transformed during his military service into "Old Pete." He had been wounded during the Mexican War carrying a battle flag over the wall at Chapultepec Castle during the capture of Mexico City. General Lee viewed Longstreet as his most capable subordinate and confidant, and frequently referred to him as his "old war horse."

James Ewell Brown "Jeb" Stuart was the youngest of Lee's subordinate commanders. He was born in 1833 and graduated from West Point in 1854. Some of his West Point classmates referred to Stuart as "Beauty," and he epitomized the historic image of a chivalrous cavalier, but many of his contemporaries also considered Stuart terribly vain. Lee and Stuart had known each other for many years prior to the war, and it appears Stuart viewed Lee as a mentor. While Lee had been West Point's superintendent, Stuart had been a cadet at the academy and had frequently visited the Lees' home as a close friend of Lee's son. Stuart also served as Colonel Lee's aide-de-camp when they were sent by General Scott to Harpers Ferry in 1859 to recover the federal arsenal from the control of the abolitionist John Brown.

Richard Stoddard Ewell was born in Washington, DC, in 1817 and graduated from West Point in 1840. Although decorated for heroism during the US war with Mexico, he served an undistinguished career on the western frontier prior to the war. In twenty years of military service, he never rose above the rank of captain and company-level command. However, resigning his commission in the US Army at the outbreak of war, he proved to be a good division commander under the direction Stonewall Jackson during the Valley Campaign of 1862. He was described as having a "bomb-shaped" head with bulging eyes, which gave him a "bird-like" appearance. Ewell had begun losing his hair as a young man and was frequently referred to as "Old Baldy." He spoke with a high-pitched lisp and often appeared extremely nervous.

Perhaps these characteristics contributed to Ewell's longtime bachelorhood, significant consumption of alcohol, and use of profanity. One of his officers observed "his profanity did not consist of single or even double oaths but was ingeniously wrought into whole sentences. It was profanity which might be parsed and seemed the result of careful study and long practice."[8] Ewell had been badly wounded at Groveton, preceding the Battle of Second Manassas in August 1862. His left leg was amputated below the knee. He did not return to the army until shortly before the onset of the Gettysburg campaign. During the convalescence from his wounds, he married his cousin Lizinka, whom it is believed he had loved since childhood. But Lizinka had spurned his affections and married a man named Brown, who had been killed during the war. The marriage to the widow Brown gave Ewell religion and moderated both his language and consumption of alcohol, which some of his fellow officers later insisted had "ruined" him. Oddly, Ewell would forever introduce his wife as "the widow Mrs. Brown."

Ambrose Powell Hill was born in 1825 and graduated from West Point in 1847. His roommate at the academy had been George McClellan, who would later command the Union Army of the Potomac. Prior to the war, Hill had served in the Mexican War and fought the Seminole Indians in Florida. Hill was pugnacious and aggressive as a division commander and had distinguished himself during the Peninsula Campaign in 1862. Many historians agree that Hill saved the Army of Northern Virginia from destruction at the Battle of Antietam by moving his division rapidly to the battlefield at a critical moment. He had performed well at Chancellorsville and taken command of Jackson's corps when Stonewall was wounded. Unfortunately, Hill suffered from chronic health problems. It was rumored that he had contracted syphilis as a West Point cadet, and the disease plagued him for the rest of his life. Many observers believe he was not effective at Gettysburg due to this illness.[9]

Problem solving and wicked problems. Furthermore, leaders must also consider whether they are facing a "problem" or a "wicked problem." A "problem" is a situation confronting an individual or organization that presents difficulty and demands resolution. Normally, a leader when confronted by a problem will consider alternatives, apply resources—people, money, capital items, and time—in an effort to seek resolution. But once the problem is solved it remains so.

A "wicked problem" involves incomplete or even contradictory information and the requirements or conditions may change as the problem is addressed. The problem continues to evolve or change as the leader attempts to solve it. Lee knew that he and his army were faced with a "wicked problem." The Union army and its leadership might react in an unpredictable fashion. In addition, his army would be operating on "foreign" soil and have imperfect information with respect to road networks, supplies, enemy disposition, and so on. Lee also realized that the Yankees got a "vote on his strategy" whether he liked it or not. As he developed his strategy and plans, his Union opponents would develop their own in an effort to defeat him. And so, the famed general faced a "dynamic" problem, rather than a "static" one. As he and his subordinates prepared their operational and tactical plans, the Union army would do so as well in order to defeat him. Modern leaders must recognize that, when they are confronted by an adversary or competitor in the marketplace, circumstances may change quickly and their "enemy" will actively try to "win." Consequently, it is imperative to be prepared to adapt planning at all levels quickly and empower subordinates to do so as well.

Lee's army was on the south side of the Rappahannock River near Fredericksburg, Virginia, as planning for the campaign was completed. North of the river was the Army of the Potomac under the command of General "Fighting Joe" Hooker. Hooker had been soundly defeated by Lee at Chancellorsville and was frequently at odds with both Lincoln and the president's senior military advisor, General Henry Halleck. Many in the administration believed Hooker was incompetent and an alcoholic.

On June 3 the first Confederate division departed Fredericksburg and moved west. Lee planned to move his army across the Rappahannock River and Blue Ridge Mountains prior to turning north and advancing into Maryland and Pennsylvania through the Shenandoah Valley. This route of march ensured that the mountains would protect the eastern flank of his force as the Army of Northern Virginia advanced north.

In preparation for the campaign, Stuart planned a grand review of his cavalry on June 8 at Brandy Station, Virginia, which was attended by General Lee. That evening a ball was planned for Confederate officers at a local plantation. Hooker had received reports of initial Confederate movements and ordered his cavalry commander, Major General Alfred Pleasonton, to attack Stuart's cavalry. On June 9 Pleasonton's cavalry corps, reinforced by an infantry brigade, surprised Stuart at Brandy Station, in central Virginia. The ensuing battle was the largest cavalry engagement in the war where both sides were mounted, but it essentially ended as a draw, and Pleasonton's forces retreated safely northward.

Stuart was clearly embarrassed by this and was roundly criticized in the Southern press for his lack of preparation. Obviously, this was a serious blow to Stuart's ego and vanity. Many historians believe this motivated him to request permission from Lee on June 23 to conduct a raid and reconnaissance around the Union army, as he had done during the Peninsula Campaign and prior to the Battle of Antietam. It is widely judged that Lee somewhat reluctantly agreed to this plan but told Stuart that he had to do two things: stay in contact with the main body to provide Lee with the intelligence he needed as the army advanced north, and place someone in command of the cavalry brigades that remained with the main body. Stuart failed to accomplish either task. The route of march he took on his "expedition" took him out of contact with Lee for over a week. The instructions he gave to cavalry commanders William E. "Grumble" Jones and Beverly Robertson for the remaining cavalry were at best misunderstood or at worst disregarded. Stuart and three of the best cavalry brigades departed in the early morning hours of June 25 and due to the intervening movements of the Army of the Potomac, he lost contact with Lee until July 2—the evening of the second day of the three-day battle. The Army of Northern Virginia advanced northward across the Potomac River and into enemy country blind.

Though Union General Hooker was aware of the Confederate movements, he did not pursue initially. Rather, Hooker proposed to Lincoln on June 10 that he cross the river and attack Fredericksburg prior to advancing on Richmond. Lincoln vetoed this proposal and ordered Hooker to pursue Lee while keeping the Army of the Potomac between Lee and Washington. Loss of the Union capital would have been a disaster. The initial elements of the Union army began moving northward in pursuit of Lee on June 11.

Hooker clashed repeatedly with both Lincoln and Halleck in correspondence during the ensuing days. Fighting Joe argued that federal troops deployed for the defense of Washington should be transferred immediately to his command, since he believed Lee vastly outnumbered him, which was untrue. On June 27, he went to Harpers Ferry, West Virginia, to inspect the federal garrison. When Virginia seceded from the Union in 1861, Western Virginia, where few slaves were held, applied for statehood in the Union. West Virginia was admitted to the Union only one week prior to Hooker's visit there.

While he was there Hooker received an order from Halleck informing him that he could not withdraw the garrison under any circumstances. Hooker angrily offered his resignation as commander of the Army of the Potomac. Later that evening Colonel James A. Hardie of the army staff in Washington was dispatched by Lincoln and Halleck on a special train from Washington to Hooker's headquarters in Frederick, Maryland, and relieved Hooker of command.

At 3:00 a.m. on June 28 Colonel Hardie arrived at the tent of Major General George Meade, commander of the Union V Corps. Meade's troops had been on the march northward through Virginia for the past seventeen days. Meade was at his headquarters encampment near

USAMHI

*Major General
George G. Meade, USA,
Commander, Union
Army of the Potomac*

Frederick some thirty miles south of Gettysburg. Asleep in his tent, Meade was awakened by the headquarters guard and told he had a visitor from the army staff. Hardie entered the tent, and Meade recognized him from the old army. Hardie told Meade that he had brought him trouble. Meade reportedly believed he was being arrested, but Hardie replied "No sir, it is worse than that. You are now commander of the Army of the Potomac."[10] Meade then assumed command of the Army of the Potomac, where he remained for the rest of the war.

George Gordon Meade was born in Cadiz, Spain, in 1815. At the time of his birth his father was a once prosperous, but later impoverished, American merchant in Spain during the Napoleonic Wars. George graduated from West Point in 1835 and served as a topographical engineer on the staff of General Winfield Scott during the Mexican War. Scott's staff at that time also included another engineer—Major Robert E. Lee. Meade was placed in command of a brigade during the Peninsula Campaign in 1862 and had assumed command of a division at Antietam and Fredericksburg. He assumed command of the Union V Corps prior to Chancellorsville, and his unit performed well despite the Northern defeat. Still, many of his officers found that he had a quick blistering temper and did not take bad news well. Consequently, they privately referred to Meade as "Old Snapping Turtle."[11]

Lincoln's selection of Meade to assume command was based largely on his performance as a division commander. It was widely known throughout the army, however, that Meade was not the president's first choice. Lincoln had offered command of the Army to Major General John Reynolds, commander of the Union I Corps, in early June. But Reynolds informed Lincoln that to take command he would require the freedom to conduct operations with no interference from the president or General Halleck. Lincoln refused to agree. As a result, Reynolds declined the command but recommended Meade, who he argued was a more suitable candidate.

Some historians have argued that Meade's place of birth may have played a role in his selection for command of the Army of the Potomac. They point out that Lincoln was clearly a very shrewd politician and fully realized that he faced a very difficult reelection in 1864. The president might have considered that even if Meade was successful and

*Major General John
Reynolds, USA*

defeated Lee, he posed no political threat. He could not run for the
presidency in 1864, since Meade was born outside the United States and
was ineligible from seeking the presidency.

On June 28 Meade made an initial assessment of the Union army's
situation. He had roughly 95,000 troops under his command organized into seven infantry corps, each with as many as 12,000 men and
as few as 9,000, a cavalry corps of nearly 12,000 troopers, and 362 artillery pieces.[12] In addition to Major General John Reynolds, two of his
subordinate commanders—Major General Winfield Scott Hancock,
commander of II Corps, and Major General Daniel Sickles, commander of III Corps—were especially notable.

Hancock was born in Pennsylvania in 1824 and graduated from
West Point in 1844. He was called "The Superb" by some of his peers
and was widely admired as both an inspiring and commanding figure
on the battlefield. A lieutenant wrote that if Hancock had given orders
to troops who did not know him while dressed in civilian clothes that
"he would likely be obeyed at once, and without question as to his
right to command." He was decorated for heroism during the Mexican
War and later campaigned against the Seminoles and during the Utah
Expedition against the Mormon settlers. Hancock led a brigade during
the Peninsula Campaign and at Antietam, and commanded divisions
at Fredericksburg and Chancellorsville. Shortly before the Gettysburg
campaign, Hancock was placed in command of the Union II Corps
and would be badly wounded during the battle. After the war he was

Photos: USAMHI

Major General Winfield Scott Hancock,
USA

Major General Daniel E. Sickles, USA

narrowly defeated during the 1880 campaign for the presidency by James Garfield.[13]

Sickles, meanwhile, is considered one of the more notorious Union commanders in the entire Civil War—more for his political past than his leadership style. He was born in 1819 in New York City and was the only corps commander on either side who neither went to West Point nor was a professional soldier. Sickles was a politician and a member of the Tammany Hall Democratic "machine" in New York City. Lincoln named several politicians—including Democrats—as generals as the federal army rapidly grew at the onset of the war. The president—always an astute politician—knew that appointing Democrats like Sickles as generals would serve to maintain their support for his efforts to end the rebellion.

Sickles had been a well-known New York attorney and congressman prior to the Civil War. He had become even more famous nationally in 1859 when he shot and killed his wife's alleged lover in Lafayette Park in front of the White House. The man killed by Sickles was Philip Barton Key, who was not only the US attorney for the District of Columbia, but also the son of Francis Scott Key (composer of the US national anthem, "The Star-Spangled Banner") and the nephew of Chief Justice of the Supreme Court Roger B. Taney. Almost immediately after the slaying, Sickles was imprisoned and tried for murder. The trial and ensuing legal circus received national coverage, but Sickles was acquitted. His attorney and friend Edwin Stanton—who later served as Lincoln's secretary of war—devised a new, and novel, legal defense that would be used for years to come: temporary insanity. Sickles was badly wounded in the fighting on the second day at Gettysburg and lost his right leg. He would later be awarded the Medal of Honor for his actions during the battle.[14]

On the evening of June 28, a Confederate civilian scout named Henry Thomas Harrison, then in the employment of General James Longstreet, reported to Generals Longstreet and Lee that the Union army had crossed the Potomac River south of Frederick, Maryland, and was advancing northward rapidly. Lee immediately sent an order to Ewell, whose corps was near Harrisburg, to turn south and march toward Cashtown—west of Gettysburg. He would send a similar order to Ambrose Powell Hill, whose corps was much closer to Cashtown. Lee's order also carried an admonition that, as they moved, they should not precipitate any engagement with the enemy until the entire Confederate army was brought back together on the eastern side of South Mountain, west of the village of Gettysburg.

Local intelligence gathering made Union General Meade aware that the Confederate army was moving in the general direction of Gettysburg. The town's geographic significance was largely due to the ten roads that passed through it. With time running short, Meade conducted his own immediate planning and assessment. He believed the Army of the Potomac had three options: move his lead forces with all speed to contest the crossroads at Gettysburg, establish defensive positions near Emmitsburg, Maryland, and challenge Lee to attack, or fall back farther south to defensive positions along Pipe Creek, thus ensuring the absolute defense of the capital.

By June 30 Union Brigadier General John Buford's lead cavalry force entered Gettysburg. At 1:00 a.m. on July 1 Meade sent a message to Reynolds, commander of both I Corps and the entire left wing of the

Union army. Meade ordered Reynolds to prepare to defend along Pipe Creek if necessary but gave Reynolds the authority to decide whether or not to fight at Gettysburg. The battle was on.

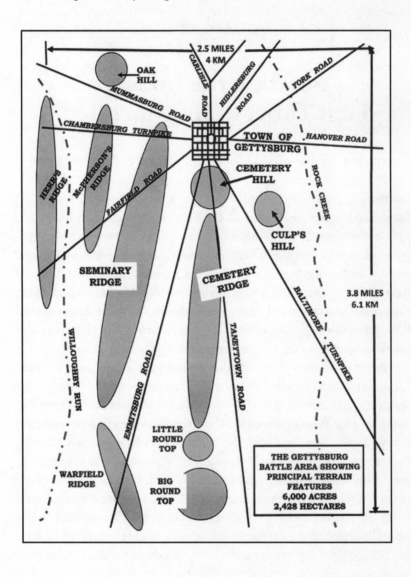

THE GETTYSBURG
BATTLE AREA SHOWING
PRINCIPAL TERRAIN
FEATURES
6,000 ACRES
2,428 HECTARES

CHAPTER 2

"Send Up the Infantry
First Thing in the Morning!"

Late on the morning of June 30, 1863, Brigadier General John Buford rode at the head of his 2,600-man Union cavalry division through Gettysburg's streets, full of local citizens cheering the arrival of the federal army. Confederate infantry under Jubal Early's command had passed through Gettysburg three days earlier but did not stay—continuing their march east toward York, Pennsylvania, and the Susquehanna River beyond. With the Confederates temporarily gone, the townspeople were relieved to see federal government protection at hand.

Buford felt some apprehension about what might soon happen. He knew the Confederate Army of Northern Virginia under the command of General Robert E. Lee had crossed north of the Potomac River on June 16 and entered the Cumberland Valley of Maryland and Pennsylvania. Ten days later the Northern leadership knew that the Confederate army was well into central Pennsylvania as far north as the outskirts of the state capital at Harrisburg thirty miles north of Gettysburg. By June 28, the main body of General Lee's army was believed to be only twenty miles west of Gettysburg in the Cumberland Valley near Chambersburg. Furthermore, several roads intersected Gettysburg, making these crossroads a likely location for the Confederate army to consolidate.

But Buford did not know the exact size and location of Lee's invading force, nor their intentions. Those unanswered questions made the

USAMHI

*Brigadier General
John Buford, USA*

thirty-seven-year-old Union general feel uneasy about the task ahead, which he knew would be difficult.

Despite his relatively young age, Buford was a veteran campaigner of the small, 16,000-man Regular Army prior to the war. Kentucky-born but raised in Illinois, he graduated from West Point, class of 1848. His family fought on both sides, with the Buford name appearing in both Confederate and Union ranks. Most of Buford's pre–Civil War service took place on the western frontier, away from the sectional politicking that led to the national divide. Spending his entire military career in the cavalry, he typically was on constabulary duty and saw action against the Native American tribes, and he also served in the army's expedition against the Mormons in Utah 1857–1858. Through all that, John Buford had developed the skills and a reputation among his peers, his superiors, and his soldiers as one of the best cavalry officers in the army.

Setting aside the standard army-issue uniform for his rank, Buford chose instead an old hunting shirt and corduroy pants tucked into his standard-issue cavalry boots. He was known well enough by his men to forgo all the flair of the standard-issue uniform and rank insignia. To the unacquainted, his bearing was of the proud, professional soldier. Fellow officer Lieutenant Colonel Theodore Lyman described Buford as "of a good-natured disposition and wry sense of humor, but he was not to be trifled with." Complementing his soldierly bearing, he was "possessed with a tawny moustache and one triangular gray eye, which gave him an expression that appeared determined, if not to say, sinister."[1]

Establishing his headquarters at the Eagle Hotel a block west of Gettysburg's town square, Buford set out for the business at hand. Two questions still lingered in his mind. First, where exactly were the Confederates, how many did they number, and what were their intentions in Pennsylvania? Second, if a battle was to be fought here, what was the key terrain his army must occupy ahead of the enemy?

In search of answers, Buford ordered his two subordinate commanders Colonel William Gamble, commander of his First Brigade, and Colonel Thomas Devin, commander of his Second Brigade, to send out mounted patrols to gather the necessary information. Because of their experience and expertise, Buford held both officers in high regard, trusted their judgment, and extended to both wide discretionary powers within the intent of what he thought needed to be done.

William Gamble was an Irish-born civil engineer, coming to the United States in 1838. He served five years in the US Army cavalry, seeing action against Native American tribesmen. In 1843 he resigned his commission to continue his work as a civil engineer in the area around Chicago, Illinois. At the start of the war, he reentered the army, serving as drill master for the volunteer 8th Illinois Cavalry, which he would ultimately come to command before earning another promotion to lead one of Buford's three brigades.[2]

Thomas Devin was born in New York City in 1822 of Irish-immigrant parents. Before the war he partnered with his brothers as house painters and retailers of paint and varnish, but his true vocation was along military lines. Once he was old enough, Devin joined a local militia company and advanced rapidly in rank. At the start of the war, he was appointed lieutenant colonel of the 1st New York Cavalry Regiment and was soon promoted to colonel—earning the command of the 6th New York Cavalry Regiment.[3]

By the beginning of the third year of the war, the soldiers commanded by Buford, Gamble, and Devin were veterans. They included men in state-formed regiments from New York, Pennsylvania, Indiana, Illinois, and even the soon-to-be-recognized state of West Virginia.

Still, despite the veteran status of those regiments from the beginning weeks of the war, Buford missed the presence of his reserve brigade at Gettysburg. His reserve brigade of US Army Regulars—the old army, which he previously commanded—was detached from him under the orders of Cavalry Corps commander Alfred Pleasonton as Buford approached Gettysburg. General Pleasonton ordered this well-trained brigade to remain in Maryland to guard the cavalry corps wagon trains and reshoe their horses, leaving John Buford to arrive at Gettysburg with only two-thirds of his total force.

The patrols, dutifully sent out by Gamble and Devin, soon galloped back to Gettysburg to report their findings. Yes, the Confederates were concentrated on the east side of South Mountain, just west of Gettysburg and might advance on the village and its crossroads at any time. But, more importantly, civilians north of Gettysburg reported rumors that additional Confederate troops were on the march from near Harrisburg and were also headed for Gettysburg.

In the meantime, Buford, the professional soldier, studied the surrounding terrain with his practiced eye. Ten major roads converged in the town. West of the town were two north-south trending ridge lines—McPherson's Ridge and Seminary Ridge. The latter was nearer the town center and dominated by the Lutheran Theological Seminary. The main seminary building was Old Main, today called Schmucker Hall, which was adorned with a cupola on the roof that provided an excellent observation vantage point. The center and southern portions of Gettysburg were dominated by a hill known as Cemetery Hill, unimaginatively named for the village graveyard. Extending south from Cemetery Hill was Cemetery Ridge, a slight ridge of high ground with two higher elevations on the southern end, Big Round Top and Little Round Top. To Buford, those three hills and the intervening ridge line were the key terrain should a battle be fought in the area of the small town of Gettysburg, Pennsylvania. They had to be held at all cost until the main portion of the federal army arrived.

Buford removed his hat and wiped his brow. Colonels Gamble and Devin looked at him nervously, in anticipation of their orders.

LEADERSHIP MOMENT   You are now Brigadier General John Buford. You know time is of the essence. You fear that early the next morning—July 1, 1863—your cavalry might well be attacked by a Confederate force six times their size before the rest of the army can arrive to relieve you. You quickly reassess both the situation and your options:

- Establish a defensive line on McPherson's Ridge west of the town and its road intersections and potentially "trade space for time."
- Fall back eastward to the edge of Gettysburg. Prepare your primary defense on Seminary Ridge, taking advantage perhaps of the three buildings of the Lutheran Seminary then on the ridge.
- Move your cavalry back to Cemetery Ridge, which you have identified as the key terrain in the area. Prepare positions there and await the arrival of the Union infantry.

Given the information you have gathered on your own reconnaissance, combined with the reports from your subordinates, what do you do now and why?

WHAT CAN WE LEARN FROM THIS VIGNETTE ABOUT LEADERSHIP?

Buford ordered Gamble and Devin to deploy most of the available Union force initially along McPherson's Ridge, which is roughly a mile west of Gettysburg and runs north-south. He hoped that this would allow him the opportunity to trade "space for time," as he might be able to slow any Confederate advance and, if pressed, his cavalrymen could fall back to Seminary Ridge—the second north-south ridgeline just west of the town and site of the Lutheran Seminary. If this approach was successful, he would preserve Union control of the key terrain in the area—Cemetery Hill, Cemetery Ridge, and the Round Tops—until his boss, General John Reynolds, could arrive with the infantry and artillery from the Union I Corps. Buford knew that Reynolds and his troops were roughly a half-day's march from Gettysburg.

Buford also directed his subordinates to deploy a cavalry reconnaissance screen north of Gettysburg that stretched eastward from

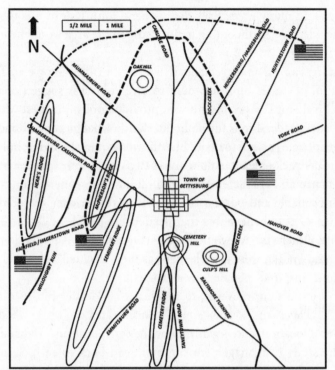

Map 2.0 Late afternoon on June 30. Brigadier General John Buford establishes cavalry
outposts and delaying positions on the ridge lines west and north of the town of Gettysburg.

Oak Hill, which was on the northern end of McPherson's Ridge. This
was accomplished by using several so-called cavalry "videttes," or
mounted outposts. A few cavalrymen were positioned at these videttes
to conduct continuous scouting and observation north of the town in
case the rumored Confederate forces' advance proved to be true.

Finally, he sent General Reynolds a short, terse message, "I have
identified a large Confederate force west of Gettysburg. I believe
the enemy to be here in force. Send up the infantry first thing in the
morning." Buford had accomplished his mission up to that point. He
had identified the key terrain (Cemetery Hill, Cemetery Ridge, and
the Round Tops) and found the enemy. He then deployed his forces
to block any Confederate advance on the town and preserved control
of the key terrain south of Gettysburg. Finally, Buford provided his
boss critical information that allowed Reynolds to make informed

decisions. In many ways, Brigadier General John Buford was the man who decided any forthcoming major battle in the area would be fought at Gettysburg.

Leadership vs. management. If we were to use Google to find a definition of leadership, we would receive countless suggestions. But again, President Dwight Eisenhower provided one of the best when he observed, "Leadership is the ability to decide what has to be done, and then get people to want to do it." Eisenhower would also agree, however, that the bedrock of leadership requires two important characteristics—competence and character. People will follow someone if they believe they are capable and possess the knowledge/experience required. But they also want to believe that their leaders are people of character and integrity. Otherwise, we would have to conclude that Adolf Hitler, Josef Stalin, and Pol Pot were great leaders, as they "decided" what had to be done and "inspired" people to want to do it.

It is important, however, to reiterate that "leadership" is distinct from "management." Management concentrates on work standards, resource allocation, and organizational design. Some historians suggest that the study of management can be traced back to early Sumerian traders or the artisans who built the pyramids of Egypt. Machiavelli wrote about what made organizations effective and efficient in his *Discourses* (1531). Still most would agree that it was not until the Industrial Revolution in the eighteenth and nineteenth centuries that we encountered large, complex organizations and the split between owners versus day-to-day managers. With the arrival of mass production in the early twentieth century, colleges and universities created management degrees for both undergraduates and graduate programs in order to study this phenomenon in greater detail.

There is no doubt that there is some overlap between management and leadership, and any organization must be well managed if it is to succeed. But leadership is distinct. It is focused on vision, motivation, and trust. Effective leaders must move people and organizations into the future. They must deal with change. Buford's actions on June 30, 1863, illustrate both leadership and management. He "decided what had to be done" with his decision to position his forces west of Gettysburg to secure the Union army's control of key terrain for the future.

Buford discussed options with his subordinates, Gamble and Devin, to ensure not only that they fully understood what he had determined but also to solicit input. He then "managed" his organization effectively by allocating most of his force to confront the immediate problem of Confederate forces that were massing just west of the town while placing a smaller force north of the town to confront additional rebel forces that had been reported to be advancing from the vicinity of Harrisburg.

Modern leaders have this same challenge of managing their organizations as well as leading them. Former Chicago Cubs baseball manager Joe Maddon led his team to their first World Championship in over one hundred years in 2016. He and Cubs' president of baseball operations, Theo Epstein, are credited with rebuilding the Cubs and ending the so-called "curse" that had bedeviled Chicago baseball fans for over a century. Epstein accepted his position with the team in the fall of 2011 and announced from the onset his vision of duplicating the success he enjoyed with the Boston Red Sox, where he had also overseen the development of a championship team in 2004. In his first year, however, the Cubs would lose over one hundred games. Epstein convinced Maddon to join the Cubs in 2014.

Following the 2016 championship season Maddon was frequently interviewed about baseball, management, and leadership. He observed that in baseball massive amounts of data are constantly reviewed to "manage" a team. Known as "sabermetrics," a word derived from the acronym for the Society of American Baseball Research (SABR), it is the empirical analysis of baseball statistics to evaluate and compare the performance of individual players and includes such things as the speed of the pitch, how fast a player runs to first base, distance covered by outfielders, velocity of the ball coming off the bat, and so on. Maddon noted that successful leaders must use "data" effectively and determine which is the best data to make crucial day-to-day managerial decisions.

But, while this was necessary, it was not sufficient to build a world championship team. Maddon argued that championship teams required effective management but also leadership, which was all about "heartbeat"—or the human factor. Heartbeat is what determined whether a particular player was focused on himself and his performance or the greater good of the team. A player might have tremendous individual talent and associated "data" but not be an effective team member. Consequently, Maddon, like Buford before him, realized that management is a science, but leadership is an art form. Both are necessary if an organization is to maximize performance and achieve success in any endeavor.

Leading the boss. The majority of literature about leadership focuses on the relationship between the boss and the subordinate. What actions does the leader take to inspire their employees or team for maximum performance? How does he or she prepare their organization to meet the challenges of the future?

These are daunting tasks and an organizational hierarchy normally exists that describes "who works for whom" to facilitate decision-making! But successful leaders allow themselves to be led by their subordinates or employees at crucial moments. Furthermore, a leader's willingness and ability to create a climate of "leading the boss" so they can be led is invaluable. "Leading up" requires courage: courage from an employee/subordinate who is willing to speak up, as well as courage from the leader who is willing to allow himself or herself to be led.

Buford's brief message to Reynolds is in many ways a classic example of "leading the boss." The final sentence—"Get the infantry up here first thing in the morning"—is unambiguous. In essence, Buford is seeking to "lead his boss" at a crucial moment for the Army of the Potomac. When Reynolds received this message, he did not hesitate, seek clarification, or order Buford to meet with him to discuss this recommendation in greater detail. John Reynolds acted and ordered the left wing of the army, led by the Union I Corps to proceed toward Gettysburg at all haste. These two men knew the other to be a solid professional of high reputation. Reynolds clearly believed that Buford was a trusted subordinate. If it was good enough for John Buford, then it would be good enough for Reynolds. Consequently, decisions could be made at the "speed of trust" between the leader and the subordinate.

There are numerous examples where failure to do so, or a leader's unwillingness or inability to accept either recommendations or key information from below, has resulted in disaster. Enron Corporation was an American energy and services company founded in 1985. By 2000 it had grown to over 20,000 employees with revenues in excess of $100 billion. *Fortune* had named Enron "America's Most Innovative Company" for six consecutive years. In December 2001 Enron collapsed under a series of accounting scandals.

Ken Lay was the CEO of Enron and highly respected by members of the company. He had been CEO of Enron for most of its existence and by 1999 was one of America's highest paid CEOs, with an annual compensation package of more than $42 million. Following the collapse of Enron, Lay was indicted by a grand jury and found guilty of ten counts of securities fraud and making false statements. During his trial, it was further revealed that Lay had liquidated more than $300 million in Enron stock from 1989 until the corporation's collapse, mostly from stock options. He would do so while continuing to urge his employees to invest in the company as part of their retirement planning. The company's demise would be the largest bankruptcy in American history, and the employees would not only lose their jobs but, in many cases, their life savings.

During his trial Lay claimed he was unaware of the accounting misdeeds that permeated the organization and that Enron's failure was due to a conspiracy by short sellers, rogue executives, and the news media. Lay died of a heart attack on July 5, 2006, and his conviction was vacated since pending appeals existed at the time of his demise. *Conde Nast Portfolio*, which is published by American City Business Journals, later rated Lay as the third worst American CEO in history. His actions also resulted in fundamental corporate reform in standards of leadership, governance, and accountability.

Throughout the Enron investigation, it was also revealed that a serious effort had been made to "lead the boss," but it had failed. Sherron Watkins, Vice President of Corporate Development at Enron, had attempted to alert Lay of accounting irregularities in financial reports beginning in early 2001. In one email message, she told Lay, "The company will implode in a wave of accounting scandals." But this was to no avail. Lay either ignored her efforts out of greed or had created a "bubble" around himself that only allowed good information to reach him. Successful leaders—like General John Reynolds—establish bonds of trust with key subordinates that encourage them "to lead the boss" at critical moments. They also ensure that they do not consciously or unconsciously create a climate that either discourages this from occurring or creates barriers between them and potentially critical information.

Effective communication and initiative. Buford's decision to deploy his force and send the brief message to Reynolds is a classic example of both effective communication and initiative. "Initiative" is critically important for successful organizations as time is often short and opportunity is fleeting. Most sources agree that "initiative" is the ability to judge what needs to be done and take action, especially without suggestions from others.

Currently, Americans are better connected than at any moment in our history. Very few people do not have a cellphone, and many have more than one. A large number have another wireless device—tablet, iPad, or other—that helps them stay in continuous contact and allows them to rapidly access information. Today there are more wireless devices than humans in the United States. We might, therefore, assume that our ability to quickly access information and be in immediate contact with each other will always lead to better and faster decisions, but this is *not* always true today, nor was it in 1863.

Consider the situation of the two protagonists at Gettysburg with respect to being in contact with their respective "bosses." Lincoln made extensive use of the telegraph and would normally position himself in the army telegraph office in Washington when it appeared a major battle was imminent or ongoing. This allowed him to be in direct communications with his general and provide immediate "guidance and advice." Shortly after General George Meade, commander of the Union Army of the Potomac, arrived in Gettysburg, a telegraph line was connected to his headquarters so he could be in immediate contact with Washington. Robert E. Lee was in a very different position with respect to his boss, President Jefferson Davis. Davis could only contact Lee by courier, and it would take several days for a message to travel from Richmond to wherever Lee's headquarters might be north of the Potomac River.

Consequently, Lee knew he had to make decisions absent any input from his superiors, but Meade received frequent "advice, assistance, and inquiry" from an anxious Washington. The interconnected world of the twenty-first century may slow decision-making and exacerbate this problem. Frequently, employees or subordinates fully believe that they know what action to take when the boss is absent or just unavailable. But the fact that they can immediately contact their leader suggests to many that they should contact them, so they will phone, text, email, fax, and so on, to seek guidance on what may be rather routine decisions. If they fail to reach their boss quickly, they will wait for instructions and valuable time is lost. Consequently, the leader must establish a climate whereby his or her team is encouraged to act. Otherwise, modern communications technology can rob the organization of initiative, and all decisions will be "pushed up" to the top of the organization.

Adapt, innovate, and overcome. In the modern world, all leaders want to believe that they are leading organizations that continuously seek to innovate and can adapt to changing circumstances. Peter Drucker, an Austrian-born American management consultant, expert, and educator, once observed, "Innovation is change that brings on a new level of performance." As a result, "innovation" differs from "invention." Many credit the Wright brothers, for example, with the "invention" of the airplane. But air travel and the use of aircraft to transport goods or the mail were the actual "innovations" that the invention of the airplane allowed to occur. Organizations can innovate in three ways— their products, processes, and organizational structure. "Adaptation" is behavior in any organization or living organism that helps it to survive and function better in its current environment. Leaders will often draw on their experiences from the past to adapt and innovate particularly during challenging moments for themselves and their organization.

Clearly, General John Buford would "adapt, innovate, and overcome" with his actions on the first day of the battle of Gettysburg. As previously suggested, Buford had spent most of his military career prior to the Civil War against the Indian tribes on the western frontier of the United States and had learned that his cavalrymen were far more effective firing their weapons when placed on the ground than when they were mounted on a prancing, nervous horse. Buford ordered his men to dismount in preparation for the defense of McPherson's Ridge even though this meant that roughly a quarter of his force (one soldier out of each four) would now have to be occupied caring for the horses while the others were on the firing line. He knew from experience that the carbine his men were equipped with offered them some important advantages that outweighed the loss in manpower.

Infantrymen during the Civil War were largely equipped with a standard rifled-musket that fired a .58-caliber Minié ball with a maximum effective range of roughly three to four hundred yards. Most of these weapons were either the Springfield Model 1861 or the Enfield 1853. A well-trained infantry soldier could load and fire three rounds per minute, but his weapon could only be loaded from the muzzle one round at a time. The length of the weapon—fifty-six inches—meant that he had to stand to reload effectively and was thus fully exposed to enemy fire while doing so.

Cavalry carbines fired a smaller cartridge and had a shorter maximum effective range, but the carbine could be loaded from the breech of the weapon. This meant that the rate of fire was normally six to seven rounds per minute, and a soldier could load and fire his weapon while kneeling or lying flat on the ground behind a fence, tree, or other protection. Buford believed that his men would mount a better defense if placed on the ground and perhaps also confuse the Confederates into believing that they were confronted by Union infantry as they moved toward Gettysburg. Buford "adapted and innovated" at a critical moment to provide his organization a greater chance to succeed in attaining its goal of slowing the Confederate advance.

Time may be the most important resource that a leader manages. As previously mentioned, in developing strategy for their organization any leader must consider three variables: ends, ways, and means. Ends are the objectives that we have articulated for the organization and must be consistent with our stated mission and vision. Ways are plans, policies, and procedures that the leader establishes/approves. Means are the resources employed to execute and move the organization into the future. These are normally described as people, money, and capital items—buildings, heavy equipment, information management systems, and so on. But frequently leaders fail to realize that the most important resource they manage for their organization is time. Furthermore, "time" is often the most inelastic of all the resources available. Leaders can put more people on a job or use additional funds and/or equipment, but they may not be able to expand the amount of time available to them.

Consequently, when a leader decides is often as important, or even more important, than the decision itself. The leader is the ultimate manager of the organization's clock. Too often leaders take excessive time to review varying alternative courses of action or in refining plans. They seek to make the perfect decision or create a flawless plan. This frequently means that their subordinates or employees receive instructions at the last minute and are expected to begin execution without sufficient time to review, determine second order effects, communicate the plan effectively throughout their teams, or initiate subsequent decisions that must be made at their level. In essence, the "perfect plan" is never executed because the leader is spending all the available time making it perfect. As a result, many options will no longer be available or cannot be realized based on a failure to manage time effectively.

Buford, as an experienced soldier and commander, understood the importance of time. He made his decisions and quickly passed out instructions to Gamble and Devin so they could execute and position their forces. But Buford also realized he had an opportunity to "expand the time available" for his boss, General Reynolds. By choosing to defend McPherson's Ridge initially he could potentially trade space for time and redeploy his men back to Seminary Ridge if they were pressed hard by the impending Confederate attack. This would hopefully ensure that the Union army maintained control of Cemetery Ridge and the Round Tops, which were the key terrain in the area, until Reynolds and his men arrived. Union success in the days ahead might well depend on his unit's ability to prevent the advancing Rebels from capturing them.

Early on the morning of July 1, 1863, Lieutenant Marcellus Jones from the 8th Illinois Cavalry and his men were manning an outpost on Knoxlyn Ridge, roughly two miles west of where Buford had deployed his main defense. Jones and his men detected a column of Confederate infantry marching east on the Chambersburg Pike toward them. Jones quickly borrowed a carbine from one of his men and fired one round at the approaching Rebel force. He would not hit anyone, but the Confederates halted and began to redeploy their force from a column on the road to a line of battle in the fields on either side of the road in preparation for an infantry assault. Buford had just bought additional time for General John Reynolds to get his forces to Gettysburg. But by making that decision, the battle had begun.

CHAPTER 3

"Forward, Men, Forward. For God's Sake, Drive Those Fellows from Those Trees!"

The Confederate troops identified by Buford's scouts on that fateful June 30 were the same troops Lieutenant Jones fired at the morning of July 1 as Lee's men began marching toward Gettysburg. The big question in Buford's mind the morning of July 1 was whether his men could delay this large Confederate advance long enough for Reynolds to bring up the infantry and additional artillery.

Upon assuming command of the Army of the Potomac on June 28, Major General George Gordon Meade found that the seven infantry corps of his army were spread out across Maryland from the base of the Catoctin Mountains eastward to Manchester, an area over thirty miles wide. At the same time Buford's scouts were tracking Confederate movements, Meade issued orders for the advance of the army northward out of Maryland into Pennsylvania to confront them.

With Buford's cavalry division as a screening force, the I and XI Corps were ordered to Gettysburg, Pennsylvania, with the III Corps to follow and support. A subsequent circular issued by Meade's headquarters on the same date directed that "Three Corps, the I, III and XI, are under the command of Major-General John Reynolds."[1]

From his years of army service prior to the US-Mexican War of 1846–1848, Meade knew he alone could not effectively command this

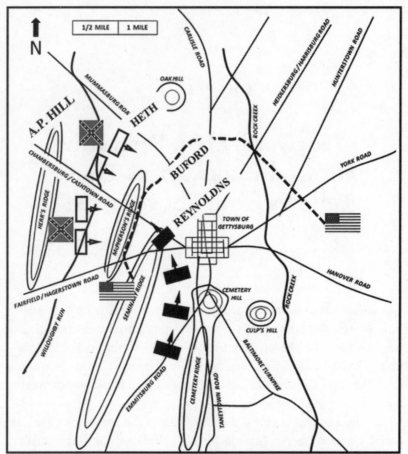

Map 3.0 Confederate infantry attack Buford's dismounted cavalry on McPherson's Ridge while Reynolds brings the Union infantry onto the field at mid-morning.

army of over 90,000 men. He must delegate authority in implementing those measures necessary in confronting the enemy forces. It is significant that with his initial orders, Meade placed one-third of his forces available under the command of his immediate subordinate, John Reynolds.

Meade knew he needed expert assistance from carefully selected subordinate commanders, or direct reports. He knew of John Reynolds's background and excellent reputation and, as far as he was concerned, Reynolds was just the man he needed at the right time and in the right place.

John Fulton Reynolds was born September 1820 in Lancaster County, Pennsylvania, only some fifty miles from what would become the battlefield at Gettysburg. He graduated in 1841 from the US Military Academy at West Point, ranking in the middle of a graduating class of fifty-six cadets.

After serving in the war with Mexico, Reynolds received decorations for gallantry and for meritorious conduct. Twice crossing the Great Plains of the American heartland, he spent several years prior to the Civil War on constabulary duty with the army in the western United States. At the outbreak of the Civil War, Reynolds was serving at West Point as an instructor of military tactics and commandant of cadets. Temporarily setting aside his Regular Army commission as a major, he was promoted to brigadier general of Pennsylvania Volunteers in August 1861. He served as infantry brigade commander in 1861 and 1862, seeing combat on the Virginia Peninsula.

In June 1862, the division to which his brigade was attached was overrun by a Confederate attack. Reynolds was captured, serving time as a prisoner before being exchanged in August 1862 for a Rebel officer held by the Union. He was quick to return to his post in the army and became a division commander in the Pennsylvania Reserves. Later he was made commander of the I Corps, which he commanded in the December 1862 Battle of Fredericksburg.[2] It is curious that during the Fredericksburg Campaign, one of Reynolds's principal subordinates was division commander George G. Meade, who seven months later would serve as his superior in the 1863 Gettysburg Campaign.

The June 30 order that named John Reynolds as the commander of the "Left Wing"—the I, III, and XI Corps—is significant. Reynolds's I Corps, now temporarily under the command of senior division commander Abner Doubleday (later of baseball fame), contained approximately 12,200 soldiers. General Daniel Sickles's III Corps had an engaged strength of 10,600 soldiers. The XI Corps, commanded by Major General Oliver O. Howard, had just over 9,200 soldiers. Thus, the combined force then under the command of Reynolds as of June 30 totaled approximately 32,000 infantrymen plus artillery.[3]

At the end of the day, June 30, the I Corps was camped astride the Emmitsburg Road along the banks of Marsh Creek some six miles south of Buford's position at Gettysburg. Reynolds had established his headquarters at Moritz Tavern, a couple of miles north of the village of Emmitsburg and a mile to the rear of his advanced troops at Marsh Creek. This unassuming countryside public house soon served as the nerve center for Reynolds's operation. Communications, information flow, and decision cycles all came through those doors, as it was at the Moritz Tavern that Reynolds received messages and reports from the field. Two of those sending messages and reports to Reynolds are of particular importance.

The first messenger to consider is commanding general George Meade. In a message to Reynolds dated 11:30 a.m., June 30, Meade advised Reynolds of the general position of the rest of the army and potential responses to enemy movements. In a postscript to the message, Meade told Reynolds, "If, after occupying your present position, it is your judgment that you would be in better position at Emmitsburg than where you are, you can fall back without waiting for the enemy or further orders. Your present position was given more with a view to an advance on Gettysburg, than a defensive point."[4] Thus, Meade delegates authority to Reynolds and empowers him to make decisions as to where the coming battle might take place.

The second messenger to consider is cavalry commander John Buford. While commanding the force screening the movement of the left wing, Buford continuously kept Reynolds—and other senior leaders of the army—informed of his assessment of the situation at Gettysburg. The strength of the information provided by Buford, his steps at "leading the boss," combined with his excellent professional reputation within the army, was of great assistance to Reynolds in his actions and orders in bringing the infantry up to Gettysburg the morning of July 1. But the question remained—would they arrive in time?

Due to confusion in orders from acting I Corps commander Abner Doubleday, it was 8:00 a.m. before the infantry of the left wing began their march to Gettysburg up the Emmitsburg Road from Marsh Creek. At a march rate of two and a half miles an hour, it would take nearly three hours before the entire force arrived at the field in support of

Buford's dismounted cavalry on McPherson's Ridge. Luckily, noting that a crisis was at hand, the men of the leading infantry brigade made the march in two hours with Reynolds on his horse in the lead.

Upon Reynolds's arrival at Buford's position on the Seminary and McPherson's Ridges west of the village, the two commanders spoke briefly. They affirmed Buford's original plan to continue to fight forward of the key terrain of Cemetery Hill and Cemetery Ridge south of the town and protect that high ground for occupation by the remainder of the army.

On horseback, Reynolds personally directed the placement of his leading infantry brigade into positions on the north side of the Chambersburg Road along McPherson's Ridge. He then rode to the south side of the road to guide the next infantry brigade coming into line of battle along the ridge. The timing of their arrival could not have been more fortuitous. Buford's men had been battling since near sunrise to hold back the Confederate advance. Some of their wounded were sheltered in the nearby bank barn of Edward McPherson's farm—the barn is still standing to this day.

That second infantry brigade coming into line, "the Iron Brigade," advanced across the McPherson farm and the John Herbst farm to the edge of Herbst Woods, a woodlot on the summit of the ridge. The 302 men of the 2nd Wisconsin Volunteer Infantry Regiment, commanded by Colonel Lucas Fairchild, could see the Confederate line of battle on the far side of the woods advancing toward them. Reynolds also saw the Confederate line coming through the woods. At that moment he rode behind the regiment and encouraged the men forward with the words, "Forward, men, forward. For God's sake drive those fellows from those trees."[5]

As Reynolds then turned his attention to his left to encourage the next regiment coming into the line of battle, a shot from the Confederate line struck him just below his right ear. He slid off the left side of his horse and died in the arms of his immediate staff members. Left wing commander John Reynolds, the commander of over 30,000 soldiers, was killed in action in the presence of the 302 men of the 2nd Wisconsin Regiment.[6]

USAMHI

*Colonel Lucius
Fairchild, USA*

Colonel Lucius Fairchild was the commander of the 2nd Wisconsin that Reynolds ordered to advance at the time of his death. His regiment was part of the famed Union Iron Brigade and included additional units from Wisconsin, Michigan, and Indiana. Fairchild's men and the other units of the Iron Brigade would go on to follow the last order given by John Reynolds and stopped, at least for the time being, the Rebel attack. Confederate Brigadier General James Archer's brigade would retreat across Willoughby Run toward Herr's Ridge. Fairchild was badly wounded in this attack, and his left arm was amputated at a Union field hospital later that day.

....

LEADERSHIP MOMENT   You are now Colonel Fairchild. The battle has concluded, and you are a patient in a hospital the Union army established in Gettysburg recovering from your wounds. Time hangs heavy as you reflect on what has happened to you, your unit, and the federal army in the past few days. You learn that your regiment suffered 26 men killed, 155 wounded, and 52 missing or captured of the 302 men who arrived in Gettysburg on July 1. The cost has been very high—233 total casualties, or three of every four soldiers.

As you lie on your cot, your thoughts go back to the moment when General Reynolds arrived on the field and ordered your men to advance. You think to yourself as the overall Union commander on the field at the time of his death was Reynolds in:

- The right place at the right time?
- The wrong place at the wrong time?
- Or the right place but the wrong time?

WHAT CAN WE LEARN FROM THIS VIGNETTE ABOUT LEADERSHIP?

Where should the leader be? The leader's physical presence is fundamentally important, though some today seem to discount it. Even in the twenty-first century when we are living in an ever more connected world where a leader physically goes—particularly when their organization is in a crisis—speaks volumes about their style and what they think is important. In July 1863 General John Reynolds was a corps commander. Furthermore, he had been given operational command over the entire left wing of the Army of the Potomac as it advanced north toward Gettysburg. On July 1 he was responsible for over 30,000 soldiers, or roughly one-third of the entire Union Army of the Potomac. Despite that huge burden, less than an hour after he arrived on the battlefield Reynolds was killed giving orders to 302 soldiers assigned to the 2nd Wisconsin regiment.

This could be characterized as a high-stakes version of "micro-management," which would be fair and is one of the main criticisms employees frequently levy against their bosses in modern organizations. Reynolds was at least three levels of command above a regimental commander. Clearly, Colonel Fairchild, veteran commander of the 2nd Wisconsin, found himself in the difficult position of having his ability to operate as the leader of his organization taken away from him—at least temporarily—by a more senior leader. Furthermore, if Reynolds was, at that moment, in command of a regiment—a tactical organization—then who was thinking operationally or strategically for his corps and the left wing of the Union army?

While this is all true, it is also appropriate to consider some additional factors that may have weighed on this fateful choice by Reynolds. Did he believe that this was an "existential moment" for his entire organization that demanded his presence? Could he have thought that it was critical for him to inspire the 2nd Wisconsin at that moment to ensure the Union line was not compromised? Gettysburg historian Edwin Coddington writes: "Personal leadership of this kind, though considered unduly rash by many people, conformed to Reynolds' temperament and his philosophy of command. Volunteer troops, he felt, were better led than driven."[7]

Still, the question remains—at that moment should he have held his gaze at a strategic level and sought to maintain "the big picture" of what was occurring? What was to be gained by focusing on a very small portion of both the battlefield and his force at what he may have thought was a crucial moment? Ultimately, there is no right or wrong answer to the dilemma faced by Reynolds, or any leader confronted with a sudden crisis in their organization—only the eventual outcome.

Some modern leaders believe that in the twenty-first century our ability to monitor what is occurring throughout the organization and contact others via modern technology—computers, cellphones, think pads, fax machines—is more than sufficient. Some modern leaders may believe they can sit in their office, close the door, pull down the blinds, and "lead." But the ancient Greek philosopher Aristotle observed thousands of years ago that this might not be the best tactic. "Man is by nature a social animal—an individual who is unsocial naturally and not accidentally is either beneath our notice or more than human," he wrote.

Technology has changed dramatically, but people have not. Human beings crave interaction particularly when under stress, and the presence of a leader during a crisis or at a critical moment can be crucial to success or catastrophe. At those times the leader must step forward, calm the team if necessary, and take full charge of the situation.

On April 13, 1970, Apollo 13 astronaut Jack Swigert radioed NASA Mission Control Headquarters in Houston, "uh, Houston, we've had a problem here." When headquarters asked the astronauts to repeat, mission commander James Lovell repeated, "Houston, we've had a problem."[8] An explosion had occurred aboard the *Odyssey* space-craft that had destroyed one oxygen tank and damaged another. The three astronauts were 200,000 miles from Earth and closing in on the moon. Clearly, the fate of the mission and the lives of the astronauts were at risk.

The mission director, Eugene Kranz, was an experienced leader and had been mission director of Apollo 11, which had successfully landed Americans on the Moon. He had been an Air Force fighter pilot during the Korean War and joined NASA as an engineer during Project Mercury. In 1965 he was made a mission director during the Gemini program. On January 27, 1967, tragedy struck the American space program. The three astronauts assigned to Apollo 1 were killed when a fire broke out in their spacecraft during a test on the launch pad. In the aftermath, Kranz addressed his team and stressed his three principles—honesty, purpose, and perfection.

In the mission control room for the endangered Apollo 13, Kranz immediately took charge of the crisis as fear gripped his team." Kranz immediately took charge of the crisis as fear gripped the control room. He told those on duty, "OK. Let's everybody keep cool.... Let's solve the problem.... Let's not make it any worse by guessing."[9] In the days ahead Kranz assumed full control of the crisis and adapted quickly to the rapidly evolving situation. He placed his most experienced team members on the consoles, exuded confidence that his team would be successful in getting the astronauts safely back to Earth, sought advice from outside experts, demanded accuracy, and quickly reorganized the team to ensure optimal decision-making. On April 17 the crew touched down safely. Apollo 13 commander Jim Lovell declared the aborted mission a failure, but he added, "I like to think it was a *successful* failure."[10]

Amid rapid technological change, contemporary leaders must constantly consider what they can do *with* new technology and developments to maximize the performance of their team or organization. At the same time, however, wise leaders must also reflect on what technological advances do *to them* and their organization in terms of encouraging or discouraging initiative especially at moments of great stress.

We must realize that the ubiquitous nature that modern communications afford us may inadvertently rob organizations of initiative. Senior leaders must continually encourage a climate of empowerment whereby mid-level managers feel comfortable making decisions consistent with broad guidance provided from above. Otherwise the fact that "I can" contact my boss will quickly translate into "I must" contact my boss for nearly every decision, especially when things do not go according to plan. The result is a loss of the most precious resource every leader should constantly measure—time. The senior leader—like Reynolds—becomes too frequently involved in making decisions that should be made several levels below them. This also means that as the senior leader becomes too closely involved in "tactical" or direct decisions, they have less time to devote to forestalling or responding to crises or working strategically.

This may sound both logical and simple, but it is extremely difficult because our increasing closeness through that mass communication encourages decisions to be "pushed up" in the hierarchy of any organization. Every leader will strongly agree that they are in favor of more initiative throughout their organization, they likely verbally endorse the concept of "empowerment," but their actions may suggest otherwise. Empowerment means the leader must embrace and accept mistakes and errors by their team. If a leader consciously or unconsciously allows their personal leadership style to suggest a "zero-defects" mentality, subordinates will immediately revert to pushing most decisions upward. Consider for a moment if Reynolds had been several miles away, but both he and Fairchild had had cellphones. Should Fairchild have called him or not prior to making a decision? Should Reynolds have expected him to?

WHAT ELSE CAN WE LEARN FROM THIS VIGNETTE ABOUT LEADERSHIP?

Understanding the impact of technological change. The arrival of amazing new technologies such as the steamboat, railroad, and telegraph was as remarkable to an American in the nineteenth century as the latest iPhone may be to someone today. Leaders should constantly feel pressed to be on the lookout for new technologies that may improve the overall performance of their organization, if not transform it. But they also must be aware of how the arrival of a new technology may affect the environment in which they are operating and further demand rapid change in how their organization performs.

Even small changes in technology that may be almost imperceptible can at times have a dramatic impact on organizations. Prior to the Civil War infantry soldiers were armed with smoothbore muzzle loading weapons that required a rifleman to quickly measure a charge of gunpowder and pour it down the barrel. A small round musket ball that was roughly .69 caliber was then dropped down the barrel, and a piece of cotton or cloth was shoved down on top to hold everything in place. The shooter then used a long metal ramrod to force everything to the bottom of the barrel prior to raising the weapon and firing. Even an expert marksman could manage only about three rounds per minute of sustained fire, and the weapon was relatively inaccurate beyond one hundred meters. Ulysses S. Grant once wrote, "At a distance of a few hundred yards, a man—with a flintlock smoothbore rifle—might fire at you all day without you finding it out."

In the early 1840s a French military inventor, Claude-Étienne Minié, came up with a revolutionary new idea for a bullet. It was a cylindro-conical shaped lead bullet. What would later be called the "Minié ball" was perfected in 1848 and officially adopted by the US Army as a .58-caliber bullet in 1855. American munition manufacturers followed the original design by including rings at the base of the projectile that were filled with grease to ease the bullet down the barrel as well as collect powder residue. The projectile was fired from a rifled bore as opposed to smoothbore gun barrel. The rifled gun barrel had longitudinal spiral grooves cut along the interior length of the barrel. The soft lead of the bullet expanded when fired, creating a tight seal inside the barrel. The bullet would seat in the grooves and spin as it moved down the barrel, further stabilizing it in flight. Consequently, the Minié ball was extremely accurate out to ranges of three hundred meters or more. A small, almost invisible change in technology had dramatically improved the lethality of an individual soldier's weapon.

The US-produced Springfield Model 1861 rifled musket and the British-produced Pattern '53 Enfield Rifle Musket were the most common rifled muzzleloaders, and both fired a Minié ball that was more than a half-inch in diameter. More than two million of these weapons saw service in the Civil War on both sides—the British sold their weapons to the North and the South. The Confederate infantry that advanced on John Buford's position on McPherson's Ridge in long lines would have halted when within range of the enemy line and initially fired their weapons on command in order to mass their fire. This was also the tactic General Reynolds employed when he ordered the 2nd Wisconsin to advance. It would be the case throughout this battle and most of the Civil War. Sadly, the arrival of the much more accurate Minié ball, such a small change, and the decision to maintain the same approach on the battlefield resulted in dramatically higher casualties on both sides than the nation had witnessed in prior wars.

That's why leaders must be aware of technological change that may have a profound effect on the environment in which their organization operates—even if such changes are very small. Modern leaders must recognize that the pace of change today includes dramatic developments in robotics or gene therapy, as well the impact of "nanotechnology." This study of extremely small things that can have a profound impact in chemistry, biology, physics, material science, and engineering, nanotechnology affects everyday consumer products, from clothing to skin lotion. For example, silver nanoparticles are now placed in fabric to kill bacteria, thus making clothing odor resistant. Skincare products are also using such particles to deliver vitamins deeper into the skin.

Today nanotechnology allows scientists to produce machines from protein that are microscopic. Consider the fact that in the past communication satellites could be as large as a small school bus and weigh up to six tons, according to the Federal Communications Commission (FCC). In fact, most satellites now in orbit weigh several tons. But NASA is now discussing the possibility of so-called "nanosatellites" that might weigh no more than ten kilograms but can still accomplish the same tasks as their much heavier predecessors. Clearly, this will have an enormous impact on the size of launch vehicles or the opportunity to use a single rocket to place thousands of satellites into orbit with a single launch. As a result, global sales of nano-related technologies are now in the hundreds of billions of dollars. In an era of rapid change, leaders must constantly consider the impact of even very small technological changes on both their organization and their environment.

Organizational culture, change, and social pressure. If "leadership" is about dealing with change, then it is important to consider how organizations "change" and what barriers exist to effective change. From the perspective of the twenty-first century we might question why both Union and Confederate officers continued to order their men to advance in long lines and engage opposing units at close range with withering fire enhanced by the new technology of the Minié ball until almost the end of the war. Why didn't they change in the face of this carnage?

Sadly, both sides were prisoners of the past. In training and directing their armies both sides still used a series of tactical manuals developed by the American Army in the years following the War of 1812. These manuals were derivatives, with only modest modification, of the 1791 *French Tactical Manual.*[11] Tactics described in the manuals directed officers to train infantry units to stand in lines, advance, and fire at the enemy at relatively close ranges using disciplined volleys. Obviously, this was driven in part by two factors—the slow rate of fire of a single shot musket and the relative inaccuracy of smoothbore weapons firing a musket ball. "Change" in procedures did not occur with the arrival of the Minié ball despite rising casualty rates because these armies—like most organizations—were inherently resistant to change.

Many of us can perhaps relate to this. We have had the experience of joining a new group, team, or organization and asking why they conducted themselves in a particular fashion that, as a new member, we found dysfunctional. Frequently, we heard the following response, "We have always done it that way!" One of the great difficulties in effecting change in any organization is that the leader must often do so through those who have been most successful in that organization, no matter how faulty systems, or the overall organization, might be.

Individuals as well as entire organizations can also be resistant to change for social reasons. Consider the story of the famous basketball player Wilt Chamberlain. Chamberlain was over seven feet tall and weighed 265 pounds, and was considered one of the greatest basketball players of all time, especially during the 1960s and early '70s.

This proved true early in his career as a player for the Philadelphia Warriors. Though Chamberlain was only in his third season, his new coach, Frank McGuire, vowed to get the ball to Chamberlain two-thirds of the time and play him every minute of the game. But Chamberlain had one enormous flaw—he was a terrible free throw shooter and only made about 40 percent of his free throws. For comparison, LeBron James has averaged over 70 percent of free throws throughout his career. That weakness meant at the end of a close game, Chamberlain became a liability to his team, as opponents would try to foul him over and over again.

At one point in the season, a teammate convinced Chamberlain to shoot his free throws underhanded, using what is popularly known as the "granny shot." (This was later perfected by Rick Barry, who was one of the very few NBA stars to use this shot for free throws. Barry would make over 90 percent of his free throws throughout his fifteen-year NBA career.) As a result of this change, Chamberlain's free throw shooting improved dramatically, approaching nearly 80 percent during the '62 season.

That would come to have huge consequences when Chamberlain's Warriors played the New York Knicks in Hershey, Pennsylvania, on March 2, 1962. Wilt scored one hundred points during this game— widely considered one of the greatest records in professional basketball history—and made twenty-eight of thirty-two free throw attempts.

Yet the most amazing part of this story may be what happened at the onset of the 1963 basketball season. Chamberlain decided to go back to the accepted method of shooting free throws overhanded and, as a result, returned to being terrible at free throw shooting. When asked why he did that, Chamberlain replied that shooting free throws using the "granny shot" made him look and feel "silly." Fans and opposing players had teased him about it, and he succumbed to the "social pressure."

Many Civil War historians would agree that the willingness of Union and Confederate commanders to stick with infantry tactics that were over fifty years old by the time of Gettysburg was due in large measure to organizational resistance to change. But it may have also been due to "social pressures." Many Civil War officers believed that it was the "manly" thing to directly face one's enemies on the battlefield. To do otherwise seemed dishonorable.

Albert Einstein is supposed to have said, "The definition of insanity is doing the same thing over and over and expecting different results." The wise modern leader might well consider Einstein's advice when considering whether or not change is needed in their organization because:

- Change cannot occur if the thinking of its people remains unchanged.
- Transformation and change in any organization require persistence from the top.
- Change may require modifications to the organization's culture.
- Changing processes, technology, or structure may not be sufficient.

Leadership and innovation. "Innovation" is change that brings on a new level of performance. Effective leaders seek to encourage innovation throughout their organization and create a climate that underscores its importance. Organizations "innovate" by introducing changes in organizational structure, new products, or new processes. Colonel Fairchild from the 2nd Wisconsin may have directly benefitted from innovation in the Union army in the aftermath of being wounded.

Successful organizations innovate when placed under stress. An army at war is no exception, and wars historically bring about rapid innovation in treating injuries. Since the onset of the war on terrorism the American military has undergone dramatic innovation in treating wounded soldiers. This has included the ability to rapidly evacuate casualties, treat mental disorders such as post-traumatic stress disorder (PTSD), develop prosthetic devices to replace lost limbs, diagnose and treat traumatic brain injury (TBI), and so forth.

This was also true during the American Civil War. A graduate of Philadelphia's Jefferson Medical College, Jonathan Letterman joined the Regular Army as an assistant surgeon in 1849. In April 1862 he was named medical director for the entire Army of the Potomac with the rank of major. Commanding General George McClellan gave

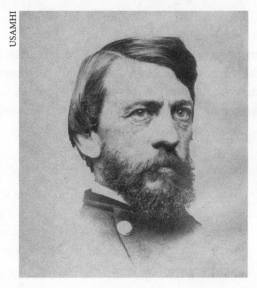

USAMHI

*Major Jonathan
Letterman,
Chief Surgeon,
Army of the
Potomac, USA*

Letterman broad authority to do whatever was required to revamp the poor medical services that troops were receiving.

Letterman came up with numerous innovations and is now known as the "Father of Modern Battlefield Medicine," and he effected all the changes inherent in innovation—new product, new process, and new organizational structure. In terms of "new products," he reinvented the then current horse-drawn field ambulance to the extent that it was a new product. His improvements to the vehicle included installing a spring suspension system between the wheel axles and the body of the vehicle and adding a rigid canvas-covered overhead wooden framework from which stretchers could be suspended to further cushion transportation of patients over rough roads or fields.

His "new organization" was the reorganization of the Ambulance Corps, placing the ambulances and evacuation system under control of the army's medical department rather than civilian contractors. Under his organizational design, this allowed wounded soldiers to be more efficiently and quickly evacuated, from collection points behind each regiment to field dressing stations at each brigade or on to field hospitals established behind the line of battle for each division and army corps.

Finally, and perhaps most importantly, Letterman came up with a "new process" that revolutionized the treatment of mass casualties. It became known as "triage" and is a method of sorting out the arriving injured based on their need for immediate medical treatment as compared to their chance of benefiting from such care. In essence, casualties are sorted into three groups: (1) soldiers who are clearly going to die and should be consoled; (2) the wounded whose injuries might require some minimal effort so they can await more in-depth treatment; and (3) casualties who, if operated on quickly, stand a good chance of recovery. Triage is still used today in hospital emergency rooms and during wars or disasters. It allows medical resources to be efficiently allocated to maximize the number of survivors. During World War II American General Omar Bradley declared triage to be the most important innovation in modern medicine.

Letterman's name is not as well-known as Ulysses S. Grant, but Letterman played a significant role in the Union's success during the Civil War. Fairchild may or may not have been evacuated and treated more quickly due to the innovations Letterman inaugurated. But the Union army clearly benefitted overall. At the onset of the war the North enjoyed several significant advantages over the South. Sixty percent of the nation's total population lived in the North, and 70 percent of the white population resided there. Due to Letterman's innovations the Union army began to see more of its soldiers survive their wounds and eventually return to the ranks. This was not the case in the South. For example, upon withdrawal of the Confederate army after the Gettysburg Battle, Robert E. Lee was forced to leave behind 5,000 soldiers as prisoners of war due to the inability of the Army of Northern Virginia to evacuate and treat their wounded.

Still, whatever leadership conclusions we draw from the fighting on McPherson's Ridge that hot July day, we must realize that due to the courage and efforts of General John Reynolds and his soldiers, the Union line would initially hold and possibly change the outset of the battle. But nothing was decided. The day was far from over, as more Confederate troops were headed to Gettysburg.

CHAPTER 4

"Take That Hill
if Practical to Do So!"

Reynolds arrived atop McPherson's Ridge with his infantry at mid-morning. Arriving just in time, his troops were successful in holding back Confederate advances through the remainder of those morning hours. Once replaced by the infantry, Buford's previously dismounted troopers, having succeeded in their covering force mission, remounted their horses and assumed positions on the ends of the Union defensive line to prevent flanking movements by the still advancing Confederate forces.

A lull in the battle occurred just prior to midday. Both sides attempted to reinforce their positions from widely dispersed units marching to the sound of the guns. It is important to understand that this battle started not as a planned battle by either commander but as a coincidental engagement between two smaller portions of two much larger but dispersed armies. The commanders, Lee and Meade, were drawn into a battle here by the actions of their subordinate commanders. Once started, the battle loomed larger over the coming hours and days as yet even more troops arrived on the field.

Over the course of the day, the remainder of the Union I Corps arrived and assumed positions on McPherson's Ridge. Meanwhile, troops of the XI Corps under the command of Major General Oliver O. Howard arrived on the scene around noontime. After Reynolds was

USAMHI

*Major General
Oliver O. Howard,
USA*

killed in action near midmorning, command of all Union forces on the field immediately fell to his senior division commander, Abner Doubleday. But Howard had rank over Doubleday by service time. In the formality of the time, Howard now had command of the field on the Union side.

Upon his arrival, Howard delegated command of the XI Corps to his senior division commander, Major General Carl Schurz. In the early afternoon Schurz positioned the two XI Corps infantry divisions on the broad plain north of the town in a line running a mile wide from near the Mummasburg Road, northwest of Gettysburg, across the Carlisle Road to where the Harrisburg Road entered the town from the northeast. Under Howard's direction, a brigade of infantry and some artillery were left by Schurz on Cemetery Hill south of the town as a reserve position.

In the early afternoon the situation began to change rapidly on the Confederate side. Entering the battle area from the north were soldiers of the Second Army Corps under command of General Richard Ewell. The first to arrive was an infantry division commanded by Major

USAMHI

*Major General
Carl Schurz, USA*

General Robert Rodes. He commanded five brigades of nearly 8,000 men and began arriving on Oak Hill, an area at the right flank of Union I Corps then fighting on McPherson's Ridge. Forward of the ridge, Confederate General Dorsey Pender's fresh 6,600-man infantry division of A. P. Hill's First Corps occupied a position behind and in support of Henry Heth's now depleted infantry division, which had fought since early morning against Buford's dismounted cavalry and then the infantry of the Union I Corps.[1]

Confederate division commander Rodes ordered three of his five brigades to advance against the exposed right flank of the Union I Corps. His remaining two brigades were held in reserve, to see how the situation further developed. Pender's division—in position behind Heth—was ordered by Third Corps commander A. P. Hill to pass through Heth's lines and attack in order to break the defending Union line farther south on McPherson's Ridge.

The men of the Union I Corps were then fighting for their lives on McPherson's Ridge and Oak Ridge west and northwest of the town against reinforced Confederate attacks. But what of the Union XI

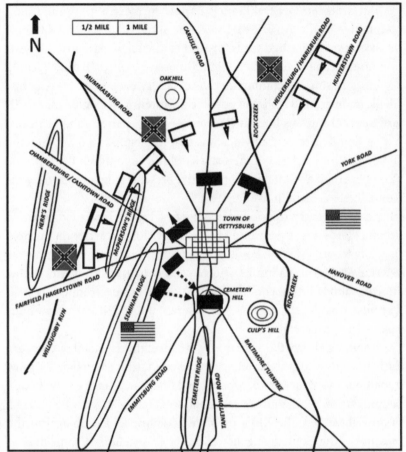

Map 4.0 Confederate infantry attacks in the afternoon force the Union defenders in retreat through the streets of the town to a reserve position on Cemetery Hill.

Corps deployed north of the town by Howard and Schurz? Upon initial deployment north of the town, Carl Schurz—former German revolutionary, personal friend of Abraham Lincoln, and future US secretary of the interior—specifically anchored the right end of the XI Corps line among a group of buildings where the Harrisburg Road entered the town from the northeast. This attempt aimed to protect the right end of the XI Corps line—or the right flank of the entire Union army—from being enveloped by any advancing Confederate forces.

But Brigadier General Francis Barlow, former attorney and future co-founder of the American Bar Association, advanced his infantry division several hundred yards forward of his assigned right-flank position on the edge of town to a slight hill now known as Barlow's Knoll. Second-guessing his commander's orders, Barlow sought to deny this small rise of ground from the possible positioning of Confederate artillery to shoot into his lines at close range. This seemed good tactically, but an unintended consequence was that in the process of moving the right of his line forward of the security of the buildings in the town, he also opened up a vulnerable right flank, presenting an opportunity for Confederate General Jubal Early.

Early's infantry division, a segment of Ewell's larger Confederate Second Corps, was the second of Ewell's divisions to arrive on the field that afternoon. A West Point graduate, class of 1837, Mexican War veteran, and former Virginia attorney, Early battled it out with fellow attorney and military commander Barlow. This courtroom, however, was now a battlefield, and lives of several hundred, if not a few thousand men, were at stake.

Booming down the Harrisburg Road with his infantry division, Early was quick to take advantage of the open flank created by Barlow's impetuous move forward of his assigned line. Early's men easily slipped behind Barlow's line, and the calls soon went out—"they are behind us." From right to left, the XI Corps mile-wide line folded up against the pressure of the Confederate attacks. As at Chancellorsville, the lives of the soldiers in the ranks of the Union XI Corps were compromised by the ineptitude of their commanders.

As if in a chain reaction, the folding-up of the XI Corps line continued right to left along the I Corps line. On McPherson's Ridge, Dorsey Pender's division advanced through Heth's now fought-out division. The Union I Corps defenders were pushed back from McPherson's Ridge. They initially sought the protection of the buildings on the ridge of the Lutheran Seminary, but they could not hold there. In their subsequent withdrawal, the remnants of the Union I Corps were joined by what remained of the XI Corps retreating through the streets of the town to the established reserve position on Cemetery Hill. They were closely pursued by the advancing Confederate soldiers from both A.

P. Hill's Third Corps and Richard Ewell's Second Corps. Many Union soldiers were taken prisoner by Confederate troops in the streets and alleys of Gettysburg. The Confederate advance west and north of the town was overwhelming but at a high cost in energy and blood, and their forward momentum gave out at the south end of the town.

General Lee arrived on the battlefield about midafternoon in time to witness the advance of Pender's and Rodes's divisions and the retreat of the Yankees through the town to Cemetery Hill. Even then he was greatly disturbed that, contrary to his orders, his subordinates had initiated a battle at a time—well before his army was consolidated—and at a place not of his choosing. He thought perhaps they had misunderstood or ignored his orders. Perhaps he had not made his vision for the coming battle clear?

This was a potential moment of crisis for Lee. His army still dispersed in enemy territory on ground unfamiliar to him. Moving forward behind his advancing troops, as far forward as Seminary Ridge, he could see his troops in the town, and he could see Cemetery Hill and part of the enemy force retreating to it. He could see the high ground of the ridge to the right of the hill. Were the troops he could see all of the enemy force in the near vicinity? Intuitively, he knew they were not. But where were the rest of them? How many of them were there? He hadn't a clue. Major General Stuart and his cavalry, his eyes and ears for information gathering, particularly in enemy territory, had still not rejoined the main body of the army. Where was Stuart? For the time being the questions in his mind went unanswered.

For those astute enough to recognize it, like Lee, crisis and the unknown represent both danger and opportunity for any organization. As he studied the situation before him, Lee recognized that, in spite of his many questions, his men now had the momentum while the enemy was in disarray. His confidence returned as he realized the opportunity which lay before him with his men in the right place at the right time to occupy the high ground to their front and finish off what appeared to be a defeated enemy.

Not fully knowing the condition of Ewell's troops in and about the town, Lee turned to his assistant adjutant general, Major Walter H. Taylor, and told him to go to Ewell and tell him that "it was only

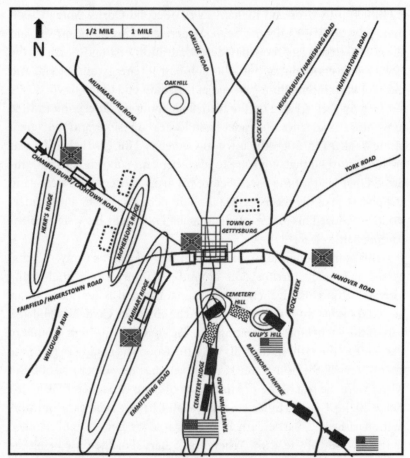

Map 4.1 In the late afternoon of July 1ˢᵗ, Confederate attacks force the Union defenders back to their reserve position on Cemetery Hill and Cemetery Ridge.

necessary to press 'those people'—the enemy—in order to secure possession of the heights" and that, *if possible*, that is what Lee wanted Ewell to do. Taylor went immediately to Ewell and delivered that discretionary order from Lee.[2]

....

LEADERSHIP MOMENT   You are now Confederate General Richard Ewell. You have been a corps commander for only a few weeks, having returned from a long recovery after losing a leg ten months ago in a previous battle.

In response to General Lee's order of three days earlier, you have marched your corps south from the vicinity of Harrisburg and Carlisle to Gettysburg and arrived on the field by midafternoon. As the day progresses—General Rodes's and General Early's divisions attack Union forces along the general axis of the Carlisle and Heidlersburg-Harrisburg Roads. The Yankee line north of Gettysburg is broken, and the Union troops retreat to reserve positions on Cemetery Hill. Your soldiers pursue them through the town and take many prisoners. Late in the afternoon you receive this subsequent order from General Lee to continue the attack through Gettysburg to seize the high ground in front of you, "if you find it practical to do so." The intended point of this attack would be Culp's Hill and Cemetery Hill. The sun will set in three hours. Only two divisions of your corps have arrived on the field, and your third division will not arrive until well after. What actions do you take and why?

....

Ewell decided not to continue the attack. He made this decision for a number of reasons. Ewell later wrote in his after-action report that "I could not bring artillery to bear on it—the hill—and all the troops with me were jaded by twelve hours marching and fighting."[3] Additionally, only two of the three divisions assigned to his corps had arrived on the battlefield. The last division would not get to Gettysburg until after dark. Lastly, his troops were now in the town following their pursuit of the Yankees and were "disordered"; that is to say their officers did not have full command and control at that moment. They had pursued Union forces rapidly into the Gettysburg, and it would take some time to get them reorganized in order to conduct a coordinated attack.

Furthermore, Ewell knew he only had a few hours until sunset around 7:30. Commanders on both sides during the Civil War were averse to fighting at night due to the difficulties of commanding and controlling forces during hours of darkness.

Many historians describe Lee's message to Ewell as the "discretionary order," as it clearly gave Ewell the ultimate decision. Some have even argued that it was the most controversial decision taken during the battle and perhaps even the entire war. In retrospect, some have argued that had Ewell continued the attack as Lee had suggested he would have captured Culp's Hill and Cemetery Ridge. The Battle of Gettysburg would have been a one-day battle and a stunning Confederate victory on northern soil. What might have happened in the aftermath is obviously open to speculation.

This argument is buttressed by several facts. Ewell had assumed command of his corps following the death of General Stonewall Jackson. Jackson was perhaps Lee's most aggressive subordinate and, consequently, would have very likely continued the attack without further orders from Lee. Furthermore, there are additional reasons to believe that an attack at that moment might well have been successful. Union General Winfield Scott Hancock arrived on Cemetery Ridge late in the day as Union forces were retreating toward it. He had been directed in writing by General Meade to proceed to Gettysburg and assume overall command of the federal forces that were engaged. That evening Hancock wrote to his wife and in the letter allegedly observed that had the Confederates pursued the attack late on the afternoon of July 1 he believed the Union would not have been able to hold Cemetery Ridge.

Furthermore, in a January 1878 letter to former Confederate General Fitzhugh Lee—nephew of Confederate commander Robert E. Lee—Hancock said that upon his initial arrival on Cemetery Hill the afternoon of July 1, it was his "opinion that if the Confederates had continued the pursuit of Howard—the retreating Union troops—they would have driven him over and beyond Cemetery Hill."[4]

WHAT CAN WE LEARN FROM THIS VIGNETTE ABOUT LEADERSHIP?

Leadership style. Lee's use of a "discretionary order" is consistent with his leadership style. He had always preferred to provide his subordinates broad guidance, which is often referred to as "mission command" by military commanders and can be used by the leader of any organization. The leader who follows this concept gives general direction to his subordinates consistent with the organization's stated mission and vision. Subordinate leaders are expected to operate within the guidance, but it allows them significant discretion and is designed to encourage initiative. Lee discussed his leadership style with Captain

Justus Scheibert on the afternoon of July 2. Scheibert was a Prussian officer who along with several other European officers was an observer with the Confederate army during the campaign. Lee observed, "My interference in battle would do more harm than good. I have, then, to rely on my brigade and division commanders. I think and work with all my powers to bring my troops to the right place at the right time, then I have done my duty. As soon as I order them into battle, I leave my army in the hands of God."[5]

This "mission command" style had worked for Lee since assuming command of the Army of Northern Virginia in June 1862, but by the summer of 1863 that may have no longer been true. When he assumed command of the Rebel army Lee had been blessed with both outstanding and experienced subordinate leaders in Stuart, Jackson, and Longstreet, as well as a great deal of good fortune. Up until this moment Lee had been clearly superior to the Union commanders he had confronted.

Richard Ewell had been a good if not outstanding divisional commander but had experienced a far different relationship with his previous boss, General Stonewall Jackson. If Lee's style of leadership emphasized "mission command," Jackson's style was "watch my lips." He issued very explicit orders to his subordinates on what he required their units to do, how he wanted it done, and when he desired it accomplished. Jackson allowed little to no room for initiative or creativity, and he further expected his subordinates to seek additional guidance when the task was completed. Some have suggested that Jackson was conscious of the *moral of his command*. He firmly believed that nothing ever fully excused failure, and it was very rare that he gave an officer a second chance. "The service," he said, "cannot afford to keep a man who does not succeed." As a consequence, he never felt restrained from changing leaders for fear that it would make things worse. His motto was "get rid of the unsuccessful man at once, and trust Providence for finding a better."[6]

Clearly, Jackson's leadership style did not create a climate of initiative throughout the corps he commanded. He was reported to have placed officers under court-martial charges for withdrawing from the field when their units were out of ammunition. He even relieved an officer who allowed his troops to burn fence rails when his unit was encamped on property that the officer owned.[7] Jackson had ordered that private property not be appropriated, and despite his generosity, the officer was suspended from duty on the charge of giving away his own property! On that fateful afternoon General Richard Ewell was newly in command of a corps and a lonely, conflicted figure.

Each leader must determine an individual leadership style that is appropriate for them. In many ways our leadership style exists on a continuum that stretches from *broad guidance* to *direct command*. This is based on a leader's individual "comfort level," their willingness to accept risk, and how experienced their subordinate leaders are. Effective leaders must also adjust their style as conditions change. If an organization is experiencing an existential crisis or has undergone a significant change in mid-level leadership, then a leader might likely assume more direct control over decisions. Still, every leader should be able to adjust their style based on the overall competency, confidence, and experience of the leaders who work for them.

Many historians have held General Ewell accountable for this decision, which they contend set the stage for the eventual Confederate defeat at Gettysburg. This is unfair in many ways or at a minimum incomplete analysis. Still the events during the afternoon of July 1, 1863, raise several interesting leadership questions. When Lee sent Major Taylor with the so-called "discretionary order" to Ewell was he *really* communicating with Richard Ewell, a new corps commander in the middle of his first major engagement? Or was he perhaps *still* communicating with the now dead General Stonewall Jackson, who Lee knew would do what he actually desired and continue the attack? Following Jackson's death, Lee lamented to one of his officers, "I had such implicit confidence in Jackson's skill and energy that I never troubled myself to give him detailed instructions. The most general instructions were all that were needed."[8]

The need for a leader to adjust his or her leadership style can also be seen in contemporary examples. General David Petraeus is a widely respected and experienced twenty-first century military leader who commanded the 101st Airmobile Division during the initial invasion of Iraq in 2003. He maintained close control of the deployment of his brigades during the invasion, but this was during a conventional war. The goal was to destroy Iraqi ground forces and topple the regime of Saddam Hussein.

Petraeus returned to Iraq in 2007 as commander of all coalition military forces in the country. This was during "the surge" that resulted in a significant increase in the overall level of troops deployed. He altered his previous leadership style and adopted a broad use of "mission command." Petraeus knew the situation had changed dramatically. Rather than engaging the Iraqi army and measuring success based on the capture of enemy territory, his troops were now facing terrorists and insurgents. They had to be deployed in small units throughout Baghdad to secure the city and provide reassurance to the population. A new environment demanded a change in leadership style.

The nature of crisis. The Chinese symbol for "crisis" combines two symbols—danger and opportunity. Every leader should consider this, as they will undoubtedly undergo both personal and organizational crises that are large and small. How do we contend with the danger? But perhaps of equal or greater importance—is there an opportunity here that we can now exploit?

When Robert E. Lee arrived in Gettysburg on the afternoon of July 1, he was initially angry at what had occurred. He had directed his corps commanders—Ewell, Hill, and Longstreet—not to become decisively engaged with the enemy until the entire Confederate army had arrived. Lee knew that his forces were operating on enemy territory and so there was the very real possibility of being defeated in detail if a major battle occurred before the entire army was assembled. General Hill's precipitous advance on the town had resulted in a major battle, and two of Lee's three corps were now engaged. General Lee quickly surveyed the situation and realized that there might be an opportunity for a quick but decisive victory over the Union army on northern soil, which could have an enormous political and military impact. With this in mind Lee issued that "discretionary order" to General Ewell.

Modern leaders will inevitably experience crises in their organizations. For example, a major corporate leader was interviewed about the impact the 2008 recession had on his organization. His corporation had over 6,000 employees and an annual budget in excess of $350 million.

He recounted that he was forced to take a 20 percent cut in his operating budget in a single year in response to this crisis.

"Wow," the interviewer remarked, "that must have been terrible!"

"It was hard," the executive replied, "but it was also great!"

"How is that possible?" the interviewer responded.

"Well," the executive said, "I had only recently taken over the corporation, and there were a significant number of major changes that I wanted to effect. I figured it would take me perhaps three to five years to accomplish all of them due to resistance from within the organization and my board. But I got them all accomplished in a single year by 'blaming' the need to change on the recession."

Effective leaders see "opportunity" in the "danger" of a crisis and while dealing with the immediate consequences seize that opportunity for the betterment of their organization.

Succession planning. Planning and executing leadership succession in any organization is difficult. By the end of the day on July 1, 1863, the Union army had had five different overall commanders on the battlefield. Cavalry commander, Brigadier General John Buford, was initially in command because his forces were the first to arrive and occupy McPherson's Ridge on the evening of June 30. Major General John Reynolds assumed overall command of all forces on the field when he arrived around midmorning, on July 1, but then he was killed shortly after his arrival. Major General Abner Doubleday then assumed overall command, as he was the most senior of Reynolds's divisional commanders. But Doubleday was replaced later in the day by Major General Howard upon his arrival on the field with his unit. This occurred since Howard was both a corps commander and also senior to Doubleday based on the fact that he had held the rank of major general for a longer period. Late in the afternoon Major General Winfield Scott Hancock reached the field with a letter from General Meade placing him in command of the Union army at Gettysburg until Meade arrived on the scene.

This obviously appears both confusing and disruptive, but military culture has an established succession plan that all soldiers know and accept. The senior officer present assumes command but in the event of his or her demise, and—as in this case—the two succeeding officers have the same grade, then whichever has the most senior date of rank is in charge. This is a long-standing cultural norm that soldiers are taught to understand and embrace. This serves to smooth transitions under difficult circumstances. Consequently, despite the fact that the Army of the Potomac was forced to retreat from the initial positions occupied by Buford's cavalry, move through the town, and occupy Cemetery Ridge, it did so in fairly good order. The organization's "succession plan" worked during a moment of crisis.

A. T. Kearney, an American-based global management and consulting firm, conducted a study in 2011 of the weaknesses in major corporations in concert with the Kelley School of Business at Indiana University.[9] The final report noted that many corporate boards fail when it comes to succession planning. This was frequently due to the fact that they did not have an effective or even existing succession plan should the CEO suddenly depart or become sick.

The report further noted that thirty-six Standard & Poors 500 companies that had stable leadership for roughly three decades were remarkably successful. They represented twenty-five different industries and included such well-known names as Abbott Laboratories, Caterpillar, Colgate-Palmolive, DuPont, FedEx, Honda, Johnson Controls, McDonald's, Microsoft, Nike, and United Technologies. These corporations consistently outperformed their competition in six measurable metrics: return on assets, equity and investment, revenue on assets, revenue and earnings growth, earning per share growth, and stock-price appreciation.[10] They also all had clear succession plans and further sought to develop "home grown leadership." This underscored the need for consistency during periods of rapid change as well as the fact that a CEO needs to know more about his or her organization than how to run a business. Success requires a firm understanding of the organization's unique culture, brand, and how to inspire their team. The report further stressed that as organizations mature there is an increasing demand to focus on leadership development and create a pool of internal qualified candidates to assume the overall future leadership of the company.

A Danish consulting company did an ancillary study. They examined what happened to large for-profit organizations when the CEO suffered a major personal disaster and was unavailable for an extended period. This included such things as major injury, disease, death of close family member, loss of a spouse, divorce, and more. In every case they examined the corporation's profits suffered in the quarter following the sudden loss of the CEO.

Effective organizations must be resilient, which scientists describe as "the capacity of a system to absorb disturbance and still retain its basic function and structure."[11] As a result, effective leaders and boards must ensure that clear succession plans exist and everyone is aware of them in case the leader is unavailable at a moment of crisis or suddenly departs. In addition, steps should be taken to develop those within the organization who may be called upon at a time of crisis to move up to higher positions of responsibility, as well as being potential "home-grown" leaders for the future.

Far too many organizations suffer from the "indispensable man" syndrome. Often times the "success" of a leader is solely measured in how well his or her organization functioned while they were in charge. But their most important leadership contribution may be how well they prepared their organization for their inevitable departure. Did they retain and develop highly qualified leaders who could assume greater responsibilities even during moments of crisis or change? Or were they so consumed by short-term success that they left the organization unprepared? Jack Welch is held in high esteem by many management theorists for his leadership of General Electric for more than 20 years, but GE clearly suffered in the transition to new leadership upon his departure. In comparison, many argued that Apple's Steve Jobs was "too good to replace," but in 2011 Jobs selected Tim Cook as his successor. Since then Cook has led Apple to even greater heights.

Most people are familiar with "Murphy's Law." It is normally summarized as "anything that can go wrong, will go wrong, and usually at the worst possible moment." The loss of the leader at a precarious moment for an organization is worthy of Murphy's admonition. But the critical importance of succession planning might suggest that leaders consider "Schultz's Corollary"—"Murphy was an optimist!"

The first day of the Battle of Gettysburg had come to an end. It had largely been a Confederate victory as the Rebels had pushed the Union forces through the town and up onto Cemetery Ridge. But it had not been decisive. Historical evidence supports the fact that, even prior to Lee sending "the discretionary order" to Ewell, Confederate Generals Isaac Ridgeway Trimble, Jubal Early, and John B. Gordon had encouraged, if not begged, Ewell to continue the attack from the town to seize the heights south of it.[12]

Ewell demurred while forestalling Trimble's suggestions with petulance, saying, "When I need advice from a junior officer, I generally ask for it." But again, Trimble, unshakable in his convictions, came back, this time more forcefully, asking for his command of a division to take those heights. Ewell remained silent in reply. Trimble then asked for a brigade and then one good regiment to take those heights. At each entreaty, Ewell bowed his head in silence.[13] Ewell had become paralyzed by indecision.

In a fictional scene portrayed in the 1993 movie *Gettysburg*, General Isaac Trimble, the oldest Confederate general on the field, visited General Lee at his headquarters late on the evening of the first day of the battle. Trimble related his encounter with Ewell to Lee and then told the elder general that in losing his temper, he had thrown down his sword in front of Ewell in utter disgust of his lack of leadership. In this perhaps fictional portrayal Trimble continued with the prediction that tomorrow "many good Southern boys will die taking that hill." Fiction or not, those words proved to be true.

CHAPTER 5

"If Those People Are There Tomorrow, We Will Attack Them..."

Late in the day of July 1, just before sunset at 7:30

As General Lee stood on Seminary Ridge observing the Union army attempting to rally on Cemetery Hill while also sending Major Taylor to deliver Ewell that discretionary order, James Longstreet, Lee's "old war horse," arrived at his side. Longstreet, commander of Lee's First Corps, had ridden ahead of his marching troops, who were still six miles west of Seminary Ridge trudging over South Mountain's Cashtown Gap on the Chambersburg Pike to the village of Cashtown.

Longstreet was an important figure for Lee, more important than most others. Since Lee took command of the army in June 1862, Longstreet, Jackson, and Stuart had been Lee's principal subordinate commanders and had been there for all his victories. However, at Gettysburg, Jackson was now two months in his grave, after being mortally wounded at Chancellorsville. Stuart had been out of contact with Lee and the main body of the army for the past week. But thankfully, Longstreet was now here with him.

Born in South Carolina in 1821 but raised in Georgia on a plantation owned by his uncle, Judge Augustus Longstreet, James Longstreet received his appointment to the US Military Academy at West Point from Alabama and maintained his true Southern flair. At West Point his classmates maintained his old family nickname for him—"Old Pete." He graduated West Point in the class of 1842, ranking fifty-four of fifty-six cadets.[1] While no academic genius, he proved to be a competent military professional, leader of men in battle, and excellent equestrian. His biographer William Garrett Piston wrote that, because of his low academic class rank:

> Longstreet was not allowed to choose his assignments, as were distinguished cadets. He was sent to the infantry where prospects for advancement were slow except in wartime. Actually, the infantry suited him. He had little use for the elite branches such as the engineers, or artillery. Courtly and well-mannered when the occasion demanded, his rustic upbringing left some rough edges which never entirely disappeared, and he was quite at home with the common foot soldiers.[2]

The class of 1842 was an exceptional class, producing ten future Confederate generals and seven future Union generals.[3] Two of Longstreet's classmates, Lafayette McLaws and Richard H. Anderson, fought at Gettysburg under his command. Four of his classmates—George Sykes, Abner Doubleday, Seth Williams, and John Newton—fought against him at Gettysburg. Yes, it truly was a civil war.

Longstreet proved to be an above average leader and commander in "the old army" prior to the Civil War. He earned two brevets for gallantry in the US war with Mexico 1846–1848, where he fell wounded in action while he, George Pickett, and men of the Eighth Infantry Regiment, breached the enemy defenses at Chapultepec. The following years included distinguished service on the western frontier in both command and staff positions. At the outbreak of the Civil War he resigned his commission as a major in the Regular Army and joined the Confederacy, where he served as a field commander starting with the first major land battle at First Manassas in July 1861.[4] Promoted upward through the ranks and positions for his demonstrated abilities and competency, he was Lee's senior corps commander at the outset of the Gettysburg Campaign.

Joining Lee at a vantage point somewhere along Seminary Ridge near the Seminary campus, Longstreet surveyed with his field glasses the enemy position on Cemetery Hill a mile to the east. For the moment Lee was busy with questions and requests for orders from his staff. Longstreet studied the Union position for five to ten minutes and was soon troubled by what he saw of the enemy rallying on the strong position of Cemetery Hill. With Lee's preoccupation now ended, Longstreet turned to the older general and told him that by morning the enemy position would be so well defended that they could not attack successfully.

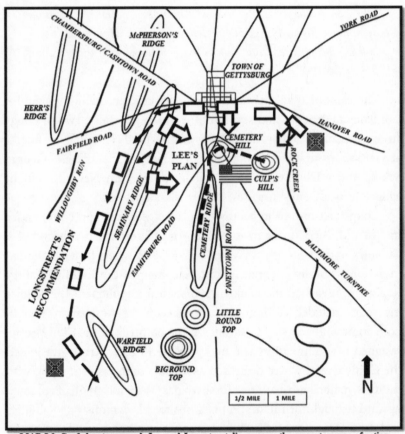

MAP 5.0 Confederate generals Lee and Longstreet disagree on the correct course of action in confronting the Union Army of the Potomac on the second day of the battle.

From here accounts vary as to what was said next as there were no firsthand witness to the conversation. The two senior leaders stood together, their staff members respectfully standing a discreet distance from them. In his memoirs Longstreet recalls telling Lee, "We could not call the enemy to a position better suited to our plans. All that we have to do is file around his left and secure good ground between him and his capital."

Lee then responded, while pointing to the enemy on Cemetery Hill, "No, if he is there tomorrow, I will attack him."

Longstreet in turn responded, "If he is there tomorrow, it will be because he wants you to attack."[5]

To which Lee finally said, rejecting Longstreet's recommendation, "No, they are in position and I am going to whip them, or they are going to whip me."[6]

Early in the morning of the second day of the battle, Lee ordered a reconnaissance conducted of the enemy lines, paying particular attention to the left of that line. Lee's staff engineer Captain Samuel R. Johnston; Longstreet's staff engineer Major J. J. Clarke; and two or three other men rode out before sunup. They allegedly rode all the way over to the two Round Top hills and back to Seminary Ridge with a couple of near intercepts by enemy patrols along the way. At eight o'clock in the morning, Johnston, finding Lee at the Seminary, reported his findings to include a vulnerable open flank on the Union left.

That was good enough for Lee. In the presence of corps commanders Longstreet and Hill, among others, Lee issued his orders for the day. Longstreet with his two infantry divisions then available was to go to the south end of Seminary Ridge and Warfield Ridge and establish attack positions there. He was to then conduct the main attack to the north-northeast, which would roll up the left of the enemy defensive line on Cemetery Ridge. The attack would commence as soon as Longstreet could get his men into position. At the same time, a secondary attack was to be conducted by Ewell's Second Corps to take the heights on the right of the enemy line, which he had declined to seize some hours earlier. Also, A. P. Hill's Third Corps was to conduct a supporting attack to the east from Seminary Ridge against the center of the Union line on Cemetery Ridge to pin enemy troops in position there and be turned into a general advance should the situation allow.

....

LEADERSHIP MOMENT   You are now General Robert E. Lee, commander of the Army of Northern Virginia. You have convinced the Southern leadership in Richmond to follow your recommendation and conduct an invasion of the North. Privately you fear that the South cannot sustain this conflict indefinitely, and this campaign may be one of the last opportunities to achieve victory. The first day of the Battle of Gettysburg has been successful but not decisive. You have met General Longstreet in the vicinity of the Lutheran Seminary. He is not only the most senior corps commander in the Army of Northern Virginia but also your most trusted subordinate. Longstreet's corps was not engaged on the first day of the fighting, and most of his units arrived either in the late afternoon or overnight. But Longstreet strongly disagrees with your plan to directly attack the enemy on Cemetery Hill and Cemetery Ridge. He recommends that the army march around the Union left flank and maneuver them off their strong defensive position. What should you do to get your primary subordinate commander to buy into your plan?

....

WHAT CAN WE LEARN FROM THIS VIGNETTE ABOUT LEADERSHIP?

Getting buy-in. Lee had a difficult challenge, which all leaders will experience. He knows that he needs Longstreet's full support if the Confederates are to be successful. In his own mind, Lee has "decided what has to be done," so he now needs to determine "how to get Longstreet to want to do it." But his challenge is further complicated by the pressure of time. How much time should he spend trying to get buy-in from Longstreet before he simply issues a direct order?

This is critical for any organization and its leaders. It is essential not only for mission success but to also maintain a sense of "alignment" within the team. Alignment is the understanding or sense that everyone is moving in the same direction consistent with the organization's overall mission, vision, and values. Furthermore, each member of the team needs to fully appreciate how his or her job contributes to that overall effort.

The actual details of this crucial conversation are clouded in the fog of history. But Lee rebuffed Longstreet's objections and directed him to move his troops into position for the planned attack as soon as possible. It seems clear that he hoped the attack would commence before more enemy troops arrived on the field and further strengthened their defensive position. Lee could have sought to achieve buy-in from Longstreet by pointing out to him that the goal of this campaign was not to win a battle but rather to win the war—the ultimate mission of the Confederacy. He might have also disclosed to his trusted subordinate his own nagging fears that despite the Army of Northern Virginia's victories over the previous year the Confederacy was in danger of losing everything. The South did not have the manpower or the industrial strength to continue the conflict indefinitely, but it appeared that the North did. He also knew Longstreet shared those views but wanted to gain the victory in a different way with hopefully fewer casualties. This might be the last and best chance the Rebels had for overall success.

Lee departed after issuing orders to both Longstreet and Hill, and rode to the left end of the line. He now saw it necessary to give General Ewell detailed instructions for his portion of the attack, and this time he was not going to allow Ewell any discretion. He returned to the area of the Seminary around midday only to discover that Longstreet's corps had not begun moving toward its attack positions. Lee was incensed and confronted Longstreet about the delay. Longstreet argued that he was still waiting for remaining units of his corps to arrive and did not want to go into battle "with one boot off." Lee ordered Longstreet to begin the movement immediately.

As Longstreet's corps began marching south a mile to the west of Seminary Ridge, he was notified that their selected route of march would soon bring them into view of Union observation posts on the high ground of Cemetery Ridge and the Round Tops. Longstreet ordered a countermarch, which meant that his column of two infantry divisions—approximately 14,000 men—had to turn around and return nearly to its initial departure point from which a different covered and concealed avenue of approach to their attack positions was taken. It was around 4:00 p.m., only three and one-half hours before sunset, when Longstreet's men occupied the positions from which they could begin their attack.

Chris Nassetta, CEO of Hilton Worldwide, discussed the problem of getting organizational "buy-in" and the critical importance of alignment within the Hilton team during an interview in the *New York Times* in 2012.[7] Nassetta observed that Hilton had over 300,000 employees worldwide, and he discovered upon his arrival as CEO that large segments of the company operated very independently. "We had massive amounts of duplication and fragmentation. We needed alignment." He further described a requirement to get "buy-in" by first ensuring everyone on the "team" understood who the organization was, what it stood for, and key priorities. Once that was accomplished, he needed them "to get their oars in the water and head in a common direction." As a result, he spent his first year travelling around the globe talking to employees about the importance of the mission of Hilton and using that as a vehicle to build a revised culture and getting that sense of alignment.

Nassetta's use of the metaphor of rowing for both building and aligning his team is instructive. Some have described the sport as a "symphony of motion." This is underscored brilliantly in the book *The Boys in the Boat* by Daniel James Brown, a compelling story of nine young college students from the University of Washington who joined the rowing team when they arrived at the college in the early 1930s. These young men came from farms, logging communities, small towns, and fishing villages from across the state of Washington. Their families had struggled through the Great Depression, and each of them had overcome enormous personal obstacles and demonstrated resilience. None of them had ever rowed prior to arriving at the university but being a member of the rowing team provided each a modest scholarship that helped them achieve their personal goal of a college diploma.

Al Ulbrickson was the Washington rowing coach at the time, and he saw his role not in growing individual rowers but rather developing a team. Ulbrickson worked closely with the boat. or "shell," master builder George Pocock. Both believed they were growing men and served as mentors to the boys. They sought to focus each member of the team on the most important goal—"the ability to disregard his own ambitions, to throw his ego over the gunwales, to leave it swirling in the wake of his shell, and to pull, not just for himself, not just for glory, but for the other boys in the boat."[8] They had both worked with many rowing teams and were convinced that several had been very good, but the "great teams" were those that did not necessarily have the strongest individual rowers but achieved complete alignment of effort. This resulted in an exponential improvement in overall team performance.

The Washington team would win the NCAA eight-man rowing championships in the spring of 1936 and become the American representatives to the Olympic games, which were held that year in Berlin. This was the so-called "Hitler Olympics," as the Nazi leader sought to use the games to demonstrate the superiority of the Aryan race. In the finals the boys from Washington faced both Nazi Germany and Fascist Italy, who were considered the favorites. The Americans got off to a very bad start, but in the final mile they began to close the gap. With 75,000 Germans screaming "Deutschland!" and Hitler accompanied by the Nazi leadership looking on, the American boat defeated the Germans by less than one second, winning the gold medal. The power of the "team" and complete alignment had triumphed.

All leaders want strong teams and strategic alignment in their organization. In the military, paradigms are used and emphasized by the leadership to underscore the importance of this. In the US Navy entering sailors or Midshipman are told repeatedly to reflect on the mantra "Ship, Shipmate, Self" in determining priorities, focus, and effort. The US Army uses a similar model: "Mission, Men, Me." Both suggest the critical significance for each member of the team to fully understand the organization's mission, vision, and values. This can only occur if the leadership of the organization frequently emphasizes these during individual or team meetings, planning sessions, or other gatherings. They are critical to getting buy-in from the members of the team.

Where does my loyalty lie? Longstreet had a problem that most subordinates will confront at some point—where does my ultimate loyalty lie? Is it with my boss, whom I truly admire, or with what I firmly believe is best for the organization? Longstreet's affinity for his soldiers and their lives was noted earlier. Some historians have described this moment as a moral dilemma for Longstreet. He and Lee had been through many battles over the previous year and been successful in almost every case. There is little doubt that he had enormous respect and admiration for Lee, but at this critical moment they disagreed. He had had an opportunity to disagree with his boss and offer a different course of action. But did he aggressively carry out his orders or allow his opposition to frame his actions?

Effective leaders want to achieve buy-in for the direction they wish the organization to take but know that they can only devote so much time to accomplishing this task. As previously suggested, time is perhaps every leader's most precious resource, and the one that is the most inelastic. Organizations operate in a dynamic environment. Consequently, extensive delay in decision-making can translate into missed opportunity or even stasis.

Some historians have criticized Longstreet for translating his disagreement with Lee's plan into getting the "slows" or even "slow-rolling" the execution of a decision the boss had made. They argue even though Lee had issued his orders Longstreet found excuses not to begin deploying his forces and wasted precious hours that had a significant effect as the day progressed. All followers will experience this challenge, and leaders must be attentive to it. Leaders must ask themselves several critical questions when making difficult decisions. Have I allowed my team to describe their alternative plans within the constraints of time and listened to them prior to making key decisions? But does resistance to a particular decision translate into a half-hearted response and undermine the organization's overall efforts?

The potential "tyranny" of planning. Dwight Eisenhower once said, "Planning is everything, the plan is nothing." What he meant by this was that leaders create plans for their organization based on their analysis of the environment in which they are operating. The plan has a clear goal, and even the path to get there may seem obvious. Planning helps us to synergize efforts between different parts of the team, determine an appropriate allocation of resources, and establish timelines for execution.

Smart leaders must pay attention to two potential problems. First, as Eisenhower suggests, and is often said in the military, "no plan survives the first round fired." The environment in which we are operating is dynamic and not static. Conditions are continuously changing, and effective organizations must adapt accordingly. Our opponent or competitor is not inactive but rather dynamic and also making decisions that have a direct effect on the possible success or failure of our efforts. The plan provides critical guidelines and analysis, but smart leaders have to be prepared to adapt along the way.

Second, "the perfect plan is never executed." Too often leaders and organizations are excessively risk averse or consumed by getting buy-in from every member of the team or stakeholder. As a result, they become consumed by creating a flawless plan that describes every possible alternative, resource shortfall, or other relevant information. Such an effort can lead to either inertia or an expectation that the team must execute the plan almost immediately since most available time has been consumed in the planning cycle. Subordinate leaders are deprived an opportunity to digest the plan thoroughly, brief their teams, and devise complementary efforts to ensure effective execution. A method to avoid this is the "one-third/two-thirds rule." The leader must determine when he or she wants their organization to begin execution of a new effort. One-third of the available time belongs to the leader and is devoted to planning. Two-thirds of the time belongs to his or her subordinate leaders and is reserved for briefing the plan throughout the organization, marshalling resources, considering minor adjustments, and so on. But the leader's job is not done when the plan is completed—it has only begun. He or she now has to provide oversight without micromanaging, supply additional guidance, and lead their organization in adapting to emerging conditions.

Based on the start of the second day of battle, we might judge that Lee had issued the plan and provided Longstreet (his subordinate) sufficient time. But that time was sadly wasted, and the environment on the battlefield would soon change.

CHAPTER 6

"Lieutenant,
Do You Have Orders?"

Major General George Meade, commander of the Union's Army of the Potomac, arrived on the battlefield in the overnight hours between July 1 and 2, missing all of the first day's fighting. When messages from Buford and Reynolds reached him on June 30 of the probability of a coming battle at Gettysburg, he resisted the natural temptation to rush to the scene. He chose instead to remain at his headquarters in Taneytown, Maryland, some thirteen miles south-southeast of Gettysburg. He knew the developing situation at Gettysburg was in the trusted hands of Buford and Reynolds while the bulk of his force was still with him in Maryland with orders to move toward Gettysburg. Moreover, he probably wished to leverage from his Taneytown headquarters the new technological advantage of the electric telegraph in sending and receiving information on the enemy force in Pennsylvania. Thanks to the work of the US Military Telegraph Service, he had good long-distance communications with army headquarters in Washington, from which he received intelligence on the size, location, and activity of the Confederate army. While remaining temporarily in Taneytown, Meade sent forward to Gettysburg in his place II Corps commander Winfield Scott Hancock and Chief Engineer Gouverneur K. Warren. Hancock was to take temporary command of the forces at Gettysburg until Meade could get there, and Warren was to begin a topographic survey of the terrain there.

USAMHI

Brigadier General Gouverneur K. Warren, USA

Upon his arrival at Gettysburg under the cover of darkness, Meade met with his senior leaders and asked his first question: "Is this good ground for a battle?" They assured him it was. At first light the next morning, Meade conducted a mounted survey of the positions his forces occupied and should occupy. He then gave his orders for the organization of the defensive position that historically has become known as "the fishhook." On the right, XII Corps was to occupy the heights known as Culp's Hill. To their left, the remnants of the XI Corps and I Corps, survivors of the first day's fighting, were to occupy the ground connecting Culp's Hill with Cemetery Hill, as well as Cemetery Hill itself. Even farther to the left, II Corps, under Hancock's command, was to extend the defensive line southward down the upper half of Cemetery Ridge. The III Corps, under the command of Major General Daniel Sickles, was then to extend the line farther southward down Cemetery Ridge to the heights now known as Little Round Top. The V Corps and, upon its arrival, the VI Corps were initially to be held in reserve behind Cemetery Ridge.[1]

Little Round Top in 2014

Photo courtesy of Tom Vossler

As noted in the previous chapter, early on the morning of July 2, Robert E. Lee ordered General James Longstreet to move the two divisions of his corps then present on the field to attack positions on the south end of Seminary Ridge and prepare to conduct an attack that he hoped would envelope the southern end (left flank) of the Union line on Cemetery Ridge. Lee wanted this attack to begin as soon as Longstreet could get his troops into their attack positions, but Longstreet moved slowly. His forces were not in position until around 4 p.m. that day and conditions had changed markedly on the Union side, exactly as Lee had feared.

On the Union side General Daniel Sickles's III Corps did not occupy the southern end of the Cemetery Ridge line as General Meade had ordered. Instead, around midday Sickles decided to move his corps of 10,000 men three-quarters of a mile forward of the assigned line and occupy what he believed was better terrain along the Emmitsburg Road centered on the Peach Orchard. Although Sickles had sought permission from General Meade to make adjustments to his line, the

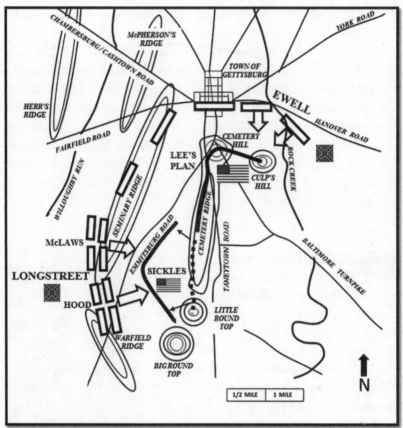

MAP 6.0 Confederate attack as it was conducted on the second day of the battle.

commanding general never granted it. But Sickles did so anyway, and the changes he made were a major shift in positioning of the left end of the Union defensive line. This created a bulge, or salient, in the Union line and a gap between Sickles's northernmost unit and the II Corps to his right along Cemetery Ridge.

General George Meade soon learned of Sickles's unauthorized movement forward and rode out to meet with Sickles near the Peach Orchard. A brief verbal confrontation ensued as Meade realized that the entire Union position was now threatened. Meade also realized it was too late to rectify the situation and, as he departed the meeting with Sickles, promised him reinforcements. Among the additional units ordered by Meade to support Sickles were a four-brigade division from II Corps and a three-brigade division from V Corps.

As Meade rode out to meet with Sickles, he directed Brigadier General Gouverneur Warren, his chief engineering officer, to conduct a reconnaissance of Little Round Top—a prominent hill on the southern end of the federal line. Upon his arrival there, Warren reconfirmed that this hill was critical to the overall Union defense, but that in his move forward of his assigned line Sickles left no troops there to defend it. Warren dispatched a courier with a message urging that reinforcements be sent immediately to defend Little Round Top from advancing Confederate forces.

Colonel Strong Vincent, USA

LEADERSHIP MOMENT You are now Colonel Strong Vincent, a brigade commander in General James Barnes's division of the Union V Corps. Your orders are to move your 1,300 troops forward to reinforce Sickles's troops that are decisively engaged in the Wheatfield and Peach Orchard. The route of march takes your troops past the northern end of Little Round Top. As you are moving forward, you encounter a courier dispatched by Brigadier General Warren. The courier is looking for General Barnes, your division commander, with a request to move troops immediately to Little Round Top. There are no federal troops on the hill, and Confederate forces are rapidly advancing toward it. But no one can find Barnes, and Warren is a staff officer with no command authority over you and your men. What should you do?

WHAT CAN WE LEARN FROM THIS VIGNETTE ABOUT LEADERSHIP?

Making critical decisions. Vincent faced an enormous leadership challenge. His orders were very clear—move his brigade forward into the Wheatfield in support of the III Union Corps. But after learning

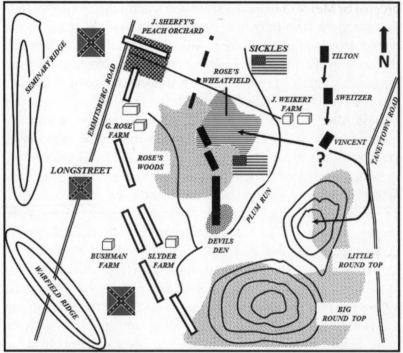

Map 6.1 Decision point for Colonel Vincent. Should he take his brigade to The Wheatfield Or to Little Round Top?

of the situation on Little Round Top, he quickly realized that this hill was critical terrain. It anchored the southern end of the Union line. If the Rebels captured it, the Union army's position on Cemetery Ridge would be compromised. Warren had no command authority over him or his men, but Vincent knew and respected him. He quickly led his brigade out of line of march to the Wheatfield and marched instead to the east side of Little Round Top, where they took an old logging trail to climb to the top of the hill.

This raises a fundamental question: How do leaders go about making critical decisions for their organization? Malcolm Gladwell in his book *Blink* argues that decisions leaders make quickly are often as good as, or even better than, those they agonize over. Gladwell underscores, however, the special value Western culture in particular places on complex, analytical decision-making approaches. Unfortunately, this method is frequently time-consuming and may be inappropriate during periods of rapid change or crisis. As a result, Gladwell argued that successful organizations must develop more decentralized decision-making processes and support the power of intuition from its experts particularly at difficult moments.[2]

Air Force Colonel (retired) John Boyd in many ways mirrored many of Gladwell's arguments. Boyd had been a fighter pilot during the Korean War, and upon his return to the United States was assigned to the US Air Force Weapons School to train future pilots. Over time he became the head of the Academic Section and developed tactics for aerial combat as well as theories for improved pilot training. Boyd later became a consultant to many large corporations and adviser to the Department of Defense upon his retirement from the Air Force.

His most celebrated concept was the OODA loop, which is the cycle of *observe, orient, decide,* and *act.* Boyd argued that all decision-making occurs in a recurring succession of observing the environment in which an individual or organization is operating, orienting on the decision-maker's mental state and key changes that are occurring in the environment, making a decision in a more timely fashion than an adversary or the competition, and acting on that decision. The OODA loop provides leaders both a framework for developing leadership within their organizations and their own decision-making methodology, particularly during difficult moments.

Clearly time is the key variable, since the OODA loop is designed to allow any entity (individual or organization) to "get inside" their opposition's decision cycle and gain comparative advantage. It requires an ability to operate at a faster tempo. Proponents of the OODA loop argue that it provides a means for organizational agility to triumph over raw power. This approach to decision-making seeks to generate disorder and confusion in opponents so that they are reacting to situations as opposed to acting upon them. That's why Boyd argued that effective organizations must develop a climate that encourages objective-driven choice, or "directive control," as opposed to "method-driven control." This allows the abilities and mental capacities of the team to be maximized. But this further requires leaders to encourage decentralization in their organizations and accept a certain level of chaos if they are going to use the OODA loop effectively.

Colonel Strong Vincent could have theoretically been court-martialed for violating his orders, though we will never know if that was a real danger since he was killed in the defense of Little Round Top. But he clearly observed the situation, oriented on the critical importance of the hill, quickly decided, and acted in a timely fashion. He was able to make his decision "inside the decision cycle" of the advancing Confederates. Many have argued that his fateful decision demonstrated "disciplined disobedience" by a leader who consciously violated what he had been directed to do by his boss because he was convinced it was best for the overall organization at a critical juncture.

Power of informal relationships and personal authority. "Power" is sometimes described as the ability to influence. Oftentimes the "personal power" of a person in an organization far exceeds their "positional power." Positional power is the authority or influence that an individual derives from their relative location in the organizational hierarchy. In very simplistic terms, those above have authority over me and those below normally receive their guidance from me.

"Personal power" is different and developed over time. People in an organization tacitly or actively acknowledge those who by their knowledge, competence, experience, and demonstrated performance are high performers. Members of the team come to trust them over time and seek their advice on routine or even complex tasks. They are frequently seen as wise, skilled, and ethical.

It is reasonable to believe that Warren's "personal authority" influenced Vincent's decision. As previously suggested, Brigadier General Warren was the senior engineering staff officer to General Meade as commander of the Army of the Potomac. Warren had been in his position since early March 1863 and had advised Meade's predecessor. A critical aspect of his duties was to advise the Union commander on the best use of terrain, which is why Meade directed him to conduct a personal reconnaissance of Little Round Top. As a staff officer, however, he had no real positional power or authority over anyone with the exception of a couple of lieutenants. He was simply a senior adviser, but highly respected throughout the Union army both for his engineering skills and his time as a former infantry brigade commander in the V Corps. Vincent knew of Warren because they both had previously served as commanders in the V Corps, Warren a brigade commander, Vincent a regimental commander. Although they served in different divisions of the V Corps, they certainly would have been aware of each other, and it does seem clear that Vincent thought well of him. This was likely key in his decision to disobey his orders and follow Warren's advice at a critical moment.

Initiative. "Initiative" is defined as the ability to assess a situation and take action independently without clear direction. It is a person's willingness to not only get things accomplished but also to take responsibility. This requires a leader's willingness to accept risk and acknowledge that subordinates may make errors while demonstrating initiative.

Dean Smith was the head basketball coach of the University of North Carolina at Chapel Hill for over thirty-six years and called a "coaching legend" by the Basketball Hall of Fame at his induction. He was once asked, "What do you look for in basketball players? People who can read defenses? Shoot? Rebound?" Smith replied that he could teach all those things, so he looked for people who were "fast because I don't know how to teach that." This is a metaphor for the challenge facing contemporary leaders when trying to develop initiative in their team. How do you teach this critical concept? Effective leaders must be conscious of this requirement during the hiring process and seek to create a "climate of initiative" within their organization. This requires a willingness to accept risk and the fact that subordinates may make errors.

Initiative was clearly demonstrated on another battlefield nearly one hundred years after Gettysburg that was critical to success. On the morning of December 7, 1941, Lieutenant Commander Francis J. Thomas was the senior officer aboard the battleship, USS *Nevada.* Thomas was a reserve officer in the US Navy and had been a member of the *Nevada* crew for less than one year. The ship's captain and other senior members of its leadership had gone ashore on a Saturday evening as the *Nevada* had only just returned on the afternoon of December 5 from a long period at sea.

As the Japanese began their attack, Thomas was below deck, as his primary duties aboard the ship were as damage control officer. The attack had only gone on for a few minutes when the *Nevada* was struck by a Japanese torpedo. Fortunately, a young ensign immediately ordered counter-flooding to prevent the ship from capsizing. Thomas made his way to the bridge, assumed command, and took initiative to get the ship underway. He hoped to get the *Nevada* to open sea where it could better defend itself. As the battleship began slowly moving down the channel, it became the focus for the second wave of attacking Japanese aircraft, which had just arrived over Pearl Harbor. The *Nevada* suffered several additional crippling hits, and there were eleven fires burning out of control at various locations throughout the ship. Thomas demonstrated initiative a second time and ordered the ship beached in order to avoid blocking the entrance to the harbor.

Malcolm Gladwell in his book *The Tipping Point* describes the importance of individual action with his "Law of the Few."[3] Gladwell argues that a few people or even an individual at a critical point can make all the difference in terms of success or failure for an organization. This was true for Lieutenant Commander Thomas and the *Nevada* crew in a number of ways. Unfortunately, they had been unable to get their ship to open water but had made an additional critical decision to beach the ship prior to its sinking and blocking the main channel to enter Pearl Harbor. Had this blockage occurred, it would have complicated recovery and resupply operations enormously.

In addition, there was 6.5 million barrels of oil stored in fifty unprotected fuel storage tanks near Pearl Harbor. These were referred to as "tank farms" and consisted of roughly two and half years of oil supplies for the American Pacific fleet. Many on the fleet staff thought these fuel reserves were vulnerable to sabotage or enemy attack and constituted the single greatest weakness to the fleet after it was moved from California to Hawaii in 1940.

Japanese pilots who participated in the attack and survived the war were later asked why the second wave did not strike these targets. The Japanese replied that they were supposed to be hit and were on every pilot's target list. Pilots in the second wave had been instructed, however, to hit the fuel tanks last, because the black smoke that would be created would obscure all other targets. But they all became distracted trying to sink the lone American battleship (the *Nevada*) as it attempted to flee the harbor. They hoped that sinking it might block the channel. Some analysts have suggested that had the destruction of the tank farms occurred, it might have taken two full years to restore the millions of barrels of fuel as well as to rebuild sufficient storage capacity in Hawaii. The loss of this fuel on December 7, 1941, might well have prolonged the war in the Pacific, resulting in thousands of additional casualties. The initiative shown by Thomas and other members of his crew likely had a greater effect than they could have ever imagined.

It can be argued that the entire battle of Gettysburg, at least for the first two days, may have come down to two leaders (Ewell and Vincent), two hills, two decisions, and two men's initiative. As previously described, Confederate General Richard Ewell received a message from Robert E. Lee on the afternoon of July 1 telling him to pursue the retreating Union forces through Gettysburg and seize the high ground—Culp's Hill and Cemetery Ridge. Ewell decided not to exercise initiative and do so. The following day Colonel Strong Vincent, a Union brigade commander, intercepted a message intended for his division commander written by Brigadier General Warren requesting troops be dispatched to Little Round Top. Vincent quickly assessed the situation and decided to set aside the previous orders he had received to advance in support of the Union III Corps. Instead he moved his brigade to Little Round Top and prevented the Confederates from capturing this key terrain. Had Southern troops captured Little Round Top, it would have compromised Union lines and likely resulted in a Rebel victory at Gettysburg. There would not have been a third day.

There are numerous reasons why each man made the decisions that he did. Both were experienced officers. Ewell had been a division commander and had been in command of his corps for a brief time. Vincent had assumed command of a regiment in June 1862 and saw action at the Battle of Fredericksburg in December. He had been promoted to brigade commander roughly six weeks before Gettysburg. Each man had seen combat in the previous two years of the war. Ewell had been a professional soldier prior to the war, whereas Vincent had been an attorney. Part of the answer to this question may not reside solely with the individual leader but rather with the climate in which Ewell and Vincent had been developed and now served. Consequently, leaders must be aware and understand that their actions on a daily basis either serve to encourage or discourage a climate of initiative in those they are leading. They need to ask themselves the question: "Are we developing Richard Ewells on our team or Strong Vincents?"

CHAPTER 7

"Fix Bayonets!"

The infantry brigade Colonel Vincent brought to the summit of Little Round Top consisted of 1,336 men in four regiments: the 20th Maine, the 83rd Pennsylvania, the 44th New York, and the 16th Michigan. All were volunteer veteran units that saw combat in previous major battles of the war. All but the 20th Maine entered military service at the start of the war in 1861. At Gettysburg the 83rd Pennsylvania—295 men—was commanded by Captain Orpheus Saeger Woodward, a schoolteacher from Harbor Creek, Pennsylvania. The 44th New York—391 men— was commanded by Colonel James C. Rice, a lawyer from New York City. The 16th Michigan—263 men—was commanded by Lieutenant Colonel Norval E. Welch, former private secretary to Michigan Senator Lewis Cass.[1]

The 20th Maine and its commander, Colonel Joshua Lawrence Chamberlain, are our focus in this chapter. At its inception, the 965 men of the 20th Maine Volunteer Infantry Regiment came into federal service on August 29, 1862. They were among President Lincoln's last call for 300,000 more volunteers in July of that year. After the war, the adjutant general of Maine wrote that of the totality of volunteer soldiers from that state, 85 percent were New England natives, the rest overwhelmingly of English, Scotch, and Irish origins. A third of Maine's volunteer soldiers were farmers, and nearly 30 percent worked in the lumber industry. Native Mainer, World War II combat veteran, and

20th Maine historian John Pullen wrote of the rural men that made up the 20th Maine:

> *With so few men from the cities and larger towns, the 20th Maine probably was composed of an even larger percentage of native stock, with farming, fishing and lumbering predominating among the occupations.*[2]

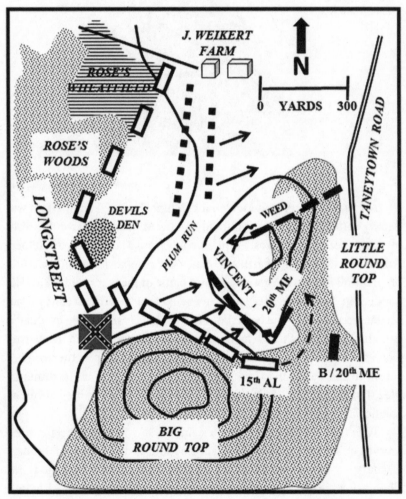

Map 7.0 Vincent's brigade defends Little Round Top

USAMHI

*Colonel Joshua L.
Chamberlain, USA*

At the war's inception Lieutenant Colonel Joshua Chamberlain was deputy commander of the regiment to a twenty-seven-year-old former merchant seaman and West Point graduate from Maine named Adelbert Ames. As a lieutenant of artillery, Ames saw combat action in the battle of First Bull Run—the first major land battle of the war in July 1861. His conduct in that battle later led to his being awarded the Congressional Medal, precursor to the Medal of Honor, for refusing to be evacuated from his guns even though he was seriously wounded. Upon recovering from his wounds and returning to active duty he saw further combat action in the Peninsula Campaign in Virginia during the summer of 1862. On August 20, 1862, the governor of Maine appointed Ames as colonel, 20th Maine Volunteer Infantry Regiment.[3]

Together, Ames and Chamberlain led the 20th Maine for nine months prior to Gettysburg, seeing action in the battle of Fredericksburg in December 1862, where they were heavily engaged and Chancellorsville in May 1863, where they saw lighter conflict. Although seven years Chamberlain's junior, Ames, having the advantage of a formal military education, served as a mentor to Chamberlain, passing on to him the leadership and tactical skills necessary to become a successful commander. Chamberlain was a "quick study" and learned his lessons well.

In the reorganization of the Army of the Potomac following the disastrous defeat at Chancellorsville, Colonel Ames was promoted to the rank of brigadier general on May 20, 1863, and given command of a brigade in the XI Corps. On the same day, Lieutenant Colonel Joshua Chamberlain was promoted to full colonel and filled the vacancy as commander of the 20th Maine Volunteer Infantry Regiment.

Apart from a very brief time as a youth in a private military school in Brewer, Maine, Chamberlain had no formal military education other than the knowledge informally passed on to him by his mentor Ames. By occupation he was a liberal arts professor at Bowdoin College in Brunswick, Maine, teaching rhetoric and foreign languages. His biographer, Alice Rains Trulock, wrote that Chamberlain's study as both student and professor allowed him to master nine languages other than English in only a few years.[4] This included Latin, Greek, French, and German. Suffice it to say, Joshua Chamberlain was a learned, intelligent man.

Chamberlain sat out the first year of the war while fulfilling his teaching responsibilities. But with President Lincoln's call for additional volunteer troops in early July 1862, many of his students set aside their studies to enlist in the army. It appears Chamberlain realized that it was past time for him to get into the fight as well.

On July 14, 1862, he wrote a letter to "His Excellency Governor Washburn" seeking a position in one of the Maine volunteer regiments then being recruited. Governor Israel Washburn subsequently offered Chamberlain the title of colonel and command of the 20th Maine. It is a testimony to Chamberlain's character that he turned down the offer in favor of starting out at a lower rank in order to, in his words, "learn the business first." On August 8, Chamberlain was appointed lieutenant colonel and on August 18 he reported for duty as the deputy commander of the 20th Maine at Camp Mason, near Portland, Maine.[5]

....

LEADERSHIP MOMENT Let's fast-forward eleven months to July 2, 1863. You are now Union Colonel Joshua Chamberlain, commander of the 20th Maine Regiment. Your regiment is part of Colonel Strong Vincent's brigade. Vincent positioned your unit on the southern end of the line that he established on Little Round Top. You are the last unit on the left end of a three-and-a-half-mile Union battlefield. Vincent tells you, "Colonel, your unit is the end of the Union line. You must hold this position at all hazards."[6] You realize this means your soldiers have to fight to the last man. Almost immediately upon your arrival on Little Round Top the Confederates begin their attack against the position. Your troops have held, but the Confederates have continued repeated assault. Your troops are now both exhausted and nearly out of ammunition. Many have been killed or wounded, and you are uncertain if they can continue to fight. You peer down the hill and see that the Confederates are preparing one more assault. What should you do?

....

WHAT CAN WE LEARN FROM THIS VIGNETTE ABOUT LEADERSHIP?

Out-of-the-box thinking. Chamberlain obviously had two clear options. He could abandon the hill and retreat, or he could stay in place but risk being overrun and defeated. The first was contrary to the orders given him by his commander, Colonel Vincent, who, unbeknownst to Chamberlain, had been mortally wounded on the opposite end of the brigade line. Sadly, Vincent would die the following day. The second was the option no leader wishes to confront—do I sacrifice my team to accomplish the mission?

Control of Little Round Top was critical to the maintenance of the Union line along Cemetery Ridge. But there was another reason that made defense of the hill critical. Roughly one mile northeast of Chamberlain's position was the Union army's reserve artillery park that held the ammunition reserve of seventy wagons, from which 19,000 rounds of artillery ammunition were issued during the second and third day of the battle.[7] If the Confederates had swept over Little Round Top and captured or destroyed this vital ammunition resupply on July 2, there would have been no artillery ammunition to support the Yankee army for a third day at Gettysburg.

Chamberlain determined there was another possible alternative. He turned to his men and ordered them to "fix bayonets" and charge down the hill to break up the Confederate attack. This was obviously *out-of-the-box thinking*, and his men may have been a bit stunned by the order— "You mean charge?" But they followed his orders, charged, broke up the Confederate attack, and ensured that the Union continued to control Little Round Top. There would be a third day at Gettysburg.

Curiously his success may have been due to Chamberlain's *emotional intelligence (EQ)* even though this concept was not even discussed until the twentieth century. EQ is largely associated with the research of Dr. Daniel Goleman of Yale University. It has to do with a leader's ability to understand their own feelings, display empathy for others, and control their emotions particularly during difficult moments. Goleman further describes EQ into five domains: (1) knowing one's emotions, or self-awareness, (2) managing emotions, (3) motivating oneself, (4) recognizing emotions in others, and (5) handling relationships often described as "empathy."[8] It is both introspective and focused on personal competence, allowing us to recognize certain tendencies and behaviors that can help move us forward. EQ also emphasizes social competence or a leader's ability not only to manage critical relationships but also to recognize how the environment can influence behavior. It does appear that Chamberlain was able to manage his emotions and remain relatively calm at that critical moment, despite the enormous strain of the battlefield, and motivate himself. He also was aware of the condition of his men and his responsibilities to them.

But Chamberlain's success at this critical moment and his emotional intelligence may have been even more clearly demonstrated a few days before the fighting on Little Round Top. Prior to the battle, on May 23, Chamberlain and his regiment were encamped when a Union Provost Guard (nineteenth century military police) arrived with around one hundred soldiers from the 2nd Maine Regiment who were prisoners.[9] These soldiers had refused to continue to fight and, in essence, mutinied, though they had apparently not committed any overt acts of violence. Most of the soldiers assigned to the 2nd Maine were heading home after having completed their two-year enlistment. These men, however, had enlisted for three years. Still they argued that they had only enlisted to fight under the 2nd Maine flag, and if the flag returned to Maine, then they should accompany it. Unfortunately, by law, they owed the Union army an additional year of service. With the 2nd Maine regiment disestablished; these men were turned over to Chamberlain only because his regiment was the closest Maine regiment to their former camp.

Chamberlain was informed by the commander of the provost guard that he could shoot the "mutineers" if he wished. Fortunately, Chamberlain had been born and raised in a town near Bangor, where these men first enlisted. They were essentially Chamberlain's neighbors. He listened to their demands and ensured they were provided both food and water. After a time, Chamberlain wisely distributed the 2nd Maine veterans to fill shortages in all the 20th Maine's companies. He also told them that he would write the governor, which he did after the battle, about the confusion surrounding their enlistments. All but three of the former 2nd Maine soldiers joined the ranks of the 20th Maine and fought at Little Round Top. Chamberlain had fulfilled several aspects of EQ. He had controlled his own emotions at a very difficult moment for a leader and demonstrated empathy for "new" members of his team.

Initially 1,000 men had initially been recruited as members of the 20th Maine. By the spring of 1863, however, that number had fallen to less than 300. The addition of the 2nd Maine soldiers to their ranks raised the regiment's strength to 386 as they arrived at Little Round Top. If Chamberlain had been unable (or unwilling) to elicit these soldier's willingness to fight he would have had to guard them. This would have been a further loss of manpower for his already depleted force. But his successful use of key aspects of EQ resulted in veteran reinforcements for his unit and was likely critical to the regiment's ability to successfully defend Little Round Top.

Some experts have suggested that EQ is the single biggest predictor of performance in the workplace as well as the strongest driver of leadership and personal excellence. Goleman has argued that his studies of outstanding performers in hundreds of organizations show that about two-thirds of the abilities that set apart star performers from the rest are based on emotional intelligence. He firmly believes that only one-third of the skills that matter relate to raw intelligence and technical expertise.

This is critical for contemporary leaders. According to one of the largest executive recruiting firms, 89 percent of executives have blind spots about themselves. Forty percent have strengths they are unaware of or are not using fully. Central to emotional health is self-awareness, the ability to grasp clearly and without self-recrimination your strengths and weaknesses. Obviously, emotional intelligence could be invaluable in closing this gap. As a result, several major American universities, including Dartmouth, Yale, and Notre Dame, have now adopted an EQ diagnostic for incoming students particularly in their business schools, as they believe it may be a better indicator of student success than IQ.

Leaders should also be aware that there are specific actions an individual can take to improve their emotional intelligence. These include the following:

- Work on social skills, or how you react/interact in social settings.
- Try to show real interest in others, and focus on them, when involved in a discussion.
- Develop both critical thinking and listening skills.
- Resist your typical "defense" mechanisms, which normally means restraining your emotions.
- Train to calm yourself when stressed.
- Let reason triumph over emotion.
- Sleep it off.
- Run it off, as exercise can be a useful antidote to stress.
- Never make an important personal or professional decision when angry.

The continued importance of time—when you make a decision—can be as important as the decision you make. Lee ordered the attack by Longstreet at roughly 8:00 on the morning of July 2, but the Confederates did not begin their attack until late afternoon for a number of reasons and individual failures previously mentioned. But if at any time throughout that day the Confederates had accelerated their schedule by thirty minutes, Vincent's Brigade, which included Chamberlain's regiment, would not have arrived on Little Round Top in time to deny the Rebels control of the hill.

Once again "time" was a critical resource that was not managed effectively on the Confederate side but was managed successfully on the Union side. Successful leaders know that *when* they make a decision is often as important—if not more important—than the decision itself. Not making a choice or deferring a decision is always an option, but it may also mean that an opportunity will be missed.

If you have your choice between being lucky or good, always pick lucky. Upon arriving on Little Round Top, Chamberlain ordered B Company, commanded by Captain Walter Morrill, to move his men to his left into the vulnerable small, narrow valley, which separates Little Round Top from the adjacent Big Round Top. Chamberlain further empowered Morrill to act as the situation might dictate to protect the exposed left flank of the 20th Maine.[10] Chamberlain's concern was that the Confederates would seize Big Round Top in order to envelop his flank. Rebel forces did advance up the western slopes of Big Round Top and then advanced down the northern slope toward the 20th Maine's position. Fortunately, Captain Morrill's men were in position behind a stone wall two hundred yards to the left and rear of the 20th Maine position defending the regiment's left flank from Confederate attack. Morrill's men began firing into the flanks and rear of the 15th Alabama Infantry Regiment that was spearheading the Confederate assault at just about the time Chamberlain began his charge down the hill. Morrill's company had also been joined by some Union sharpshooters who had retreated from Devil's Den, which added to their firepower.

Former Alabama attorney Colonel William C. Oates was the commander of the 15th Alabama regiment that had conducted the attack against the 20th Maine position. Oates recognized that his unit was confronted by a counterattack by the 20th Maine while also receiving fire from a "unit of unknown size" on his flank and rear. He would later say that the surprise fire by Morrill's men panicked his troops at that critical moment. Oates and his 15th Alabama Regiment were forced to withdraw, and the 20th Maine had prevailed.

USAMHI

*Colonel William
C. Oates, CSA*

Chamberlain had clearly been very lucky. The basis for his "luck," however, began with him empowering Captain Morrill to make decisions that could potentially have a critical impact on the entire organization. Fortunately, Morrill and his men remained in their designated position and denied the Confederates the possibility of enveloping the 20th Maine line. Otherwise, the Confederates might have not only been able to withstand the desperate attack by the 20th Maine but also sent a deadly counterattack that would have allowed them to take the hill. But Captain Morrill understood his boss's vision as to what needed to happen and fulfilled his responsibilities.

All leaders want their organizations to be lucky, particularly at critical moments. One wise sage observed, "Luck is when preparation meets opportunity." Chamberlain's men were experienced veterans of numerous campaigns and recently had been reinforced by the arrival of other veteran soldiers from the 2nd Maine. They were well-trained and led by good junior officers and noncommissioned officers (NCOs). Many members of the 20th Maine believed Captain Morrill to be perhaps the best officer in the entire regiment. In giving Morrill this special directive, perhaps Chamberlain thought so as well. It also appears that Morrill felt empowered to act when he saw an opportunity or critical moment for the organization. Success on the afternoon of July 2 may have actually been because "preparation had met opportunity."

Keep the first thing…the first thing. Peter Drucker, the famous leadership expert, once observed that effective leaders delegate many things and certainly Chamberlain had to do that in leading his regiment on this fateful day. All leaders must delegate, or they run the risk of being buried in trivia and being labeled a "micromanager." But Drucker argued that successful leaders do not delegate those things that only they can do and must do. They must focus on the *first things*—the decisions and tasks that will make a critical difference, the one thing that sets standards, or the one thing they want to be remembered for. They know *they* must do it. Chamberlain realized that at a critical moment for his organization on a fateful afternoon on Little Round Top, as he ordered and led the bayonet charge. It was a critical choice, and Chamberlain knew it could not be delegated—only he could do it.

Courage. Chamberlain showed enormous courage in leading the bayonet attack. Few executives will ever be placed in this position, but often the bigger challenge facing contemporary leaders will be issues of "moral" as opposed to "physical" courage. Moral courage has been described as having the intention to engage in moral or ethical actions in the course of doing your job. Professional moral courage requires leaders to act, despite potential adverse consequences, and resist the temptation of "easier" choices that are morally problematic.

Modern leaders often face moral dilemmas that will test their courage. Such "tests" are often more difficult to discern or analyze than events that require physical courage. In 2015 public schools in Atlanta, Georgia, were thrown into chaos in one of the largest scandals in the history of American public education. It was discovered that teachers and principals throughout the school district had conspired to cheat on state-administered student standardized tests beginning in 2009. Prosecutors argued teachers were forced to change incorrect answers on the standardized tests and students were also allowed to fix their responses during the actual conduct of examinations. The superintendent and thirty-four educators were indicted. Eleven were convicted of racketeering and other charges for allegedly facilitating a massive cheating operation on the standardized tests.

Many observers saw this as a moral dilemma. The 2001 No Child Left Behind Act mandated the use of high-stakes student testing to hold educators accountable for student progress. Many of the teachers involved in the scandal argued that inordinate pressure was being placed on them to meet targets set by the district and they faced negative evaluations or even losing their jobs if their students failed to meet the goals established. Funding for schools was also tied to student performance, so some may have believed that their actions had "helped" their students. The courage of key leaders in the organization had been tested. They had determined that the ends justified the means. In so doing they failed a moral challenge.

Chamberlain survived Gettysburg but was badly wounded during the siege of Petersburg, Virginia, in the fall of 1864. He was shot through both hips while leading his brigade in an attack, and it was believed he would die. Promoted to brigadier general on his supposed "death bed," he ultimately recovered from his wounds, but they continued to plague him for the remaining fifty years of his life. He subsequently commanded a brigade in the pursuit of the Army of Northern Virginia after Robert E. Lee abandoned Richmond. Following Lee's surrender at Appomattox Court House, Virginia, on April 9, 1865, General Grant selected Chamberlain to be the commander of troops for Union forces during the formal surrender of Lee's army.

That fateful day came three days later on April 12. The terms of the surrender required Confederate commanders to march their troops into the center of the village, stack their individual weapons, turn over their battle flags, and give up their remaining ammunition and artillery. General Lee appointed General John B. Gordon, also of Gettysburg fame, to command the Rebel forces. Chamberlain positioned Union troops on both sides of the road that the Confederates would use for this solemn occasion. As the Rebel column led by Gordon approached, Chamberlain called the Union soldiers to attention and "carry arms" as a salute to the Southerners who the day before had been their enemy and now were fellow countrymen once again. General Gordon appeared surprised at this demonstration of respect and responded with a salute using his saber. Chamberlain returned Gordon's salute and recounted this moment in his book *The Passing of the Armies*:

The momentous meaning of this occasion impressed me deeply. I resolved to mark it by some token of recognition, which could be no other than a salute of arms. Well aware of the responsibility assumed, and the criticism that would follow, as the sequel proved, nothing of that kind could move me in the least....My main reason, however, was one for which I sought no authority nor asked forgiveness. Before us in proud humiliation stood the embodiment of manhood: men whom neither toils and suffering, nor the fact of death, nor disaster, nor hopelessness could bend from their resolve. Was not such manhood to be welcomed back into a Union so tested and assured?[11]

This event further illustrates Chamberlain's emotional intelligence and ability to have understanding and empathy for others. It also is a clear expression of moral courage. Chamberlain's prediction was correct, and "criticism would follow." Many Northern politicians called for his court-martial for this act, and the award of the Medal of Honor for his courage at Gettysburg would be held up until 1893. It's worth remembering that courage isn't action in the absence of fear; rather it's action in the face of it. Ernest Hemingway once observed that in the end "courage is grace under pressure."

CHAPTER 8

"Tell Me About Your Troops…"

In what Confederate General James Longstreet later called "the best three hours fighting ever done by any troops on any battlefield,"[1] his two attacking infantry divisions had some success on July 2 against the left end of the Union defensive line. Despite his esteem for the work his troops had accomplished, it still had not been decisive. Longstreet's troops captured the Peach Orchard and Devil's Den as well as part of the Wheatfield, but they failed to seize Little Round Top and were unable to outflank the left of the Union army as a result. The attack by Ewell's Confederate troops against the Union right was too little, too late and ineffective. Lee returned to his headquarters dejected over what he believed has been poor coordination by his subordinates. After the war, Major Walter D. Taylor, Lee's assistant adjutant general, wrote of the fighting on July 2:

> *The whole affair was disjointed. There was an utter absence of accord in the movements of several commands, and no decisive results attended the operations of the second day.*[2]

And so, the battle had a third day.

The night before the soldiers would once again pick up their arms, General Meade returned to his headquarters near the center of his three-and-one-half-mile-long defensive line on Cemetery Ridge to determine what the Union army should do. At 8:00 p.m. July 2, Meade sent a telegraph message to General-in-Chief Halleck in Washington

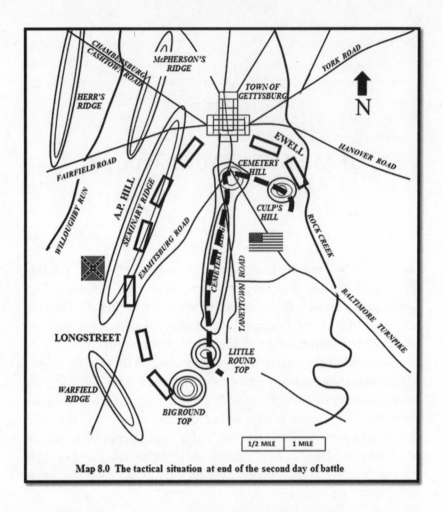

Map 8.0 The tactical situation at end of the second day of battle

in which he summarized the events of the day. Union forces had successfully defended against the Confederate attacks, and he ended the message with the following words:

> *I shall remain in my present position tomorrow, but am not prepared to say, until better advised of the condition of the army, whether my operations will be of an offensive or defensive character.*[3]

LEADERSHIP MOMENT   All leaders go through a process that they develop consciously or unconsciously when they make important decisions. Their analysis often considers key factors and consultations with experts and key subordinates. This all occurs under the pressure of time. You are now General George Gordon Meade, commander of the Army of the Potomac. You have a monumental decision to make on what your army will do on July 3. Victory or defeat in this battle and the fate of your nation may well hang in the balance. What is the process you will use to determine the condition of your army and what it will do on a third day at Gettysburg?

WHAT CAN WE LEARN FROM THIS VIGNETTE ABOUT LEADERSHIP?

Group decision-making. Our definition of leadership from the onset underscored the need to "get people to want to do it." This is frequently referred to as "buy-in" and is essential to getting maximum output from all team members. The two leaders (Meade and Lee) adopted very different decision-making approaches on that evening—a critical juncture. We previously examined Lee's efforts to get buy-in from his most trusted subordinate. Now let's consider how his opponent attempted to do that with his entire leadership team.

In this case, Meade decided the quickest and surest way to get the information he needed to make the decision was to convene a "council of war," an event not at all unusual during the American Civil War. Many of them are recorded in the official records of the war. Sometime after sending his message to Halleck in the early evening, Meade summoned his seven corps commanders, his chief of staff, his chief engineer, and two other senior leaders at his small, rustic farmhouse headquarters in the widow Leister's house on the east side of Cemetery Ridge.[4] He first inquired about the state of their units—how many casualties had they suffered? Did they have sufficient ammunition and supplies? What was the state of morale of the troops? Brigadier General John Gibbon attended the meeting. He commanded an infantry division in

USAMHI

General Meade's July 2nd Council of War

the Union II Corps, positioned in the center of the Union defensive line. He was the junior member of the "council of war," and he later described this critical meeting:

> *The discussion was at first very informal and in the shape of conversation, during which each one made comments on the fight and told what he knew of the condition of affairs…. General Meade himself said very little, except now and then to make some comment, but I cannot recall that he expressed any decided opinion upon any point, preferring apparently to listen to the conversation.*[5]

According to Gibbon, Chief of Staff, Brigadier General Daniel Butterfield, grew impatient with the length of the discussions. Consequently, Butterfield posed three possible courses of action for the Union army on July 3 for the group to consider. Butterfield's notes on the three courses of actions discussed during the council of war are recorded in the official records.[6]

1. Under existing conditions, is it advisable for this army to remain in its present position, or should it move back closer to its base of supplies?
2. If our forces stay here, should we be the aggressor or wait for the attack of the enemy?
3. If we choose the latter option, how long do we wait?

The group discussed these questions at length, but as time went on, Butterfield became increasingly impatient. He urged that a vote be taken to force the decision. This was done, but the votes were cast in reverse order of seniority in order to ensure the most junior officer was not in any way influenced by the vote of those senior to him. Brigadier John Gibbon, a one-star general, was the first to vote. The vote resulted in a unanimous agreement by the commanders that the federal army continue to defend its present position and see what the Confederates would attempt to do the next day.

Meade did not state his preference in advance, but there are clear indications that he wanted to stay the course and defend the Union army's position. He and his subordinates now had a shared vision. It is once again instructive to take further note John Gibbon's memories of the meeting:

> [J]ust as the council broke up, Meade said to me, "If Lee attacks tomorrow, it will be in your front." I asked him why he thought so, and he replied, "Because he has made attacks on both our flanks and failed, and if he concludes to try it again, it will be on our center."[7]

Thus, George Meade was inside his adversary's "decision cycle." On the third day at Gettysburg, Robert E. Lee would attempt exactly what George Meade predicted and prepared for.

By using this decision-making process, Meade was able to get "buy-in" from his team. He now had everyone in the same boat, and all of them were "rowing the boat in the same direction." Even those who outranked him were supportive. His chief of staff, however, had realized that only so much time could be used to come to a decision on what the army would take the next day. Time was of the essence, as once the decision was made subordinate leaders had to provide resources and guidance to their units. A leader "manages" the clock for his or her organization. They must decide eventually, and timing is often critically important.

Achieving buy-in was more important for Meade than Lee. It is important to remember that Meade had only been in command of the Union army for five days at this point. He probably felt that he had to seek greater consensus as two of his subordinates, Major Generals Sedgwick and Slocum, outranked him since they were promoted to major general a few months before him. But upon President Lincoln's June 28, 1863, appointment of Meade as commander of the Army of the Potomac, Sedgwick and Slocum both agreed to willingly serve under the command of their junior, as did the other major generals in the room who had the same date of rank as Meade. In many ways, Meade was leading his peer group—one of the greatest of all leadership challenges.

Meanwhile, during the afternoon of July 2, Lee observed the Confederate attack from a vantage point on Seminary Ridge in the company of Ambrose Powell Hill and division commander Henry Heth whose forces were not engaged at that time. Historian Edwin Coddington records that "for the most part he [Lee] sat alone on a stump intently observing the movements of his infantry and artillery through a field glass, anxiously moving from one stump to another to get a better angle of view. According to one observer 'his—Lee's—countenance betrayed no more anxiety than upon the occasion of a general review...' While the battle raged, he sent only one message and received only one report by courier."[8]

After the fighting concluded on July 2, sometime after 11 p.m., Hill arrived back at Lee's headquarters, then located where the Chambersburg Pike/Cashtown Road crossed over the north end of Seminary Ridge. As Hill was arriving, another visitor to Lee was departing. The late-arriving Confederate cavalry commander Jeb Stuart preceded Hill's visit to Lee.

Although the headquarters wagons were positioned on the south side of the road, there is evidence that the widow Thompson's house was taken over for the general's comfort. Lee greeted Hill warmly, and they talked together for a quarter of an hour. This was the nearest Lee came to holding a "council of war" that night.[9]

After the second day's fighting Longstreet did not, as was his custom in previous battles, personally visit with Lee to review events and discuss plans. Instead, he sent a courier with a verbal summation of events. Lee likely preferred this approach that evening. For his part, he probably did not care to listen to Longstreet's predictable opinions and objections, and so did not visit him or summon him to his headquarters.[10] Neither did Ewell put forward a personal appearance with Lee that night, sending a verbal summation of the day's activities via courier.

Historian Stephen W. Sears has this analysis of the situation: "There is no knowing what Longstreet's and Ewell's couriers may have said to Lee about the July 2 fighting, but they were surely poor substitutes for personal accounts delivered by the two generals themselves. It is thus astonishing how little General Lee knew of his own army, of the enemy's army and of the battlefield when he announced that his general battle plan was unchanged and that the attacks would continue."[11]

Because the morale of the army was still superb, because much ground had been taken, because admirable artillery positions had been won and because reinforcements had arrived—Stuart's cavalry and Pickett's I Corps division—Lee determined to renew the battle on the third day.[12]

But his determination was made outside of the situation's reality. He had not reached out to his subordinates for the true capabilities of their commands. He was yet unaware of the extensive casualties experienced by A. P. Hill's and Ewell's men in driving the Yankees back to Cemetery Hill on the first day (over 50 percent casualties in five of their infantry brigades), and he did not have a complete understanding of their logistics. How much ammunition, food, water, and fodder for the horses were available? Furthermore, he had underestimated the capabilities of his adversary. He assumed away the current challenge the Army of the Potomac presented based on his experience during the past year. He did not carefully consider their improvements as a "learning organization" that had new leadership, and the basic fact that the Yankees were now fighting on their "home ground." He also failed to recognize that his style or method of leadership in this battle was not working, given the changes in the leadership environment of two-thirds of his army after Chancellorsville. The two new senior leaders (Hill and Ewell) had not been fully up to the task. The tide was about to turn, and he had no way of knowing it.

Historian Glenn Tucker examines yet another question of "just how clearly Lee had any of his plans in mind at different stages of the battle." In large measure, says Tucker, "Lee was improvising, which is necessary in most battles, but there was a heavy amount of it—on Lee's part—at Gettysburg. Each project would likely depend on the results of the last."[13] In other words, Lee was reacting to his opponent's initiatives while relinquishing his own.

Lee made his decisions on the evening of July 2 in virtual isolation from his confidants. Having already talked with A.P Hill, Lee contented himself late that night with sending orders to Longstreet, Ewell, and General W.N. Pendelton, his chief of artillery, to renew their attack in the morning. But he provided no additional details of where and how it would be done. Thus, the momentum passed to George Meade.

As Meade worked to gain the respect of and lead his "peers," Robert E. Lee was viewed as an "icon" in the eyes of his subordinates. He had been in command for nearly thirteen months by this time and had been very successful. He had gained great renown and respect in the federal army prior to the war and served as the superintendent at West Point. Lee was even offered command of all Union forces at the onset of the war by his old commander and mentor, General Winfield Scott. He had refused Scott's offer based on his loyalty to his home state of Virginia.

While his subordinates considered Lee's history, accomplishments, and status, they struggled with a difficult question on the battlefield that day: how do you tell an icon that you think he is wrong?

Leadership is lonely, but reflection is important. Lee kept his own counsel that evening and did not call his immediate subordinate leaders together, seek their advice, or inquire about the state of their troops. Why did he do that? It appears he was extremely disappointed in his team, and it is likely that based on what had transpired during the previous two days his subordinates were reluctant to voice their views unsolicited. Lee likely believed that Hill and Ewell had let him down on the first day of fighting. Hill had gotten the army fully engaged in battle before they had been able to consolidate—disobeying Lee's specific orders. Longstreet had not moved as quickly as Lee had wanted on July 2, and this may have resulted in the Confederate army's missed opportunity to achieve victory that day. Stuart had been missing for a week.

On the evening of July 2 Lee may have finally realized that his leadership style was no longer working. As previously mentioned, he had used a style that emphasized providing broad guidance and allowing his subordinates maximum flexibility. While this had worked in the past, it had failed over the previous two critical days. Before the third day, he took time for self-assessment and reflection, which is crucially important. While this may seem counterintuitive since leadership is all about relationships, leadership can also be a solitary, lonely experience.

Many experts argue that effective modern leaders must be "thinkers," those who can take time in solitude to consider what should be done and—perhaps more importantly—why.[14] Thinkers who question the routine can formulate new ideas and directions with independence, creativity, and flexibility. Successful leaders today must have the courage to argue for ideas that may not be popular even when they don't immediately please their superiors.

This can only be achieved if the leader takes his or her own counsel but, in the end, comes to a final decision. Many people might think solitude and leadership are contradictions, but solitude in reality is the essence of leadership. No matter how many people the leader consults, he or she is the one who ultimately must have the courage to make a hard decision. Lee had used a style that emphasized guidance, and now he may have believed that he needed to be more assertive. After all, at that moment, all Lee had was himself.

This requires concentration and the ability to focus on one issue long enough to develop an idea about it. Lee had perhaps an enormous advantage over modern leaders in this regard. He was leading his organization prior to the onset of the Information Age. In the nineteenth century it was relatively easy for a leader to find solitude anytime they wanted to concentrate on a problem, as Lee did on the evening of July 2, 1863. Today leaders are saturated continuously with information, questions, and entertainment from a variety of electronic sources. They are *always* connected, even though society did not make a conscious decision to surrender the bulk of its time for reflection in favor of time spent texting, tweeting, and staring at a screen.

It is difficult today—certainly harder than in 1863—but modern leaders need to mark off sixty to ninety minutes daily for "time to think." A leader can make it known that he or she does not text and only checks email periodically—or at a certain point during the workday—and will neither write nor respond to emails on weekends. This approach will not occur without cost. Emails will go unanswered for hours rather than minutes, subordinates might have to wait for meetings with the boss, and other meetings may be postponed. But scheduling a time to think and reflect is *not* a zero-sum game. Fundamentally, a leader must decide whether reflection and hard analytical work are important.

There is a second potential price for a change like this, however. The usual social adherence to traditional organizational processes may be sacrificed to a degree in the name of nonconformity. If a leader does this without explanation, it could lead to the impression that she or he is aloof, arrogant, unapproachable, and uncaring. He or she must make it clear in as much detail as necessary that doing the organization's essential work requires time to think. It may also have ancillary benefits, as it can serve to reinforce a leader's desire to encourage initiative throughout the organization and encourage mid-level leaders to make decisions.

Intuitive vs. informed decisions. It is important to keep in mind that the one thing leaders do that makes them different from everyone else is they get to "decide" and—perhaps more importantly—"decide when they are going to decide." Effective leaders achieve buy-in and make important decisions based on the best possible information they can acquire, thorough analysis, and information processes established in the organization. Such processes must ensure wide-ranging information is gathered, analyzed, and directed to leaders in a timely fashion. This is critical since the leader must make choices within a decision cycle because, again, they manage one of the most critical resources organizations have—time.

Lee was making "intuitive decisions." He relied on his "gut" to determine what course of action the Army of Northern Virginia would pursue on July 3. He neither sought input from his subordinates nor possessed a clear intelligence picture to conduct his analysis. This approach to decision-making had largely served him well in his recent near decisive victories at Chancellorsville and Fredericksburg.

In comparison Meade was making "informed decisions" not based solely on the input provided by his corps commanders, but also from a new system of intelligence gathering/analysis instituted by his predecessor, General "Fighting Joe" Hooker. Hooker assumed command of the Army of the Potomac in January 1863 after the Union army's near catastrophic defeat at Fredericksburg. He quickly realized that he was receiving very little intelligence on the Confederates and largely "fighting blind."

As a result, Hooker recruited Colonel George Henry Sharpe, an attorney from Kingston, New York, who had volunteered for the Union army at the onset of the war to head the new Bureau of Military Intelligence.[15] Sharpe had distinguished himself as a dedicated leader who was both conscientious and efficient. He determined that in order to make good decisions the commander of the Army of the Potomac needed accurate information on the composition and disposition of enemy forces.

Sharpe approached this new task with aggressive precision and refused to base his conclusions on any single source. Consequently, he gathered information from a variety of sources and insisted his subordinates rate the credibility of each source. His men questioned Confederate prisoners, deserters, and the escaped slaves who had made their way to federal lines. Sharpe also recruited spies and sent them South to infiltrate the Confederate army, pored over Southern newspapers, and even analyzed reports provided by "spy" balloons. He was even curious about Southern railroad timetables and the price of flour in Richmond.

Sharpe ran a spy ring known as the "Richmond Underground," led by Elizabeth Van Lew, which operated in the Rebel capital. Van Lew provided food, clothing, and writing material to Union prisoners held in the infamous Libby Prison and aided several in their escape. She gathered information about Confederate troop levels and movements from these prisoners that she sent to the North. Van Lew also recruited clerks from the War and Navy Departments of the Confederacy as well as a Richmond mayoral candidate to gather intelligence for the Union. It is also believed that she convinced Varina Davis, wife of the Confederate president, to hire a servant who, unknowingly, was a member of Van Lew's spy ring.

While not all leaders have access to a "spy ring," contemporary leaders must carefully consider the following questions: Where do I get the information I need in order to make critical decisions? Am I getting it in a timely fashion? Do I have multiple sources of information? How reliable are my sources, and are new ones available as the situation evolves? Are my organization's processes for analyzing data and other information current? Do these efforts provide me an accurate picture of the environment my organization is currently operating in, as well as highlighting impending changes?

By the evening of July 2, Sharpe's men had interviewed Confederate prisoners and accurately determined that Lee had only 15,000 semi-fresh troops—largely George Pickett's division from Virginia—to commit on the third day. He was also able to provide an accurate description of the deployment of most Confederate units on the battlefield. This allowed Meade to have a complete picture not only of his own troops but also the number and morale of Confederate forces arrayed across the field. This may have been key in his decision for the Union army to take a defensive position on July 3, which set the stage for Pickett's Charge. Curiously, Meade was using data and analysis to make "management" decisions about positioning his forces while "listening to the heartbeat" of his organization, as described by his immediate subordinates, in making this crucial choice.

CHAPTER 9

"A Fateful Meeting..."

We introduced you briefly to Confederate cavalry commander Jeb Stuart in Chapter 1. In Chapter 2 you read about Brigadier General John Buford's two Union cavalry brigades fighting dismounted in their delaying action against the attacking infantry of Henry Heth's Confederate division. A few additional words on cavalry operations and on General Stuart are necessary in setting the stage for what follows in this chapter.

The forces on both sides of the battlefield at Gettysburg in July 1863 were similarly organized into units of infantry (marching foot soldiers with rifles); artillery (cannons and their firing crews); and cavalry (horse-mounted soldiers with cavalry carbines, pistols, and sabers). The infantry and artillery of the Civil War era did most of the fighting in battle. The cavalry in the nineteenth-century American model, meanwhile, fought within six basic functions:

1. They could participate directly in the battle, adding combat power to the infantry and artillery.
2. They could perform reconnaissance of local areas, providing information on the terrain, road networks, population centers, and location and movement of enemy forces.
3. They could perform counter-reconnaissance to deny enemy cavalry information on friendly forces and the terrain they occupied.

4. They could delay enemy advances by falling back slowly from point to point, as Buford's men did on the first day of the battle.
5. They could pursue, harass, or finish off a retreating enemy force.
6. Moving at twice the pace and distance of infantry in a given period, they could raid enemy positions and lines of communications.[1]

But cavalry forces were limited, and so there never were enough on either side to do all six functions at the same time. In a given campaign, commanders had to decide which two, or in a stretch three, functions they wanted their available cavalry force to perform.

For the first two years of the war, Confederate cavalry was superior to their Union counterparts because of better organization and tactics. While Union cavalry units were often fragmented and restrained in their operations by non-cavalry experienced senior commanders, the Confederate cavalry operated in a bolder, more aggressive role. By the third year of the war, there were many good cavalry leaders on both sides but few so bold and aggressive as the Confederate General Jeb Stuart.

In the summer of 1863 Jeb Stuart was thirty years old. He had graduated from the United States Military Academy at West Point in 1854, ranking thirteen in a class of forty-six. Robert E. Lee had been superintendent of the academy at that time, and Stuart was both a classmate and friend of Lee's eldest son, George Washington Custis Lee, who ranked first in the class of 1854. Stuart visited the superintendent's home numerous times during his time as a cadet, and Lee befriended him as well.

The West Point connection began a long-term relationship between Lee and Stuart. Many experts believe Lee looked upon Stuart almost as a son, and the younger man viewed Lee as both an idol and mentor. In 1859 Stuart served as a volunteer aide-de-camp to then Colonel Robert E. Lee when he was dispatched with a company of United States Marines by President James Buchanan and General Winfield Scott to capture the insurrectionist John Brown following his seizure of the federal arsenal at Harper's Ferry, Virginia. Stuart, like Lee, was a native Virginian and both, in the greatest loyalty test of the time, resigned from the US Army after the Virginia state convention voted to secede from the Union on April 17, 1861. Stuart resigned his commission as a captain in the US Army on May 14, 1861. Two months later he was appointed colonel of the 1st Virginia Cavalry Regiment and distinguished himself from the very onset of the war.[2] He led a charge by his unit that shattered part of the Union lines at the Battle of Bull Run in July 1861.

Jeb Stuart was a good officer and excellent cavalry commander. He often described his men as knights, and he often wore elaborate cloaks, ostrich plumes in his hat, and decorative spurs. He may not have exhibited extreme hubris, but there was no doubt that he had a strong self-image as a bold cavalier from the time of seventeenth century English history. Stuart clearly wielded a relatively sizable ego. A contemporary described him as follows:

> Stuart was a gallant figure to look at. The gray coat buttoned to the chin; the light French saber balanced by the pistol in its black holster; the cavalry boots above the knee, and the brown hat with its black plume floating above the bearded features; the brilliant eyes, and the huge mustache, which curled with laughter at the slightest provocation—these made Stuart the perfect picture of a gay cavalier.[3]

Stuart and the cavalry of the Confederate Army of Northern Virginia performed very well before and after Lee assumed command in June 1862. The cavalry raid Stuart led around General George McClellan's Union Army of the Potomac on the Virginia peninsula in June 1862 stood out as a major feat of arms. In a strange twist of irony, one of the Union cavalry commanders chasing Stuart's men in the wake of their plundering was Stuart's father-in-law. Colonel Philip St. George Cooke was a native of Leesburg, Virginia, and veteran Union cavalry commander. He had written the US Army cavalry tactics manual that was then in use. The war had split Cooke's family. While he remained in the Union and pursued his Confederate son-in-law, he also had one son serving as an infantry brigade commander in Lee's army.

As previously told in chapter 1, prior to the Gettysburg campaign, Stuart had invited General Lee to attend a cavalry review on June 8 at a plantation near Brandy Station, Virginia. Stuart wished to hold the event before the Confederate army crossed the Rappahannock River and began its march north toward Pennsylvania. He had planned not only a parade of his troops, but also wanted to combine this with a grand ball at a neighboring plantation. Lee remarked in a letter to his wife that when he arrived at the parade site "Stuart was in all his glory."[4]

Unfortunately for Stuart, uninvited guests showed up for the grand review the next morning. A large force of federal cavalry and infantry, under the command of Union General Alfred Pleasonton, crossed the river and conducted a surprise attack on Stuart's forces. The ensuing Battle of Brandy Station was the largest cavalry battle in the American Civil War and was basically a draw. Still it is not difficult to imagine that Stuart was greatly embarrassed by this turn of events. Southern newspapers publicly excoriated him for his lack of preparation and allowing his troops to be taken by surprise and nearly defeated at Brandy Station. This criticism rankled Stuart, and he desperately wanted to reestablish his reputation. As a result, he crafted a plan and presented it to Lee and Longstreet on June 18. Stuart proposed to conduct the raid with three cavalry brigades and ride around the federal army. Clearly, Stuart was motivated at least partially by a desire to assuage his damaged ego and restore his image in the eyes not only of his soldiers but also the wider Southern public.

Stuart believed that by operating to the east of the main body of the advancing Confederate army, this raid (he later referred to it as "an expedition") would confuse the Union army commanders as to the location and intentions of Lee's army while also harassing the movements of the enemy and cutting their lines of communications. He also saw that by placing his men in enemy country, he then would have precise information as to the location and activity of the Union forces to send to Lee.[5]

Stuart's after-action report covering all of the Gettysburg Campaign reveals that he and three brigades of cavalry totaling over 5,000 men and horses, six cannon with caissons, and an unspecified number of horse-drawn ambulances left Salem Depot, Virginia, at 1 a.m. on June 25, headed east.[6] Over the course of the next eight days their "expedition" traveled approximately 230 miles around and in some cases through the Union Army of the Potomac. Each day they rode north-ward, the presence of enemy forces tended to push them farther to the east of their intended line of advance and farther from Lee and the main body of the Confederate Army. There was some limited fighting along the way but nothing so big as to turn back their advance. Enemy facilities were destroyed, and food, animal feed, and other supplies—particularly horseshoes—were seized. Many prisoners were taken that would further slow Stuart's movements.

Two days after setting out, Stuart's cavalry crossed the Potomac River at Rockville, Maryland. The Chesapeake and Ohio Canal, a major supply route for the Union Army of the Potomac, paralleled the north side of the Potomac River. Gates to canal locks were broken up, and canal boats, with the supplies they carried, were seized. Also, at Rock-ville, Stuart's men captured "more than one hundred and twenty-five best United States model wagons and splendid teams"[7] as well as their cargoes of food, animal feed, and other supplies.

Continuing the advance northward from Rockville on June 29, Stuart said he "found myself now encumbered by about four hundred prisoners, many of whom were officers. I paroled nearly all at Brookev-ille that night and the remainder next day at Cookesville."[8] Now unencumbered by the large number of prisoners, the expedition arrived at Westminster, Maryland, on June 29. Westminster was the major supply depot for the Union Army of the Potomac. Yankee cavalry were now on the hunt, and after a brief fight there, with little damage to the supply base, Stuart and his men rode northward where they were inter-cepted by Union cavalry at Hanover on June 30. After their heaviest engagement with the enemy thus far, Stuart and his men then moved on toward York, Pennsylvania, which was on the Susquehanna River. In York Stuart expected to link up with Jubal Early's division of Ewell's Second Corps. But Early and his men were not there.

Early's division had been at Wrightsville on the Susquehanna River just east of York trying to secure river crossings there. Having failed to do so, on June 29, Early and the rest of Ewell's Second Corps responded to General Lee's orders of the previous day to consolidate just west of Gettysburg on the east side of South Mountain in anticipation of a major battle. By the time Stuart arrived at York, Early was long gone.

Out of contact with his boss, behind enemy lines, Stuart had no idea where Early, or the rest of the army for that matter, was located. Lee also had no idea where Stuart was.

Still wishing to fulfill General Lee's directive to "feel and protect" the right flank of Ewell's II Corps, Stuart advanced to Dover, Pennsylvania, on the morning of July 1. Stuart and his force continued north arriving at Carlisle—former home of the US Army Cavalry School—later that day. He did not find Ewell's troops there either; they had already gone to Gettysburg, unknown to Stuart. At this point the ride was not pleasant. In Stuart's words: "Whole regiments slept in the saddle, their faithful animals keeping the road unguided. In some instances, they— the soldiers—fell from their horses, overcome with physical fatigues and sleepiness."[9] Some of the soldiers were secured in their saddle with ropes in hopes of avoiding accidental casualties from sleep-induced falls from their mounts.

On the night of July 1 scouts sent out by Lee to search for Stuart found him in Carlisle and gave him Lee's instructions to proceed immediately to Gettysburg. Stuart finally arrived with two of his fatigued brigades near sunset on July 2. His third brigade rejoined the main body of the army very early the next morning. Stuart was elated and reported to Lee that his raid had been "successful." His cavalry had captured a significant number of wagons and served to disrupt Union forces, but Lee was visibly angry. He probably believed Stuart had violated his guidance and failed to provide him critical intelligence on the movement of Union forces or their composition. This had endangered the entire operation. Several senior Confederate leaders openly called for Stuart to be relieved of command and replaced.

....

LEADERSHIP MOMENT   It is late on July 2, and you are now General Robert E. Lee. Your cavalry commander, General James Ewell Brown Stuart has just returned from a raid around the Union army and reported to your headquarters. You have not seen nor heard from him since June 23. Stuart has been your cavalry commander since you assumed overall command of the Army of Northern Virginia in the summer of 1862. He has distinguished himself in previous campaigns and is in many ways a favorite of yours. But your army is now on Northern soil, and the absence of his cavalry has deprived you of critical intelligence on the enemy. You also know that had Stuart and his troops been present the chances for a Confederate success during the past two days of fighting would have significantly increased. Many Rebel senior officers are complaining that Stuart has endangered the entire army and let them all down. They are quietly calling for him to be relieved of command. But tomorrow will be decisive. What do you do and why?

WHAT CAN WE LEARN FROM THIS VIGNETTE ABOUT LEADERSHIP?

Counseling and controversies. Many if not most leaders have either experienced this situation or will at some point. You have a subordinate who has worked for you for a significant period. This individual has performed very well and in many ways is one of the "go-to people" you turn to when things are difficult or you have a particularly tough problem. It is also widely recognized throughout the organization that you have known this person for a long time, perhaps even prior to their joining your organization and coming to work directly for you. Everyone knows you view this subordinate as a favorite, and he or she may personally look upon you as a mentor.

Unfortunately, this person is either absent or fails at an especially difficult moment for the entire organization. Many of his or her peers are outraged and expect you as the leader to act. The leadership challenge is determining what you can do that is best for the organization. Do you need to replace the person? Can some other action be taken that takes into account the needs of the organization while still acknowledging this person's loyalty and numerous past contributions?

There is much controversy about Stuart's meeting with Lee upon his arrival at Gettysburg. Major Henry B. McClellan, Stuart's adjutant, provided one of the very few accounts of the conversation, describing the encounter at Lee's headquarters as "painful beyond description."

Upon seeing Stuart approach, Lee immediately inquired in a very sharp tone, "General Stuart, where have you been?"

Stuart replied with a glowing description of the raid that he had conducted for the previous eight days.

Lee quickly responded, "I have not heard a word from you for days, and you the eyes and ears of my army!"

Stuart immediately defended himself and pointed out that "I have brought you 125 wagons and teams, general."

Lee was obviously disturbed and retorted, "Yes, general, but they are an impediment to me now." Abruptly changing his tone, the older man continued, "Let me ask your help now. We will not discuss this matter longer. Help me fight these people."[10] Lee's written reactions are officially recorded in his report on the battle. He confined himself to the following mild statement, "[T]he movement of the army preceding that Battle of Gettysburg had been much embarrassed by the absence of the cavalry."[11]

No executive should want to be described as a "zero-defects leader." Such a leader is someone who routinely fires or publicly humiliates a subordinate when an error is made or something bad happens for the organization. As one wise sage observed, "The search for blame is always successful," and the zero-defects leader is constantly on the lookout for someone to shoulder the blame. Sadly, there are far too many leaders like this in organizations today. Some mistakes, particularly if they violate the values of the organization, are cause for immediate dismissal. Still, the leader who routinely removes people if they err or fail will find that trust and a willingness to take initiative throughout the organization will suffer. Robert E. Lee was not a zero-defects leader and may have also realized that he had perhaps provided Stuart too much discretion during a campaign that would take him deep into enemy territory. Many experts believe at least some of the responsibility rested with Lee.

Lee did not relieve Stuart, and Stuart would distinguish himself during the retreat of the Confederate army back to Virginia, which began on July 5. He remained in command of the Confederate cavalry until his death at the Battle of Yellow Tavern on May 11, 1864. A member of Lee's staff wrote that Lee "was greatly affected" when he received a message informing him that Stuart had been mortally wounded. In an army circular announcing Stuart's death, Lee wrote, "Among the gallant soldiers who have fallen in this war, General Stuart was second to none in valour, in zeal, and in unflinching devotion to his country." A week later Lee further observed in a letter to his wife, "A more zealous, ardent, brave, and devoted soldier than Stuart the Confederacy cannot have."[12]

Mentoring. Stuart looked upon Robert E. Lee as a mentor from the onset of his career. Mentoring is one of the most important elements of individual leadership development. It serves as an opportunity for a personal relationship in which a more experienced (normally older) mentor acts as a guide, role model, and sponsor for a less experienced (usually younger) mentee. Mentors provide mentees with knowledge, advice, challenges, counsel, and support in their career. Effective leaders want to not only offer themselves as a mentor to people in their organization but also to frequently talk about its importance and encourage other senior members of the team to do so.

Mentoring is key for any organization to develop leaders who have the individual character and competence to make the right choices at difficult moments. An organization that is known to encourage the mentoring of its rising leaders will not only attract more talent but also experience greater retention. The *Harvard Business Review* once observed that a study of the top 1,250 executives listed in the *Wall Street Journal* at that time found that 65 percent said they had an important mentor. The importance of mentorship for modern executives has only continued to increase.[13] A study of mentored executives also reported they believed having a mentor resulted in higher salaries, more rapid promotions, greater achievement of career objectives, and higher overall job/life satisfaction.

Three Google executives—Eric Schmidt (a former director of *The Economist*), Jonathan Rosenberg, and Alan Eagle—further confirmed the critical importance of mentors and the counsel they provide in *Trillion Dollar Coach*, the book they wrote in praise of their coach and mentor, Bill Campbell. A college football coach prior to entering the business world, Campbell later worked for Apple and was the head of its marketing department for the original Macintosh. Campbell subsequently became chief executive of Intuit, a financial software company, but his most effective role may have been as a board member at Apple and close friend of Steve Jobs. He clearly performed the duties of a mentor in being generous with his time and providing them with his undivided attention. Campbell believed his role was not to oversee specific projects but rather to develop leaders. He was quick to publicly praise members of the Apple team in large meetings but was not a "soft touch." It appears he believed it was better to provide harsh praise in private, and some say he was usually adept enough to make the recipient of a tongue lashing grateful.

Lee had been key in Stuart's leadership development since they first met at West Point, but their relationship was not the only example of the importance of mentoring at the Battle of Gettysburg. Union Colonel Joshua Chamberlain, who gained fame through his successful defense of Little Round Top from repeated Confederate assaults on July 2, had initially refused to accept the command of a regiment when offered by Maine Governor Israel Washburn Jr. in the summer of 1862. As previously written, Chamberlain believed he needed to enter the army at a lower level in order to learn and gain experience. He was initially assigned as assistant commander of the 20th Maine Regiment under the command of Colonel Adelbert Ames.

Ames, a young Army officer, graduated from West Point shortly before the war began and was badly wounded at the Battle of Bull Run. He returned to the Union army following his recovery and distinguished himself during both the Peninsula and Seven Days Campaigns. He had assumed command of the 20th Maine Regiment in August 1862 and mentored Chamberlain as his deputy. This only lasted for a few months as Ames was selected to be a member of General George Meade's corps staff and then appointed brigade commander in the XI Corps in May 1863—only six weeks prior to Gettysburg.

Beware of "hubris and nemesis." Multiple ancient Greek philosophers warned of the *"hubris-nemesis"* dynamic, a concept that may have first been attributed to Hesiod, who lived around 700 BC. He warned that *hubris* was the capital sin of pride and, consequently, the antithesis of two ethics that the Greeks valued highly—*aidos*, humble reverence for the law, and *sophrosyne*, self-restraint and the ability to ascertain a sense of proper limits. Those exhibiting hubris or sinful conduct displayed overweening pride, self-glorification, arrogance, and overconfidence in their abilities, and ignored the feelings of others.

Leaders and conquerors in Greek literature were often afflicted by *hubris* despite having great leadership abilities. As a result, they abused both their power and authority to gratify their vanity and ambitions. According to the Greeks, acts of hubris challenged the divine balance of nature and aroused the envy and anger of the gods on Mount Olympus. In response, they would call on Nemesis, the goddess of divine vengeance and retribution, to descend and destroy the sinful leaders, teach them a painful lesson, and restore order. In modern discussions, these ancient terms are infrequently used, but the dynamics are present in Christian thinking. One need only reflect on the famous Biblical saying "Pride cometh before a fall" (Book of Proverbs, 10:16). It is also referred to in discussions of the "arrogance of power." For contemporary analysis, some might consider the decision-making of American leaders during the Vietnam War or the actions of President Nixon during the Watergate scandal as illustrations of hubris.

As for Stuart and three brigades of cavalry being absent for two of the three days of the Gettysburg Battle, Lee did approve Stuart's request and must bear some responsibility. Lee agreed at a point in time—June 22—when he knew that the army was moving deeper into enemy territory where Stuart and his cavalry would be needed the most. Lee had hedged his bet and sent Stuart a message on June 22 agreeing with Stuart's proposal but only under three conditions. First, Stuart was to ensure that he stayed in contact with Lee and the main body of the army. Second, prior to commencing the raid, Stuart must place someone in command of the remaining two cavalry brigades that guarded the passes of the Blue Ridge Mountains into the Shenandoah Valley, which served as the army's main line of communications back into Virginia. Lastly, once inside Maryland, he was to immediately move north to the Susquehanna River and guard the right flank of Ewell's I Corps.[14]

Unfortunately for Southern fortunes, Stuart failed to follow these directives. That failure will captivate historical analysis long into the future, but one fundamental question will likely remain unanswered: Did Stuart plan and execute this raid because he thought it best for his organization—the Army of Northern Virginia—or because he thought it was best for his own image?

Good leaders must be willing to conduct self-assessments and often reflect honestly about their motivation. Ultimately every leader must ask themselves the following question: What is my primary motivation for making this decision? What do I truly value the most—myself or my organization? All of us have an ego, and this is a good thing because it encourages self-confidence, but it can also be our undoing. Jim Collins in his book *Good to Great* argues that organizations that experience dramatic success are led by so-called Level 5 leaders. These are people who can subordinate their own ambitions and ego to what is best for their team and organization. Humility is one of the most important qualities a leader can carry, and although it may sound like an easy quality to acquire, it is an incredibly difficult when making a decision.

Leading yourself. The most difficult dimension of leadership is often leading yourself. Leaders must be self-aware and pay close attention to their mental preparation and emotional well-being, as well as their overall health. This is critical if they are to be in the best position to make decisions at stressful moments. It seems apparent that the Confederate leadership was "less physically" well than its Union counterparts during these dire three days. General A. P. Hill, whose corps was the first to arrive at Gettysburg, was suffering from the effects of a social disease, which made it difficult for him to move about the field. General Richard Ewell, who did not pursue the attack on July 1, had just returned to the army after being badly wounded and losing a leg.

The life expectancy of an American male in the early nineteenth century was roughly forty-five. In 1863 Robert E. Lee was fifty-six years old—he had beaten the actuary tables and was an old man. He was clearly under enormous stress, and July 2, 1863, may have been one of the most stressful days he had ever experienced as a soldier and leader. There are some reports that suggest General Lee suffered from severe back pain possibly due to a sciatic nerve problem and showed signs of the heart disease that would contribute to his death in 1870. At a minimum, several soldiers at his headquarters recorded in letters and diaries that Lee appeared to be suffering from dysentery or, as it was referred to in the nineteenth century, "the old soldier's disease."

The emotional well-being and physical health of the leaders are critical factors for any modern organization. Successful businesses now recognize that their leaders are key assets that can positively influence the entire organization. As an asset, they are either thriving and appreciating, or their health is suffering and their value to the organization is declining.

Analysis of the health of contemporary America suggests several disturbing trends. While the number of American adults between the ages of forty and fifty-five is at an all-time low, studies show the percentage of the US adult population that is overweight is climbing, cholesterol levels are stubbornly high, and a significant percentage are suffering from incipient heart disease.[15] Furthermore, there is clear evidence that the need for stress management is also growing in the United States at a dramatic pace. The American Institute of Stress reported in 2019 that 83 percent of American workers suffer from work-related stress.[16] The results are as follows:

- US businesses lose up to $300 billion annually due to workplace stress.
- Stress causes roughly one million workers in the US to miss work every day.
- Only 43 percent of American employees believe their leadership cares about their work-life balance.
- Depression in the US leads to $51 billion in increased costs due to absenteeism and $26 billion in treatment costs.
- It is estimated that work-related stress may cause 120,000 deaths annually and an overall increase of $190 billion in health care costs.

Dealing with these challenges must be viewed as more than risk mitigation and needs to be seen in terms of how the health of the leader can drive results. Far too many modern executives find themselves under enormous stress, have hectic travel schedules, and fail to get sufficient sleep or exercise. But it is more than simply improving the health of the leader. While organizations need to seek ways and provide opportunities for their employees to improve their health outcomes, many people will "model" the performance of the person in charge. If the leader takes time to exercise, eat well, and take care of himself or herself, this will more likely become an organizational norm. Numerous health studies have shown such programs can drive significant increases in productivity and employee satisfaction and engagement, as well as driving down the costs of absenteeism, disability, and prescription drugs.[17]

Stuart departed Lee's headquarters, and the general pondered the enormous challenge that the next day would present. It had been a very hard day, and Lee was undoubtedly exhausted by the physical and emotional stress. His army's leaders had failed to live up to his expectations and hopes. They had not achieved the victory that all desperately sought.

CHAPTER 10

"Home, Boys, Home! Home Is Just Over That Hill!"

Having kept his own counsel overnight, Confederate commander Lee rose early on the morning of July 3, as was his custom. He mounted his horse, and before the 5:30 sunrise, began his journey of just over two miles south along his army's occupied line on Seminary Ridge in search of his "old war horse," James Longstreet. He found him at a nearby peach orchard planted by a local reverend. On this, the third day of the battle, the meeting was not meant to be a consultation. As recorded in his after-action report, Lee had already made up his mind as to what should happen next.

> *The result of this day's operations—July 2nd—induced the belief that, with proper concert of action and with the increased support that the positions gained on the right would enable the artillery to render the assaulting columns, we should ultimately succeed, and it was accordingly determined to continue the attack. The general plan was unchanged.*[1]

That's what Lee ultimately told Longstreet, ordering him to resume the attack against the left-center of the enemy line with the two divisions he had used in battle the previous day. The difference this time was that they would now be reinforced by Major General George Pickett's division, whose men hadn't seen any combat and were well rested.

But Longstreet immediately demurred. He argued that those two divisions commanded by Generals John Bell Hood and Lafayette McLaws had been heavily handled the previous day. Six of the eight brigades had suffered over 30 percent casualties—dead, wounded, captured, or missing. The remaining men were in no condition to attack. Additionally, he told Lee if those two divisions moved forward from the ground they occupied, enemy cavalry would get around behind them and into the rear of the army. Once again Longstreet recommended to Lee that they pass around the big hill—Big Round Top—and envelop the Union left. This would force the enemy to abandon their strong defensive positions. Longstreet firmly believed this was far better than attacking the Yankees directly.

Lee bristled at the suggestion and pointed to Cemetery Ridge. He curtly told Longstreet: "The enemy is there, and I am going to strike him." Attempting a partial buy-in to the plan by Longstreet, Lee promised him two infantry divisions from A. P. Hill's Third Corps in place of Hood's and McLaws' divisions. Hill's troops would then team up with George Pickett's division in an attack against the center of the Union's position on Cemetery Ridge. As if by prophecy, this was exactly where General Meade had predicted that the Confederates would attack during his meeting with his leaders the night before.

Lee made it clear to Longstreet that he was to plan, prepare, and conduct the attack. Yet, once again, Longstreet protested, later recounting:

> I felt then it was my duty to express my convictions. I said, "General, I have been a soldier all my life. I have been with soldiers engaged in fights by couples, by squads, companies, regiments, divisions, and armies, and should know as well as anyone what soldiers can do. It is my opinion that no fifteen thousand men ever arranged for battle can carry that position."[2]

....

LEADERSHIP MOMENT You are Robert E. Lee. Would you order this attack despite the opposition of your principal subordinate leader? Was this a gamble or a calculated risk? Are they the same?

....

WHAT CAN WE LEARN FROM THIS VIGNETTE ABOUT LEADERSHIP?

Risk and the Stockdale paradox. In making decisions, leaders must calculate the risk to their organization. This is a key aspect of strategic thinking and planning. It is important, however, to realize that a *risk* and a *gamble* are different. Risk includes calculations based on resources available, the difficulty of the task at hand, and the level of opposition or competition. A gamble is simply relying on fate or the roll of dice. All leaders need to be conscious about their personal tolerance for risk.

No leader should ever place the future existence of his or her organization at risk for the possibility of minor gains. Though Confederate forces had been successful tactically over the preceding year and won a number of battles, particularly in the east, it appears Lee privately believed they could not continue the war indefinitely. The South did not have the resources in material or manpower. This was particularly true with respect to the losses of key leaders. In the aftermath of Gettysburg, a British liaison officer with the Army of the Northern Virginia lauded the prowess of the Confederate Army to a group of Southern officers. But he then ticked off the illustrious dead since the Battle of Fredericksburg in December 1862. "Don't you see?" he implored them. "Your system feeds upon itself. Your troops do wonders, but every time at a cost you cannot afford."[3] Consequently, it is clear that Lee came to Gettysburg to win the war, not just to win a battle.

It also appears that President Lincoln believed that the Confederacy, with less than half the population of the Union, could not sustain the war indefinitely. He once observed that if the Battle of Fredericksburg (a Confederate victory) had been fought numerous times with the same results, the Army of the Potomac would still be a "mighty host" but Lee's army would be "wiped out to the last man."[4]

Other leaders have had to assume enormous risk at particularly critical moments for their organizations. General Dwight Eisenhower faced a similar challenge in the days immediately prior to the Normandy Invasion. In December 1943, he assumed command of Allied forces in preparation for Operation Overlord (the D-Day landings), which was to occur in mid-1944. The mission was clear—to liberate the

*General Eisenhower
with men of the
US 101st Airborne
Division on June
5th, 1944*

European continent from Nazi control, but the scale of the planning for this operation was immense. Approximately 156,000 soldiers from five countries participated in the landings on five beaches along a fifty-mile front. The overall effort involved nearly two million soldiers, sailors, and airmen from a dozen nations. The invasion armada consisted of 6,000 ships carrying 50,000 vehicles and hundreds of tons of supplies. Overhead 11,000 Allied aircraft provided close air support and strategic bombing, as well as delivered thousands of paratroopers. The Allies had also created an elaborate deception plan on the timing and location of the invasion.

There were several critical elements to this decision that Ike and his staff had no control over—the tides, the moon, and the weather. The ideal tides and moonlight occurred on only a handful of days each month. In June 1944, those days were the fifth, sixth, and the seventh. If the Invasion of Normandy did not occur on one of those three days, Eisenhower knew they would have to wait until the nineteenth to try again. Any delay risked the security of the effort as well as reducing the time Allied forces would have to conduct subsequent land campaigns during the summer.

The invasion had initially been planned for June 5, and troops had begun boarding ships on June 4. Unfortunately, the weather forecast for the next day was threatening—cloudy, stormy, windy, and with a cloud base of zero to five hundred feet. Airborne operations would be severely hampered if not impossible. Allied air support would also be much more difficult, and the actual landings would be problematic. Eisenhower decided to delay the invasion for twenty-four hours.

Early on the morning of June 5, he reconvened his senior leaders at his headquarters at Southwick House. A British weather expert predicted that conditions would improve for a thirty-six-hour window of time, but he made no guarantees. An invasion on Tuesday, June 6 appeared possible. Eisenhower asked each of his principal British and American subordinates for their recommendation. They each recommended going ahead with the invasion despite the great risk.

Several of those who were in attendance later recounted that Ike then stood and began pacing the war room deeply in thought.[5] He pondered the most important decision he would make in his entire life and knew that the fate of millions hung in the balance. As the leader, only he could exercise the fundamental aspect of leadership. And so, he decided. He suddenly stopped, turned to those assembled, and said, "OK, let's go."

This could be described as an illustration of the Stockdale paradox for Lee, Eisenhower, or any leader who must make a very difficult decision while under great stress. This concept was coined by Vice Admiral James Bond Stockdale. His aircraft was shot down during a bombing raid over North Vietnam on September 9, 1965, and he was held as a prisoner of war (POW) for the next seven and a half years in the infamous "Hanoi Hilton." As the senior US Naval officer among the prisoners, Stockdale was one of the primary organizers of prisoner resistance, conduct, and mutual support.

He was repeatedly tortured and denied medical treatment for a badly injured leg.

Stockdale was once asked who didn't make it out of captivity. He replied,

"Oh, that's easy, the optimists. They were the ones who said, 'We're going to be out by Christmas.' And Christmas would come, and Christmas would go. Then they'd say, 'We're going to be out by Easter.' And Easter would come, and Easter would go. And then

Thanksgiving, and then it would be Christmas again. And they died of a broken heart."[6]

From this experience he created what later became known as the "Stockdale paradox." It requires a leader to have an absolute clear understanding of how difficult the situation he and his team confront, but Stockdale combined that with a fierce determination to be successful.

A more contemporary example might be Jeff Bezos, CEO of Amazon, and one of the richest men in the world. His acquisition of the *Washington Post* and Whole Foods showed his willingness to take great risks to stay at the forefront of ongoing change in the American economy. Some experts described the purchase of Whole Foods as a $13.4 billion wager to take on the $800 billion domestic American grocery business.[7] It is fair to argue, however, that the huge financial risks Bezos has taken pale compared to the dilemmas faced by Lee and Eisenhower. Still his decisions show a leader, not unlike Lee and Eisenhower, who plans carefully, assesses the environment in which his organization is operating, and has a both a high tolerance for risk and a willingness to accept short-term failure. Bezos has argued that his high level of risk tolerance is a function of the long-term perspective that he follows. He contends that modern leaders must "think in decades instead of quarters."[8] This allows a leader in a competitive environment to be willing to accept risks that the competition will avoid.

Longstreet continued his recollection of this critical meeting, "The General [Lee] seemed a little impatient at my remarks, so I said nothing more. As he showed no indication of changing his plan, I went to work at once to arrange my troops for the attack."[9] In making his "arrangements," Longstreet appointed Lieutenant Colonel Edward Porter Alexander to plan and arrange the artillery bombardment that would precede the infantry assault. But the Army of Northern Virginia had to take significant risk in terms of available resources as well as significant changes that had occurred in its leadership over the past two days of fighting.

Alexander—with the added support of cannon from A. P Hill's III Corps and its artillery chief Colonel R. Lindsay Walker—was successful in organizing a line of Confederate artillery in the middle ground

*Major General George
E. Pickett, CSA*

between the force's attack positions on Seminary Ridge and the attack
objectives on Cemetery Ridge. The assembled line totaled 136 cannon
in direct support of the coming infantry attack with another 29 cannons
in general support.[10] Alexander and Walker's challenges were two. First,
they had to move their cannon closer to the enemy's position because
they had an excess of shorter-range cannon compared to the enemy's
number of longer-range guns. Second, after two days of battle, the
Confederates had a decided disadvantage in the supply and resupply of
artillery ammunition.

As for the infantry, George Pickett's division was moved forward
from their overnight bivouac sites on the Emanuel Pitzer farm on the
western side of Seminary Ridge to the fields surrounding the Henry
Spangler farm east of the ridge. Division commander George Edward
Pickett was thirty-eight years old at the time of the battle. A native Virginian, he graduated last among the fifty-nine cadets in the West Point
class of 1846. Future Union general George B. McClellan and future
Confederate general Thomas J. "Stonewall" Jackson were among his
classmates.

Pickett was twice decorated for gallantry during the 1846–1848 US war with Mexico. He subsequently served at army posts in Texas and in the Washington Territory before resigning from the US Army in June 1861 to enter Confederate service. His division was only lightly engaged at Fredericksburg in December 1862 and was on detached duty during the Chancellorsville battle in May 1863.[11] At Gettysburg, although a favorite of I Corps commander James Longstreet, George Pickett was among the least experienced of Lee's nine infantry division commanders.

All three of Pickett's subordinate brigade commanders were veterans of the war with Mexico. Attorney James Lawson Kemper was a graduate of Washington College in Virginia and prior to the war had served five terms as a ranking member of the Virginia House of Delegates and president of the board of visitors of the Virginia Military Institute.[12] Lewis Addison Armistead attended the US Military Academy at West Point for two years, 1834–1836, but did not graduate. He had been expelled for breaking a dinner plate over the head of classmate, fellow Virginian and future Confederate general Jubal Early. Still, Armistead received a direct commission in the US Army in 1839 through family connections.

He was a decorated veteran of the war with Mexico, as well as earning accolades for his distinguished service on the western frontier between the wars.[13] During his pre–Civil War army service he became a close personal friend of future Union General Winfield Scott Hancock, whose troops occupied the Confederate attack objective on Cemetery Ridge on July 3. The third brigade commander was Richard Brooke Garnett, who had graduated from West Point in the class of 1841, ranking twenty-ninth of fifty-two graduates. Future Union General John Fulton Reynolds was a classmate. Although he saw no action in the war with Mexico, he had earned recognition for his distinguished service in the western states and territories before the Civil War. Resigning his commission in the US Army in May 1861, he commanded Confederate forces at the regimental and brigade level prior to Gettysburg and proved to be a good, if not exceptional, tactical leader. However, at Gettysburg Garnett had something more to prove.

Photos: USAMHI

Brigadier General Lewis Armistead, CSA

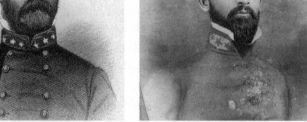

Brigadier General Richard Garnett, CSA

Brigadier General James Kemper, CSA

In the spring of 1862, Garnett was in command of the famous "Stonewall Brigade," the former command of Stonewall Jackson, who had been promoted to command a larger force. During Jackson's 1862 Shenandoah Valley campaign in Virginia, Garnett withdrew his brigade from the frontline at the battle of Kernstown when his soldiers ran out of ammunition. Jackson was furious, charged Garnett with neglect of duty, placed him under arrest, and preferred court-martial charges. But Jackson was mortally wounded at Chancellorsville before the incident could be brought to trial. Consequently, the charges had not been resolved, but Garnett believed this continued to sully his reputation.[14] He desperately wished to clear his good name, but Garnett hit another setback when he was kicked in the knee by another man's horse a few days before July 3. He could barely walk and consequently feared that he would be unable to lead his men in the charge against the federal lines.

The morning of July 3 on Seminary Ridge, Southern army commander Lee, corps commander Longstreet, division commander Pickett, and brigade commander Armistead were planning and preparing for an attack against the center of the Union line on Cemetery Ridge. It was only a mile away and defended by troops under the command of their former comrade, Union II Corps commander Winfield Scott Hancock.

Sixteen years before during the US-Mexican War, engineer officer Lee had provided General Winfield Scott the plan that brought his army to the gates of Mexico City—the enemy capital. The towering fortress of Chapultepec had been the objective in 1847. Lieutenant Lewis Armistead led the storming party and was among the first to be wounded in the assault. Near Armistead during the assault was his close friend— Lieutenant Winfield Scott Hancock. A few paces behind, carrying the American flag, was Lieutenant James Longstreet, who fell seriously wounded. As the colors dropped, they were immediately picked up by Lieutenant George Pickett. The first soldier over the parapets, Pickett unfurled the American flag over the captured enemy fortress.[15]

Time changed all that.

On July 3, General Pickett ordered his men to lie in the swales at the Spangler farm out of sight of the enemy and prepare to charge the flag they all once supported. Pickett's men were also unseen by the other Confederate forces that would make the same attack. At times the battlefield is a lonely place. Perhaps, in a sense, they were alone. They might not know whether anyone besides their unit would be making the attack. Organizational cohesion—the faith and confidence they had in their leaders, past successes, and the mission ahead of them—would now reconcile in each soldier's mind.

Pickett's brigades were only three of nine brigades positioned to make the attack. To the left—north—of Pickett's division, positioned on the protected ground on the west side of the Seminary Ridge, was Henry Heth's division from A. P. Hill's III Corps. These were the troops

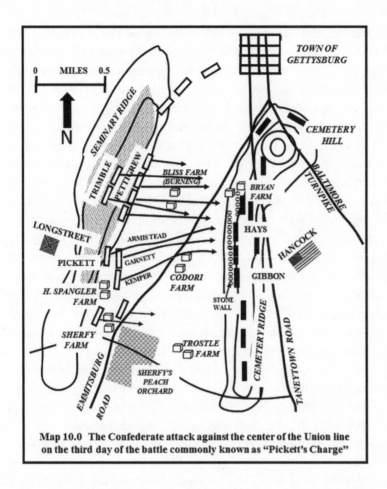

Map 10.0 The Confederate attack against the center of the Union line on the third day of the battle commonly known as "Pickett's Charge"

Lee had promised Longstreet as replacements for his two divisions commanded by Generals Hood and McLaws. With an estimated remaining strength of 5,000 men, Heth's division, organized into four brigades, remained hidden from the view of their enemy who sat a mile away on Cemetery Ridge. Also positioned to advance in support of these four brigades were two brigades from Dorsey Pender's III Corps division numbering an estimated 2,300 troops.[16]

Pickett's men were predominantly Virginians with perhaps a few Marylanders. The soldiers of Heth's and Pender's divisions were men from North Carolina, Tennessee, Mississippi, and Alabama, as well as a collection of more Virginians. These men were the survivors of the fighting on McPherson's and Seminary Ridges two days earlier. Thus, their ranks the morning of July 3 were reduced in number, in some cases greatly reduced by as much as 50 percent. When Generals Lee and Longstreet reviewed the troops in the late morning hours just prior to the attack, both were greatly surprised at the number of men present for duty in the ranks with bandaged arms, legs, torsos, and heads.

It was not just the men in the ranks who had already suffered. Neither Heth nor Pender was able to command their respective divisions on the third day. Henry Heth had been hit in the head by a spent bullet on the first day, which knocked him unconscious but did not kill him. Forty-eight hours later he was still incapacitated and not fit to command. J. Johnston Pettigrew, a classical scholar from North Carolina, was Heth's senior brigade commander and assumed command of the division on July 3. Likewise, General Dorsey Pender was also out of the fight on July 3. He had been hit by enemy artillery fire on July 2, and though they did not know it yet, his wound was mortal. Lee ordered sixty-one-year-old Major General Isaac Trimble to command the two brigades from Pender's division in the attack.

All these replacements of fallen leaders had a potential trickle-down effect in the cohesion of the units. Four of six brigades on the left end of the Confederate line that made the attack were now commanded by men who, forty-eight hours earlier, had only been good enough to command a single regiment, let alone a brigade of several regiments.

Sergeant June Kimble of the 14th Tennessee Regiment made his way to the crest of Seminary Ridge late on the morning of July 3. Prior to the attack, he wanted to get a view of the enemy position that was just over a mile away. He was awestruck by what he saw of the intended objective and the approach to it. He apparently now understood the full implication of what he and his men would be ordered to do. He recalled later that he began speaking to himself, "June Kimble, are you going to do your duty today?" As he remembered, he thoughtfully answered himself back, saying, "I'll do it, so help me God."[17]

The power of the team. When you stand on Seminary Ridge and peer across the 1.1 miles that separated the Union and Confederate lines you automatically ask yourself, why did thousands of Confederate soldiers march across the field on a sunny afternoon against Union soldiers protected behind a stone wall? What does it take to get an organization to attempt it? The answer lies in the power of any team. This is a function of the cohesion among individual team members, as well as between them and the leadership.

"Cohesion" is the act or state of a group that pulls together to get a mission accomplished. All organizations have both "horizontal cohesion" and "vertical cohesion." The former is bonding among team members at the same level within the organization, while the latter cohesion is bonding between the members of the organization and their leadership. This is another way to describe "trust," which is fundamental to long-term organizational success.

When any organization experiences a crisis, its overall cohesion is tested. Organizations with a high level of horizontal cohesion have a greater likelihood for success at difficult moments. This is because the members of a cohesive team have confidence in both themselves and their teammates. Clearly, the Army of Northern Virginia was an experienced, successful, and cohesive organization. Cohesion serves as a force that attracts members to the team, provides resistance to leaving it, and motivates the efforts of all members. High levels of cohesiveness within the team also result in lower levels of absenteeism, attrition, and turnover. The men in the ranks on that afternoon advanced because they were not going to let their fellow soldiers down.

Vertical cohesion is also placed under stress. During difficult moments for an organization three factors determine the level of trust members of the organization have in their leadership, and these are true whether the leader is Robert E. Lee or a modern corporate executive.

First, the credibility of the leader is the foundation for trust. This is based on his or her perceived competence, character, and caring. This is often described as the leader's "idiosyncratic credits," which he or she builds over time. These credits increase based on a leader's demonstrated competence, success, and record of caring for all members of the team.

Clearly, after a year in command of the Army of Northern Virginia Robert E. Lee was perceived as both an extremely competent and successful leader by his men. He had led them to major victories at

Fredericksburg and Chancellorsville. His integrity was beyond reproach, and he had demonstrated enormous caring for his troops, which they found inspirational. The men frequently cheered when he appeared at their individual units. Furthermore, Lee had many subordinate leaders at the corps, division, brigade, and regimental levels who also demonstrated these critical characteristics. As the war continued, however, a critical challenge for the Confederacy was replacing key leaders at all levels when they were killed or badly wounded.

The second factor for vertical cohesion is dependent on whether organizational systems set the conditions for success and are fundamental to cohesion. It was clear that the members of both the Union and Confederate armies had shared values, beliefs, and norms. As military organizations, they also had clear structure, policies, and procedures that had been developed over the preceding two years of combat. War is a harsh "teacher," and all organizations must learn as changes occur in their operating environment or they will invariably undergo crises. Failure to do so risks obsolescence or outright failure.

Third, the relationship that exists between the leader and his or her followers must be based on mutual respect, open/candid communications, and common purpose. The veterans of both the Army of Northern Virginia and Army of the Potomac had been through a great deal together, and they had a shared goal to win the war. As General George Pickett's division advanced across the field on the afternoon of July 3, the officers and noncommissioned officers walking behind the line of advancing troops could be heard saying the following, "Home, boys, home! Remember, home is over beyond that hill! If we can take the hill, we can win the war and you can go home!"[18]

The cohesion of any team cannot be taken for granted and only developed by the leader's concerted efforts. Some studies even suggest that over time cohesion in any organization will atrophy unless intentionally rebuilt or maintained. Even small improvements in cohesion and motivation can result in large increases in organizational performance. The opposite can also be true, and a lack of cohesion seems pervasive in many modern organizations, especially those experiencing significant change. About half of all American workers say they have been affected by organizational change, are currently being affected, or expect to be affected in the near future. As a result, they report higher levels of chronic work stress, are less likely to trust their leadership, and are more inclined to leave their organization in the near future.[19] Still the Conference Board that conducts an annual survey of job satisfaction across the United States found that roughly 51 percent of American employees felt overall satisfaction with their jobs, a measurement that is related to the strength of the American economy.[20] The report, however, also provided warning signals that many workers remain dissatisfied with recognition plans, opportunities for professional development, and communication channels within their organization.

How then does a leader increase cohesion within his or her organization? Part of the answer rests in the passage of time, as a leader must establish himself or herself when taking over a new organization. How a leader manages the transition into a new role can speed the process, and four things are of great importance. A new leader must consider carefully the "first one hundred days" on the job. He or she must set a trajectory in terms of what their priorities are. They also should ensure every member of their organization fully understands what recoverable and nonrecoverable mistakes are. The new leader must then get to know the team on their "territory" and listen to them carefully. Abraham Lincoln once observed that "God gave us two ears and one mouth because he was trying to tell us something." But upon arrival a new leader must also set the tone in the organization, particularly if change is required due to a crisis or ongoing circumstances. Finally, he or she must seek or, if necessary, demand buy-in from their immediate subordinate leaders on those issues they deem critical at the onset.

Patrick Lencioni in his award-winning book *The Five Dysfunctions of a Team* describes how members of the team must trust one another. They accept that mistakes will be made and are willing to ask for help from other team members. Cohesive teams also engage in unfiltered conflict around ideas. It is important for the leader to accept that "constructive conflict" around ideas is both normal and healthy. But members of cohesive teams can't just talk ideas out, they must commit to decisions and plans of action. They further hold one another accountable for delivering on those plans. At the end of the day, however, they have to focus on the achievement of collective results and continually ask, "How are WE doing?"

Our focus to this point has been on one team—the Confederate Army of Northern Virginia. General Lee had ordered them to launch an attack against the center of the Union defensive line on Cemetery Ridge. Despite the fact that Lee's principal subordinate—Peter Longstreet—was opposed, cohesion among the soldiers in individual units remained strong. What about the other team, the soldiers in the Union Army of the Potomac who were defending along Cemetery Ridge? They knew their cohesion was about to be tested by an attack somewhere along their lines. How had their leadership analyzed the problem and prepared them for this?

Union General George Meade had held a council of war on the evening of July 2 with his principal subordinate commanders. He did so in part to gain buy-in from his "team" to support his desire to continue to defend their present positions and see what the Confederates might do the next day. In his analysis, Meade predicted the Confederates, having been unsuccessful in their attacks against the ends of the Union's strong defensive line on the second day, would attack the center of the line on the third day under the rationale that that the center was less well defended.

The center of the line was defended by troops of the II Corps under the command of Major General Winfield Scott Hancock, a professional soldier from Philadelphia, Pennsylvania. As many as a thousand of his troops were Pennsylvanians no longer fighting in faraway Virginia. There were also nearly 1,600 soldiers from New York, 1,400 from Vermont, 475 from Massachusetts, and single regiments from Maine, Connecticut, New Jersey, Delaware, Ohio, Michigan, and Minnesota.[21] All these men were now fighting to defend their homeland from Confederate invasion—whatever had happened during the previous two years of the war no longer mattered.

Hancock was named for General Winfield Scott, the venerable veteran and hero of the War of 1812 who was still on active duty with the army at the start of the Civil War. He had graduated eighteenth in a class of twenty-five from West Point in 1844 at the age of twenty, and he and many of his former army comrades who now fought against him

Brigadier General John Gibbon, USA   *Brigadier General Alexander Hays, USA*

had been part of the successful assault against Chapultepec Castle in Mexico. He was also a veteran of the mini-civil war in bloody Kansas in 1856 and the US Army expedition against the Mormons in Utah Territory in 1857–1858.

The advent of the Civil War found Captain Hancock in Los Angeles, California, co-stationed with his friend Lewis Armistead, but Hancock soon came east to a brigadier general's commission in the Pennsylvania volunteers. He commanded at both brigade and division level in the Army of the Potomac during previous campaigns before assuming command of II Corps two weeks prior to the Gettysburg Battle,[22] and at this point had earned the respect and admiration of his men.

Two of Hancock's three infantry divisions were positioned in the center of the line on Cemetery Ridge where the Confederates were destined to strike. Brigadier Generals Alexander Hays and John Gibbon commanded these two divisions. Both men were graduates of West Point: Hays in the class of 1844 and Gibbon in the class of 1847.

One of Hays's West Point classmates was Winfield Scott Hancock, his current boss. Hays was a decorated veteran of the war in Mexico but resigned from the army in 1848. He then spent thirteen years as a civil engineer in western Pennsylvania. At the outbreak of the Civil War he reentered active duty as a captain and company commander. He proved to be a capable leader and rose quickly in rank and position.[23]

One of John Gibbon's West Point classmates was future Confederate general A. P. Hill. Like many others of his rank and position, he was a veteran of the war in Mexico and was an artillery instructor at West Point when the Civil War started. Born in Pennsylvania but raised since early childhood in North Carolina, he held true to his oath to the Army of the United States when the Civil War broke out even though three brothers entered Confederate army service.[24]

Taken together, the two divisions commanded by Hays and Gibbon totaled around 5,500 infantrymen who occupied nearly seven hundred yards of ground along a stone wall on Cemetery Ridge, which proved to be the center-point of the Confederate objective. Supporting and interspersed among the infantry regiments were artillery units of four to six cannon each—with a total of seventy-seven pieces in position along the line. Large reserves of artillery were waiting in position east of the ridge beyond the range of enemy artillery, available to be brought forward quickly to reinforce the firing line when necessary. Having made their preparations and now fighting on home ground, the Union soldiers, like their Confederate counterparts just over a mile away, optimistically waited to see what would happen.

Optimism is a force multiplier. Napoleon once said, "Leaders are dealers in hope." They can fall victim to overconfidence particularly if their organizations have enjoyed a long period of success, and many historians have argued subsequently that overconfidence is exactly what Lee suffered from. Still, all leaders must be confident in themselves and their organization, while also frequently displaying their optimism. Emotion is infectious but often best coupled with the leader's subsequent quiet confidence.

Still it is critical to remember that the members of any organization will be no more confident about accomplishing any mission or task than their leadership. They may reach that level but will rarely—if ever—exceed it. This is particularly true if the task is daunting or the organization is faced by a crisis. Former Secretary of State Colin Powell frequently said, "Optimism is a force multiplier." Ultimately leadership is about convincing a group that they can accomplish more than they deem possible. As Eleanor Roosevelt once observed, "A good leader inspires people to have confidence in the leader; a great leader inspires people to have confidence in themselves."

This is often seen in athletics. In January 1969 the New York Jets faced the Baltimore Colts in Super Bowl III. The game was the third AFL-NFL professional football championship and the first to bear the trademark name "Super Bowl." It is regarded as one of the greatest upsets in sports history. The Colts were heavily favored and entered the game with a record of thirteen wins and a single loss for the regular season, but three days before the game Jets quarterback Joe Namath appeared at the Miami Touchdown Club and personally guaranteed a victory to the astonishment of everyone present. Namath's prediction was immediately front-page news in every newspaper in America. Don Shula, head coach of the Colts, was angry but also saw this as an opportunity to inspire his team. He immediately pinned the offending articles on the team's bulletin board and in every one of his players' sports lockers.

Jets' head coach Weeb Ewbank learned of Namath's comments the next day. He was furious and confronted Namath in the Jets' locker room. Ewbank asked him if he realized he had helped motivate the Colts for the upcoming game. Namath looked at him in surprise. "But Coach," he said "it is your fault! You gave me the confidence!" Fortunately for Namath the Jets won a surprise victory by the score of 16–7 in what many still consider the greatest Super Bowl ever played.

Back in Gettysburg, as preparations for the attack continued, Lee was clearly confident that the Army of Northern Virginia would be victorious. One observer reported that when Longstreet questioned the attack on July 3 Lee replied optimistically, "There never were such men in an army before. They will go anywhere and do anything if properly led."[25] In the town, the Reverend Doctor Michael Jacobs at Pennsylvania College—now Gettysburg College—kept pace with the journal he maintained over the course of the three-day battle and its aftermath. His entry for 1:07 p.m. July 3 recorded, "After a long morning calm, the cannons begin firing again." The Confederate bombardment of their Cemetery Ridge objective had begun.

Although eyewitness accounts of the length of the bombardment vary widely, it is generally accepted that for two hours the Confederate cannon line organized by Alexander and Walker shelled the Union position on Cemetery Ridge trying to destroy or drive away the defenders. Initially, Union cannon responded with return fire. But after the first fifteen to twenty minutes, Brigadier General Henry Hunt, chief of artillery for the Union Army of the Potomac, rode along the line and ordered the Union artillery batteries to cease fire and conserve their ammunition for the expected infantry attack.

Meanwhile, on the Confederate artillery line, Lieutenant Colonel Alexander, on his knees and with the aid of field glasses, attempted to look under the building smoke cloud from the discharge of the two opposing lines of cannon to observe the strike of his rounds on the objective. Although he did not know it, faulty fuses resulted in a large number of Confederate projectiles continuing their trajectory over and beyond their intended target prior to exploding. Still, the effects of the Confederate artillery fire were felt on the Union defensive position. General O. O. Howard, whose troops were in position on Cemetery Hill itself, later wrote:

> Shells burst in the air, in the ground to the right and left, killing horses, exploding caissons [artillery ammunition carriers], over-turning tombstones, and smashing fences. There was no place of safety. In one regiment twenty-seven were killed and wounded by one shell....[26]

Nonetheless, as the minutes ticked away so did the Confederate's supply of artillery ammunition. Alexander grew increasingly anxious. According to his memoirs, he ultimately would send a note to Pickett stating, "If you are coming at all, you must come at once or I cannot give you proper support, but the enemy's fire has not slackened at all. At least eighteen guns are still firing from the cemetery itself."[27]

Pickett galloped on his horse, with Alexander's note in hand, to find Longstreet at a position on the eastern edge of the Seminary Ridge tree line where he could observe the effects of the artillery bombardment. In his memoirs, Longstreet confirmed the wording of the note Pickett handed to him. After he had read it Longstreet later recollected, "Pickett said, 'General, shall I advance?' The effort to speak failed and I could only indicate it by an affirmative bow. He accepted the duty with seeming confidence of success, leaped on his horse and rode gayly to his command."[28] In later times Longstreet wrote regarding the same incident, "I could not speak. I merely gave a nod of assent, and then the tears rushed to my eyes as I saw those brave fellows rush to certain death."[29]

Pickett rode to the front of his division and called out, "Charge the enemy, and remember old Virginia. Forward! Guide center! March!" In a battle line a mile wide from south to north on the east side of Seminary Ridge, the Confederate infantry commanded by Pickett, Pettigrew, and Trimble, marched steadily forward. Forty regiments of infantry walked into harm's way, eighteen from Virginia, fifteen from North Carolina, three each from Tennessee and Mississippi, and one from Alabama.[30]

Lieutenant Frank Aretas Haskell was a Dartmouth College graduate and a prewar attorney from Madison, Wisconsin. At Gettysburg, Haskell was aide-de-camp to II Corps division commander Brigadier General John Gibbon, whose troops were at the epicenter of the Confederate attack objective. Haskell was in a perfect position to observe the advance of the Confederate infantry and provided this account:

> None on the crest now needed to be told that the enemy is advancing. Every eye could see his legions, an overwhelming resistless tide of an ocean of armed men sweeping upon us! Regiment after regiment and brigade after brigade rapidly take place in the lines forming the assault.... [T]he dull gray masses deploy, man touching man, rank pressing rank and line supporting line.... Right on they move as with one soul, in perfect order...magnificent, grim, irresistible.[31]

As daunting as the Confederate assault appeared from the Union defensive lines, the attacking troops have their own version of approaching the gates of hell. As their overly large formation of attacking infantry crossed the 1.1 miles of open ground between the Seminary and Cemetery Ridges, they had become a "target-rich" environment for the Union artillery gunners on Cemetery Ridge, Cemetery Hill, and Little Round Top. Major Charles Peyton, destined to be the surviving senior officer of Garnett's brigade of Pickett's division, explained what happened at the midpoint of their advance across the open fields:

Up to this time we had suffered but little from the enemy's [artillery] batteries...with the exception of one posted on the mountain about a mile to our right [Little Round Top], which enfiladed nearly our entire line with fearful effect, sometimes as many as ten men being killed or wounded by a single shell.[32]

As previously mentioned, brigade commander "Dick" Garnett, unable to walk due to a leg injury, was one of four or five men to ride his horse during the attack. Walter Harrison, inspector general of Pickett's division, thought that Garnett's whole purpose was to expose himself, even unnecessarily, "to wipe out effectively, by some great distinction in action, what he felt was an unmerited slur upon his military reputation." Eppa Hunton, one of Garnett's regimental commanders and one of the few leaders who also rode his horse into the attack said of Garnett, "He was one of the noblest and bravest men I ever knew."[33]

Shaken but undeterred by the incoming artillery fire, the Confederates continued their advance. However, their original mile-wide line had become shorter due to casualties inflicted by Union artillery fire. As the casualties rapidly grew, all units closed ranks to the center of the line. They advanced as one, moving toward the Emmitsburg Road which lay roughly 250 yards west of the crest of the Union-occupied Cemetery Ridge. Lieutenant Haskell continued to observe:

All was orderly and still upon our crest; no noise and no confusion. The men had little need of commands, for the survivors of a dozen battles knew well enough what this array in front portended, already in their places, they would be prepared to act when the right time should come.... General Gibbon rode down the lines, cool and calm, and in an unimpassioned voice he called to the men, "Do not hurry, men, and fire too fast, let them come up close before you fire, and then aim low and steadily." The coolness of their General was reflected in the faces of the men.[34]

As the Confederate battle lines moved closer to the Emmitsburg Road they came within the effective range of the Union infantry behind the stone walls on Cemetery Ridge. Volleys of rifle and musket fire burst from the walls as the Yankees opened fire. Still, the advancing

Rebels attempted to push forward. But stout post and rail fences had been firmly planted on both sides of the road and slowed their advance. Men began to bunch up, the once orderly formations were broken up. Another "target-rich" environment had been created, this time for the defending Union infantry.

Once over the second fence and on the east side of the road, the attackers briefly attempted to reorganize their lines prior to pushing farther up the slope. But now the battle lines east of the road measured only a quarter mile across their front. As they advanced farther up the slope, the defenders' lines overlapped those of the attackers, and they were able to also fire into the Confederate flanks as well as their front. Union cannon were pushed down to the wall, and the infamous canister antipersonnel rounds, which turned the cannon into giant shotguns, were now double-loaded by the gunners and fired into the ranks of the attacking Confederate infantry.

As the attackers approached the wall, the target range for the defenders decreased while their accuracy increased. Men fell in growing numbers. Brigade commander Lewis Armistead led a small group of Confederate attackers, perhaps no more than two to three hundred, over the Union defended wall. He was almost immediately shot and mortally wounded, and the men who had followed him were either killed or captured.

The Confederate attack of July 3 had been defeated. Overall, the three-day battle at Gettysburg was a major military victory for the Union, and a few months later President Abraham Lincoln made it a moral victory as well. But the Union victory did not end the war, which continued for twenty more bloody months. Today there are twenty-five American Civil War campaign streamers on the US Army flag. Each is for a major campaign that was fought during the war beginning with the Bull Run campaign in 1861. The streamer for Gettysburg is number thirteen. Hence, US Army Civil War heritage is that there were twelve campaigns prior to Gettysburg and twelve campaigns after Gettysburg. As British Prime Minister Winston Churchill observed during the Second World War following the 1942 Allied victory at the battle of El Alamein: *"Now this is not the end. It is not even the beginning of the end. But it is, perhaps, the end of the beginning."*[35]

CHAPTER 11

The Aftermath

Lee's July 3 attack against the center of the Union defensive position on Cemetery Ridge failed. The surviving Confederate troops fled across the field under harassing artillery fire that knocked up dirt and debris. Lee, mounted on his horse, met them as they returned to their original attack positions on Seminary Ridge. There was no question in the mind of those soldiers as to who remained their leader and commander. Many of them called out to him to regroup and renew the attack. In reply, Lee made it clear that he accepted full blame for the failure of the attack. He was particularly solicitous to one officer who was deeply depressed. "Never mind, General," he told him taking his hand as he spoke. "All of this has been my fault. It is I who have lost this fight, and you must help me out of it the best way you can."[1] After that, beyond some minor engagements of little consequence, the fighting at Gettysburg was over. Now the soldiers and the citizens had to deal with the aftermath of three days of battle.

Of the more than 5,000 infantrymen who made up Pickett's division and the 420 men in Dearing's supporting artillery battalion, 2,655 were casualties following the charge. Nearly 500 were killed outright. The remainder were wounded or captured, a loss rate of just under 50 percent. But there were more. Of the wounded, 233 would die of their wounds over the next few days in Union and Confederate field hospitals or in US military hospitals in Baltimore, Maryland, as well as Chester and Harrisburg, Pennsylvania. Of the captured, 197 were destined to die from disease in Union prisoner of war camps at Fort Delaware and Point Lookout, Maryland.[2]

While George Pickett survived unscathed, the leadership of his division was decimated. As mentioned in the previous chapter, Brigadier General Lewis Armistead was mortally wounded leading his brigade in the charge and died the next day. Brigade commander James Kemper was wounded and taken prisoner. Brigade commander "Dick" Garnett was killed in action just before the wall that Union soldiers were shooting from behind. In one instant he was there, still mounted on his horse among his men, encouraging them forward. In the next instant he was no longer visible, his riderless black horse last seen racing at a terrified gallop back toward Seminary Ridge. Garnett's body was never identified among the dead. Years later his personalized, engraved sword was found for sale in a pawnshop in Baltimore.

All the fifteen regimental commanders in Pickett's division were casualties in one form or another. Colonel Waller Tazewell Patton, commander of the 7th Virginia Infantry, was wounded and taken prisoner. With his lower jaw shot away, he was unable to eat or speak. The only way he could communicate was to write on a slate with chalk. For two weeks he lay in the dormitory at Pennsylvania College being cared for as much as was possible given the nature of his wounds and the limited medical technology of the period. Just before dying from malnutrition, Patton instructed his nurse to write a final letter to his mother, which he dictated, "Tell my mother I died in a foreign land."

Waller Tazewell Patton, great-uncle of US Army General George S. Patton of World War II fame, died in Gettysburg on July 21, 1863, at just twenty-eight. His remains were eventually "repatriated" to his native Virginia and reinterred in Stonewall Confederate Cemetery in Winchester, Virginia, next to his brother who also was killed in the war.[3]

Casualties for the two Confederate divisions commanded by Generals Pettigrew and Trimble, the other and often forgotten half of "Pickett's Charge," are more difficult to determine since these units were heavily engaged on the first as well as the third day of the battle. Of the estimated 5,000 men Pettigrew took across the field on July 3, perhaps 40 percent became casualties in making the attack. The two small brigades commanded by Trimble mustered an estimated 2,300 men that morning and suffered 45 percent casualties.[4]

One of the survivors of Pettigrew's division was Sergeant June Kimble (previously mentioned) of the 14th Tennessee Infantry. In a letter to his mother after the attack that was later reprinted in *Confederate Veteran* magazine, Kimble confessed he began his individual retreat to Seminary Ridge once it became clear that the Confederate attack had failed. "For about one hundred yards I broke the lighting speed record." Then, thinking better of it, not wanting the dishonor of getting shot in the back running from the enemy lines, he stopped running, turned around, faced his enemy on Cemetery Ridge, and walked backwards to his starting position a mile away.[5]

Overall Confederate leadership had been decimated. For the entire army over 150 colonels, lieutenant colonels, and majors had been killed, wounded, or taken prisoner. Nineteen colonels had been killed during the fighting, the most in any single battle in which the army had been involved. A stunning example might well have been the Liberty Hall Volunteers, or Company I, 4th Virginia infantry. In April 1861, seventy-three volunteers had joined the unit and headed off to war. As it marched away from Gettysburg, only three members remained.[6]

For the successful Union defenders, the advantage of their slightly elevated position, their long fields of artillery fire across a mile of open ground, the protection of a stone wall, their ability to deliver enfilade and flanking fire on the attacking force as it drew closer, and perhaps most important, strong leadership, organizational cohesion, and individual resolution, enabled them to turn back the Confederate attack. In team sport events it is often said that the primary duty of the team coach or manager is to recognize the individual talents of their players and then place them collectively in those situations where they can win. On July 3, 1863, Confederate commander Lee failed in doing so while Union commander Meade succeeded.

Still, the Gettysburg victory was not without cost for Meade's Army of the Potomac. Of the combined force of 7,000 men in the two divisions from the Union II Corps defending at the focal point of the Confederate attack, two of every five men in Gibbon's division and one of every three men in Hays's division were killed, wounded, or missing. Included in those numbers were II Corps commander Hancock and division commander Gibbon, both wounded in action leading their troops. Both were lost to the army for several months, but they returned to duty by 1864. At the end of the battle, General Meade had to reconsider his leadership teams. In addition to the losses of Hancock and Gibbon, Reynolds was killed on the first day, and Sickles was wounded on the second day and permanently out of action. Many of Meade's fifty-one infantry brigades were now commanded by former regimental commanders, and some of the regiments were commanded by surviving company commanders. In some cases, the senior leaders in individual companies were sergeants rather than captains or lieutenants.

On July 4, the fourth day at Gettysburg, both armies expected the other to attack. It did not happen. Both armies were "fought out" and exhausted. As George Meade reflected on what had happened during the previous three days and reviewed the information supplied to him by his chain of command, he found that one of every four soldiers he had brought to Gettysburg was a casualty. While it was not yet certain, it appeared he had achieved a major battlefield victory over Lee, a victory which none of his six predecessors as commander of the Army of the Potomac had accomplished. General Meade was elated at his success and sent a message to Lincoln proclaiming that he had achieved a "glorious result."

But what should Meade have done in follow-up to this glorious result? Perhaps the better question is: What *could* he do in the aftermath? After three days of battle, over 3,000 of his men had been killed, over 14,500 wounded, and over 5,000 missing or captured. Of the survivors, most of the men had existed the last few days on scant marching rations. The survivors had to be fed, the dead had to be buried, and the wounded—both his own and the large number of wounded enemy prisoners—had to be gathered for medical care, which was now overwhelmed in capacity and capability.

At 12 p.m. on July 4, Meade sent a message to General-in-Chief Halleck in Washington, a clue as to what was, and what was not, going to happen next:

The enemy apparently has thrown back his left and placed guns and troops in rear [west] of Gettysburg, which we now hold. The enemy has abandoned large numbers of his killed and wounded on the field. I shall require some time to get up supplies, ammunition, etc., rest the army, worn out by long marches and three days hard fighting....[7]

Over the following days Meade pursued slowly while Lee moved faster in his withdrawal south. The evening of July 3, Lee convened a council of war of his senior subordinate commanders and staff officers at General A. P. Hill's corps headquarters at the Emanuel Pitzer farm on the west shoulder of Seminary Ridge. It was here that General Lee briefed his senior leaders on the who, what, when, where, and how the Confederate army was going to successfully break contact with the enemy, withdraw what was left of the force over South Mountain while encumbered by hundreds of wagons, herds of "liberated" livestock, several thousand wounded comrades, over 4,000 enemy prisoners of war, and make their way to the Potomac River for a safe crossing back into Virginia to fight again another day. There was no need for "discretionary" orders.

The first step in the process was to immediately shorten and consolidate the Confederate battle line in anticipation of a possible enemy counterattack. Ewell's Second Corps on the left and Longstreet's First Corps on the right were pulled back to Seminary Ridge with A. P. Hill's Third Corps in the center. As a result, a continuous defensive line facing Cemetery Ridge and the enemy was created the night of July 3, which ran from Oak Hill in the north down along Seminary Ridge to Warfield Ridge in the south. In creating this defensive line, Lee also sought to place his soldiers in positions from which they could readily embark upon the retreat that he now saw as the most viable course of action. He needed all good men at that moment. He did not wish to waste their energy or their time. Much more endurance would be asked of them in the coming days, and Lee understood that thoughtfulness now would avoid putting undue stress on the troops during moments of crisis. After heavy losses, Lee had a new vision that he hoped would lead his team to victory in future: withdraw and fight again another day.

Throughout the fighting Lee had been careful to protect two important roads and two key mountain passes that connected Gettysburg with the Cumberland Valley on the west side of the South Mountain range. The Cumberland Valley north of the Potomac River and the Shenandoah Valley south of the Potomac are the same valley system, but they are called different names on opposite sides of the river. This valley system served as the Confederate army's avenue approach into the north at the start of the campaign. The same valley system would now serve as their line of retreat back to Virginia.

A priority for Lee was to get his large number of wagons and wagon trains on the roads back over South Mountain and into the more secure area of the Cumberland Valley well ahead of his fighting regiments, brigades, and divisions. One such wagon train, estimated to be seventeen miles long, started out in the late afternoon of July 4. It passed through Cashtown Pass, crossed over South Mountain, and entered the Cumberland Valley carrying with it what little ammunition remained plus the burden of 4,000 enemy prisoners and 8,500 Confederate wounded.[8] Another large wagon train—fifteen to twenty miles long—departed the area using the Fairfield Road ahead of the combat component.

The last part of the retreat was the movement of the combat component of the army out the Fairfield Road, up and around Jack Mountain, and through Monterey Pass. As the sun set on July 4, it became apparent to Lee that General Meade was not going to counterattack. The wagon trains had gotten a good start, so it was time to begin withdrawing his troops. A. P. Hill's Third Corps led the way followed by Longstreet's men, then Ewell's. The artillery and supply wagons of each corps were mixed in among their marching troops. Hill's men started marching just after dark on July 4 toward Fairfield and the high ground beyond. But then the rains started.

About midday on July 5, the Union VI Corps began an advance over and beyond the abandoned Confederate positions on Seminary Ridge. Their line of march took them in the direction of Fairfield where they ran into the Confederate rear guard. The heavy rains had turned the roads and fields into a quagmire. Under those conditions, combined with the effective action of the Confederate rear guard, the Union army did not get far. Militarily it would be inaccurate to describe their

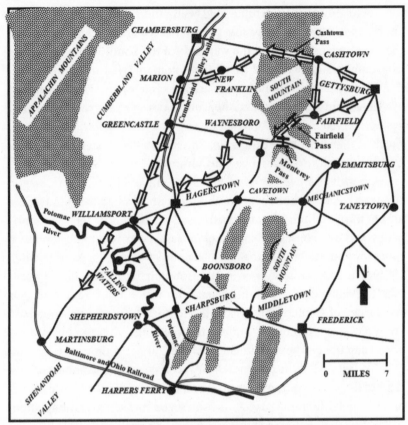

MAP 11.0 ROUTES OF CONFEDERATE RETREAT AFTER THE BATTLE.

limited and cautious advance as a "pursuit" of a defeated enemy. Lee's army had quickly moved on to the high ground of South Mountain and beyond. The Confederates had gotten away, at least for the moment.

On July 6 the retreating Confederate army, having been successful in escaping the grasp of their enemy, began reassembling near Hagerstown, Maryland. The rear guard rejoined the main body of the army the following day. However, now on the north and northeast bank of the Potomac River, they found that the post-battle rains, which up to now had aided them in disengaging from the enemy, also made the river fords impassable for their continued retreat into Virginia.

Trapped, at least temporarily, with the Potomac River to their back, a hasty defensive position was established. The Union Army of the Potomac, slowed down by the exhausted condition of its soldiers and animals—as General Meade had previously cautioned at end of the battle—was still some distance away. This allowed time for earthworks to be constructed and the Confederate defensive position to be reinforced. By July 11, a cordon defense had been established by Lee's army to protect the crossing sites at Williamsport and Falling Waters while waiting for the river's depth and flow speed to recede to safe, passable levels.[9]

On July 12 the initial forces of the Union army began to arrive. That night a council of war was held at Meade's headquarters. There was a consensus by the leadership that they did not have enough information about the nature of the Confederate defensive position. Consequently, it was decided that the Army of the Potomac would not attack the next day but allow time for a reconnaissance mission to be made and plans developed more fully. This meant the earliest Meade's army was going to attack was July 14. However, on the night of July 13 the river had receded enough for the Confederate army to begin crossing. By 11 a.m. on July 14, all but the rear guard of Lee's army were safely across the river and back in Virginia.[10]

Lincoln was disconsolate, believing that there had been an opportunity to destroy the Army of Northern Virginia. On July 4, he had received word that the Confederate army defending Vicksburg had surrendered to General Ulysses Grant. As a result, the president believed the Vicksburg success coupled with an aggressive pursuit of the retreating Confederates from Gettysburg might have brought the war to an end.

He confided to Secretary of the Navy Gideon Welles, "Our Army held the war in the hollow of their hand, and they would not close it. We had gone through all the labor of tilling and planting an enormous crop and when it was ripe, we did not harvest it."[11]

The war would continue for nearly two more long and bloody years.

LEADERSHIP MOMENT   You are now President Abraham Lincoln. Major General Henry W. Halleck, your principal military adviser, has continued to update you on Lee's retreat and his successful crossing of the Potomac on July 14. You also received a copy of the general order to the Army of the Potomac that General George Gordon Meade had written commending the soldiers (and himself) for their success at Gettysburg that had driven "from our soil every vestige of the presence of the invader." You are extremely disappointed with the results of this critical battle and your commanding general. You believe that had Meade pursued Lee more aggressively he might have been able to destroy the Army of Northern Virginia, and this, coupled with the recent victory at Vicksburg, might have brought about an end to the war in the summer of 1863. What actions do you take and why? Should you consider replacing General Meade?

WHAT CAN WE LEARN FROM THIS VIGNETTE ABOUT LEADERSHIP?

How do you define success? One of the most difficult challenges many organizations have is determining how to define success and communicating that clearly throughout the entire leadership structure. Walt Ulmer, former head of the Center for Creative Leadership, observed that the most neglected element of leadership and management in most organizations was an inability to have a clear process to determine success and modify planning accordingly.

Success for any organization—army, nonprofit, or corporation—should include both an objective and subjective calculation. This must consider hard data such as financial or material gains vs. losses, market share, effective use of critical resources, and more. It must also include a subjective analysis of stakeholder/client satisfaction as well as an honest evaluation of how the organization is performing in its ever-changing environment. This must also include a careful consideration of its comparative performance with respect to peer institutions or competitors. Subjective analysis must carefully examine where the institution is regarding its stated goals and mission. Ultimately, effective leaders understand that long-term success depends on not only the effectiveness of utilizing an organization's financial and physical resources but also—and perhaps most importantly—its human resources.

Clearly, General Meade and President Lincoln had different views on what constituted "success" at Gettysburg. Meade was newly in command—by the end of the battle on July 4 he had been in command of the Army of the Potomac for less than one week. He believed success was defeating the Confederate army led by Robert E. Lee on the battlefield and forcing the Rebels to retreat. This is logical as it was something that had not been accomplished by any of his predecessors. His elation and subsequent caution might be somewhat understandable then. President Lincoln had been the commander in chief since the onset of the war, and its burdens weighed heavily on him. Furthermore, the president knew he had to face the American people during the upcoming 1864 election. He desperately wanted to bring the war to a conclusion and preserve the Union.

Consequently, organizations must clearly understand and effectively communicate the difference between *tactical* and *strategic success*. Meade achieved a stunning tactical success by defeating Lee at Gettysburg and forcing the Confederate army to withdraw from Pennsylvania. His critics now and in 1863 argue that he failed to translate that tactical achievement into strategic success for his organization—the Union.

A story was once told about a high school science teacher who posted a banner in the classroom with a well-known expression, "What is popular is not always right, and what is right is not always popular." The same could be said for any organization public or private. Just because doing things in a certain way achieves short-term results does not mean that the accomplishment is right, sustainable, or even acceptable. Too often leaders measure success primarily in objective terms of dollars earned and immediate results produced. These measurements are further examined against a relatively short time frame of a week, month, or quarter of the calendar year. They are not considered with respect to how those things are accomplished and whether they are sustainable.

In evaluation terms, organizations too frequently focus on *performance* or the achievement of set goals, which are normally objective. They fail to also consider the full value of *process* metrics: measures of how well those same goals were achieved, which is frequently subjective. It is great for any organization to achieve its immediate goals, but this is neither strategic nor sustainable if the organization is alienating stakeholders in the process. Strategic "failure" can also result if the organization is suffering significant staff turnover because employees are stressed, overworked, and disconnected from each other as well as the organization. Consequently, calculating an organization's strategic success must be a disciplined integrated process and not merely a data solution. An expert once commented, "Leaders must carefully coordinate the dashboard and the scoreboard."

Many organizations fail to consider process metrics and as a result merely survive instead of thriving. This is the due to how their leaders define success and how they value the people who drive the organization's accomplishments. Leaders who invest in the workforce have a greater probability of achieving programmatic success while ensuring their organizations are more resilient and sustainable.

This is hardly revolutionary and has been cited by both organizational experts and successful leaders. For example, it is widely believed that Walmart's success started with the company's philosophy established by its founder, Sam Walton. He had three basic tenets that he believed were the foundation of the company, and the first was "respect for the individual." This conviction was further underscored in his "Ten Rules of Business." The top six rules for the purposes of this analysis are as follows: (1) encourage passion from employees since it will translate into their best every day, (2) share profits with your team, (3) motivate employees through development, (4) communicate everything to them, (5) appreciate their efforts since "praise costs nothing," and (6) listen to them.[12] Walton once observed, "Outstanding leaders go out of their way to boost the self-esteem of their personnel. If people believe in themselves, it's amazing what they can accomplish." This same belief was emphasized by Lee Iacocca in his autobiography as he stressed three important variables—the organization's people, product, and profits.[13]

Decision-making and emotion. On July 14, 1863, word reached Washington, DC, that the Confederate army had crossed the Potomac back into Virginia. General Halleck, President Lincoln's principal military adviser, immediately dispatched a message to General Meade expressing the disappointment that was felt throughout the White House. "I need hardly say to you that the escape of Lee's Army without another battle has created great dissatisfaction in the mind of the President...."[14] Meade clearly viewed this as a rebuke and responded that he would like to be relieved of command.

It is reported that Lincoln was literally tearing his hair in frustration and disappointment. Halleck went to the Oval Office and delivered General Meade's message requesting to be relieved. Lincoln immediately sat down and wrote a long and stinging letter to his commander. In it the president acknowledged Meade's request but continued:

> *I am very, very grateful to you for the magnificent success you gave the cause of the country at Gettysburg; and I am sorry now to be the author of the slightest pain to you. But I was in such deep distress myself that I could not restrain some expression of it.... I do not believe you appreciate the magnitude of the misfortune involved in Lee's escape. He was within your easy grasp, and to have closed upon him would, in connection with out other late successes, have ended the war. As it is, the war will be prolonged indefinitely.*[15]

The president then made a critical decision. He put down his pen and placed the letter in his desk drawer. He returned to the Oval Office the following morning—having perhaps "cooled off"—reread the letter and decided not to send it. He scribbled on the envelope: *To Gen. Meade, never sent, or signed*.[16] He probably realized that to do so would certainly result in Meade's resignation, and Meade would have joined a growing list of failed Union commanders. In Lincoln's decision is a further strategic lesson for all leaders: if possible, don't make important decisions when you are angry. Try to find time to calm down and reflect.

Lincoln may have done this for several reasons. He may have believed that even a *tactical* success was critical to both the army and the nation that had suffered so many stunning setbacks. Furthermore, the soldiers who had fought so valiantly at Gettysburg did not deserve what might have been construed as an implied reproach to their courage that the publication of the letter might have engendered.

As is often the case when leaders confront a tough decision, other problems present themselves that may have a significant impact.

Lincoln had a serious domestic crisis on his hands as he was drafting the letter to General Meade, which may have also encouraged him not to send it. The president was clearly distracted by what one observer described as the "all engrossing topic of conversation" in Washington, which was occurring in New York City.[17] On July 13 a Union army officer and some clerks had begun feeding names into a drum and turning it in at an office near 46th Street and Third Avenue in New York. Names would then be impartially withdrawn, thus beginning conscription, or the "draft" of eligible men into the Union army. Almost immediately a paving stone was thrown though the draft office window, and a mob attacked the building. The officer and clerks fled for their lives while a police guard was nearly beaten to death.

This was the beginning of the New York City draft riots that raged until July 16. This remains the largest civil disturbance in a major American city in the nation's history. The riot also had serious racial overtones. Most of the rioters were Irish immigrants who feared that free black people would compete for work. They further resented the fact that, under the conscription law, wealthy men could pay a $300 commutation fee to avoid being drafted. As the rioting spread, the mayor's home was attacked, trolley lines were ripped up, dozens of police were killed, Negroes were lynched, and a black orphanage was burned to the ground. The militia could not be called out because it had been sent to Pennsylvania. The official report listed around 120 killed and thousands injured, but many believe that the death toll was much higher. Property damage was estimated between $400,000 and $2.5 million, and mob violence did not end until soldiers who had been at Gettysburg entered the city. The conduct of the draft was suspended in New York until August 19, at which time it was protected by the presence of over 20,000 federal troops in the city.[18]

The difference between authority and responsibility. The basis of a strong organizational structure largely rests upon the relationship between "authority" and "responsibility." These two concepts are not the same though many people mistakenly use them interchangeably. Authority is the legal right to give orders or compel subordinates to perform necessary tasks. This is often a reflection of a person's position within the organization's hierarchy. Responsibility is the need for accountability or to be answerable for an obligation that the organization has undertaken. Successful leaders understand that they must give authority to subordinates, since it is not possible for them to accomplish all the tasks required of a modern complex organization. The transfer of authority also implies making available sufficient resources—people, material, and time—as well as any necessary training or development prior to tackling the new task.

A measure of responsibility certainly lies with the subordinate, but ultimate responsibility rests with the leader, particularly for those tasks critical to an organization's future. One need only think of the famous plaque that President Harry Truman placed on his desk in the Oval Office: "The buck stops here." Truman was an inveterate poker player, and the phrase is derived from this card game. It has come to mean that someone cannot absolve himself or herself from failure by denying authority or jurisdiction.

This is perhaps best illustrated in the maritime field. The captain of a ship, whether military or commercial, is ultimately responsible for its operation. Since a long voyage may take several weeks, it is clearly not possible for him or her to remain on the vessel's bridge twenty-four hours a day. As a result, subordinates are selected and then trained to be the captain's representative on the bridge in his or her absence.

In the US Navy and Coast Guard this is called the "officer of the deck" (OOD). When the ship is underway, the OOD oversees navigation and the overall safe operations of the ship. Training for this position is rigorous, and each applicant must pass numerous tests before being awarded a Surface Warfare Officer's badge. When seen on a uniform, this badge clearly identifies the wearer as someone who has been trained and certified for this critical position. If the ship strikes a rock and is badly damaged or sinks, however, the OOD will be held responsible. But since a crisis like this is an existential event for the vessel, the captain will also likely be held accountable.

Robert Half, founder of a global human resource consulting firm, once observed, "The search for blame is always successful." So why should a leader publicly accept responsibility in the immediate aftermath of a major organizational disaster? Two reasons come to mind. First, as previously mentioned, a climate of initiative is fundamental to any organization's continued success. This will not occur if members of the team believe that they are working in a zero-defects organization, or that any setback, no matter how small, will be immediately followed by the leader looking for someone to "throw under the bus." Furthermore, initiative may be fundamental to the organization's rapid recovery from a major setback.

Second, Ralph Waldo Emerson once observed, "Trust men and they will be true to you." The willingness of the leader to be a "heat shield" to his or her team when the organization suffers failure will serve to increase trust between leaders and followers. Leaders often talk about how they want their team to be "loyal" to the organization, and this is very important. But as Emerson suggested, people will be loyal to a leader who is also loyal to them particularly at difficult moments. Furthermore, this may also be critical during any team's recovery and beyond. This does not mean that the leader should subsequently avoid conducting a thorough review of what went wrong in the aftermath. These efforts over time may result in changes in processes, procedures, or even personnel, which is crucial for any "learning" organization.

A modern example might be Mark Zuckerberg, founder and CEO of Facebook. Zuckerberg has been widely credited with a transformational leadership style that focuses aggressively on innovation and growth. He founded Facebook in 2004 at the age of twenty and is estimated to now be worth $72 billion.

In the aftermath of the 2016 election Facebook faced perhaps its greatest crisis since its founding—the functional equivalent of the "ship hitting a rock." It was discovered that Facebook had failed to protect the privacy of 50 million users who were secretly mined for voter insights during the 2016 election. Millions of clients deleted their accounts, and this catastrophe caused serious damage to the organizational climate at Facebook. Numerous veteran employees sought to transfer to other divisions or left the corporation altogether. Zuckerberg was called before Congress but failed to appear at an initial staff meeting about the issue and the corporation's responsibilities. He finally admitted that "it was also a breach of trust between Facebook and the people who share their data with us and expect us to protect it."

The crisis Facebook confronted was essentially an organizational challenge of authority and responsibility in a rapidly evolving environment. Zuckerberg had displayed tremendous leadership in the creation of Facebook. He had been described by many as the quintessential twenty-first-century leader who is passionate, communicates well, solves problems, has excellent interpersonal skills, and provides a true vision for his organization. Still the long-term future of his company may depend on how he is able to handle the following questions: (1) What is the leader's personal responsibility? (2) What is organizational responsibility and how is it different? (3) Who had the authority to prevent this problem from occurring, and how did they exercise it? (4) How will the answers to these questions serve to reestablish trust and confidence in Facebook's stakeholder and employees? Zuckerberg initially was shaken by the problem:

> If you had asked me, when I got started with Facebook, if one of the central things I'd need to work on now is preventing governments from interfering in each other's elections, there's no way I thought that's what I'd be doing if we talked in 2004 in my dorm room.[19]

In the immediate aftermath of Gettysburg, Robert E. Lee accepted full responsibility for his army's defeat. He sought to console a devastated General George Pickett and told him, "This has been my fight, and upon my shoulders rests the blame....Your men have done all that men can do." After a brief pause, he added, "The fault is entirely my own."[20]

Lee could have logically blamed Stuart due to his absence. He might have also argued that Ewell's failure to pursue the retreating federal troops on July 1 was the reason for the defeat. He could have even blamed Longstreet for being slow in moving his forces into position on July 2, which prevented the South from achieving victory. But he likely realized that to do so would have shattered his organization at a critical moment.

In the weeks that followed, Confederate civilian and military leaders as well as the general public began the difficult process of analyzing the reasons for this devastating defeat. Lee continued to largely accept responsibility, as he would do for the rest of his life. He wrote a letter to President Jefferson Davis on August 8 proposing "to Your Excellency the propriety of selecting another commander" for the Army of Northern Virginia. Lee even noted "the growing failure of my bodily strength" since being seriously ill in the spring.

Davis replied to Lee's proposed resignation three days later, asking, "Where am I to find that new commander who is to possess the greater ability which you believe to be required?" He concluded with a vote of confidence, "To ask me to substitute you by someone in my judgement more fit to command, or who would possess more of the confidence of the army, or of the reflecting men of the country, is to demand an impossibility."[21] Robert E. Lee remained commander of the Confederate Army of Northern Virginia until the war's end. Likewise, George G. Meade remained commander of the federal Army of the Potomac until the war's end.

CHAPTER 12

"Four Score
and Seven Years Ago..."

By Monday July 6 the main forces of both armies had left Gettysburg and Adams County, Pennsylvania. In their wake they left carnage, destruction, and death. As the two armies departed, the roughly 2,400 citizens of Gettysburg emerged from their cellars to a horrific scene. There were roughly 8,000 Union and Confederate dead strewn across the field, and the vast majority had not yet been buried. In addition, there were over 5,000 dead horses and mules lying in the hot July sun.

The Union had also suffered over 14,000 wounded, and every building in the town was now a makeshift hospital. The Confederates had been forced to leave over 5,000 of their wounded in Gettysburg as they retreated south. They were either too badly injured or left behind due to a shortage of wagons to convey them. Many of the wounded from both sides would die in the weeks that followed.

Union brigade commander Norman Hall, whose troops had defended against the charge of George Pickett's men at Cemetery Ridge, later wrote in his after-action report, "Piles of dead and thousands of wounded upon both sides attested the desperation of assailants and defenders." Eventually, 522 dead Confederate soldiers would be buried in a mass grave in the field between Hall's defensive position on Cemetery Ridge and the Emmitsburg Road 250 yards away.[1]

But it wasn't just the fields of Pickett's Charge where the dead and wounded lay. The fighting over three days encompassed a rectangular area measuring just over three miles wide east to west by over three and a half miles long north to south with the town of Gettysburg in the upper center. The majority of the dead and the wounded left behind lay somewhere at random, within those roughly 7,000 acres of ground on thirty-eight different farms.

What of the farmers and landowners? German immigrant Johann (John) Herbst owned a 110-acre farm that had been contested on the first day of fighting. His house survived, but his barn was burned to the ground. All his farm equipment had been destroyed, and the Rebels had confiscated his livestock and produce. He ultimately filed a damage claim with the federal government detailing an inventory of his losses that totaled $2,689.36. Eventually, he received $2606.75 as the government's approved settlement—$53,800 in 2018 dollars.[2]

Other farmers were not so fortunate during the battle, nor in their dealings with the state and federal governments afterwards. George Rose owned a 230-acre farm between Little Round Top and the Emmitsburg Road, and it was his fields, barn, and house over which the Confederates attacked on July 2. After the battle George, his brother John, and tenant farmer Francis Ogden also filed damage claims with the federal government that totaled over $4,500—$92,800 in 2018 dollars. They received no payment from the government.[3] J. Howard Wert provided this account of his visit to the Rose farm soon after the battle:

> A much disgusted man was Rose when he returned [to the farm].... His house was filled with vermin, his supply of drinking water polluted with dead bodies.... Nearly 100 Confederates were buried in his garden, some 175 behind the barn and around the wagon shed....[4]

What burials took place during the battle were hasty in nature, not very deep, and intended to be temporary. Over the course of the three days most of the dead remained unburied until the fighting ceased, and the two contending armies separated. With the Confederate army in retreat, it was left to the Union army to tend to the dead. When the Union troops left Gettysburg on July 6, the local civilian population completed the burials if for no other reason than self-preservation in the July heat.

Many of the dead were "unknown." The US Army did not require a standardized individual identity system, or "dog-tags," until 1906. During the Civil War the absence of such a system was a major problem, particularly in those cases where the dead had remained exposed to the elements for several days prior to being recovered.

No matter who did the burying, the burials tended to be of two different types depending on whether the deceased was a Union or Confederate soldier. The Confederate dead were brought together in mass graves with little attempt at identification of the remains. In contrast, Union dead were often placed in temporary individual graves with rudimentary headboards inscribed with names of the soldiers if known. Wooden roof shingles did nicely as tombstones or headboards. In either case the burial details attempted to record on maps the location of mass grave sites and individual graves.

At the start of the American Civil War, there was no national system to take care of the dead and wounded soldiers. At Gettysburg, 113 improvised hospitals were established after the battle to care for the several thousand wounded Union and Confederate soldiers. Sadly, many of the wounded would die in the weeks that followed due to infection and the inability to provide them proper medical care. Consequently, Governor Andrew Curtin acted upon a February 1862 Pennsylvania law that provided for the care of the state's wounded and burial of her battle dead. In addition, the weather quickly began eroding the initial grave sites, and the citizens of Gettysburg called for the creation of a cemetery for the proper burial of the Union dead. As a result, Curtin appointed Gettysburg attorney David Wills to find suitable ground as a final resting place for the dead soldiers from Pennsylvania.

The final plan as devised by Wills and a select committee was to create an independent cemetery under the joint management of all the states interested in interring their soldiers at Gettysburg. There was one provision: Confederate soldiers and states were excluded. In 1872, under the sponsorship and funding by the Ladies Memorial Association of the South and the Daughters of the Confederacy, the remains of the Confederate dead were retrieved from their graves on the battlefield, nine years after they had been killed and buried there. Their remains were then carried south for reinternment in the cities of Richmond, Charleston, Savannah, and Raleigh.[5]

With the approval of Governor Curtin and representatives of the other seventeen Union states involved, seventeen acres of ground were purchased adjacent to the existing civilian cemetery on Cemetery Hill for just under $2,500. The irregular shape of the five lots of land purchased provided for a unique boot-shaped plot of ground within which agricultural architect William Saunders created a semicircular lot for the burials. Within the semicircle the participating states were assigned sections appropriate in size to the number of their dead to be interred.

At the contracted price of $1.59 per body, the Union dead were exhumed under the supervision of Samuel Weaver, the superintendent of exhumations. Weaver was present for every exhumation, which began October 27, 1863, and ended March 18, 1864. He reported in his after-action report:

> *The number taken up and removed to the Soldiers' National Cemetery is 3,354, and to these add the number of the Massachusetts soldiers taken up by the authorities of the city of Boston, by special contract, amounting to 158 making the total number of removals 3,512. Of these 979 were nameless, and without any marks to designate the state from which they volunteered.*[6]

Within each state plot the coffins containing the remains were laid side by side in a series of parallel trenches dug three feet deep and twelve feet apart. Within the wooden coffins the heads of the deceased faced the center-point of the semicircle where the Soldiers' National Monument was built and dedicated in 1869. The state of New York had the largest number of burials at 866. Pennsylvania came in second with 526. Three sections of the semicircle were set aside for the burial of the 979 unknowns, and a section was provided for the burial of the 138 soldiers of the US Regular Army who were killed in the battle.

David Wills also decided that a suitable ceremony needed to be conducted to dedicate the ground that would hold the Union dead. He invited Edward Everett, a distinguished orator from Massachusetts, to be the main speaker. Everett had been a close friend of American statesman Daniel Webster, and many people believed he had inherited Webster's position as the most distinguished orator in the nation. Everett was a pastor, scholar, diplomat, politician, and statesman, having served in both the House and the Senate. He had also been the fifteenth governor of Massachusetts and US secretary of state, and later served as ambassador to Great Britain. Everett had previously delivered major patriotic addresses at Lexington, Concord, and Bunker Hill.[7] Curiously, Everett had run against Lincoln in 1860 as the vice-presidential candidate for the Constitutional Union Party. Sadly, Everett would die two months after delivering his oration at Gettysburg.

Wills issued a formal invitation to Everett on September 23 for a ceremony initially planned for one month later. Everett immediately demurred, arguing that this did not provide him sufficient time to prepare. In the nineteenth century it was expected that an address like this would last several hours. Consequently, Everett firmly believed he needed more time to conduct careful research on the battle that he had been asked to commemorate. The task was complicated by the fact that official accounts of the three-day engagement had only just begun to appear. Wills agreed to delay the dedication until November 19.

President Lincoln was not invited to attend the ceremony until late October and may have only received the formal request two weeks prior to the event. This was not intended as an insult, since the dedication was viewed as a ceremony of the participating states. Wills clearly encouraged limits to the president's remarks, which hardly provided great promise for any politician. In the invitation he wrote, "It is the desire, that after the oration, you, as chief executive of the nation, formally set apart these grounds to their sacred use by a few appropriate remarks."[8]

Lincoln had shown interest in delivering a speech about the Battle of Gettysburg in its immediate aftermath. On July 7 he told a group of supporters that the defeat of the Confederate army on the anniversary of the Declaration Independence was a "glorious theme, and the occasion for a speech," but he had added that he was not currently "prepared to make worthy of the occasion."[9] Upon receiving the invitation Lincoln told assistant James Speed that he was "anxious to go to" Gettysburg.

The week prior to the ceremony was very busy for the president. He was focused on the military operations outside Chattanooga and

Library of Congress

Lincoln at Gettysburg,
November 19, 1863

the writing of his annual address to Congress. He and his wife were also both very worried about their ten-year-old son, Tad, who was extremely ill. The Lincolns had lost son Willie to disease in February 1862 and another child earlier in their marriage. John Nicolay, another aide to the president, wrote:

> It [November 1863] was a time when he [the president] was extremely busy, not alone with the important and complicated military affairs in the various armies, but also with the consideration of his annual message to Congress, which was to meet in early December. There was even great uncertainty whether he could take enough time from his pressing official duties to go to Gettysburg at all. Up to the 17th of November, only two days before the ceremonies, no definite arrangements for the journey had been made.[10]

....

LEADERSHIP MOMENT   You are President Abraham Lincoln. You have not frequently left the capital throughout the war, and your wife begs you not to go to Gettysburg. Your son Tad is very ill, and she fears the child will die, just as Willie had done in 1862. The principal speaker, Edward Everett, is in many ways a political opponent. You have been asked to make only a "few appropriate remarks," and you received the invitation just a couple of weeks prior to the ceremony. Would you go to Gettysburg or not?

....

WHAT CAN WE LEARN FROM THIS VIGNETTE
ABOUT LEADERSHIP?

Dealing with stakeholders. Obviously, Lincoln did decide to attend the ceremony. He departed Washington, accompanied by several members of his cabinet, at noon on November 18 for the journey to Gettysburg. It is reported that he was sad and depressed by the fact that Tad was too ill to eat breakfast and "Mrs. Lincoln was hysterical" with concern for her sick child.[11] Secretary of War Edwin Stanton had arranged for a special train for the presidential party, and the initial plan was to depart Washington early on the morning of the nineteenth and return the same day. Lincoln insisted that the train depart the afternoon prior to the event. "I do not wish to so go that by the slightest accident we fail entirely," he explained, "and, at the best, the whole to be a mere breathless running of the gauntlet." The president warmly greeted Governor Curtin at the train station upon his arrival, as Curtin's political support was essential for Lincoln as he approached the election of 1864. The president knew that the governor had been infuriated when Lincoln ignored his opposition and appointed Pennsylvania senator Simon Cameron as secretary of war. Lincoln then made the short walk to the home of David Wills, where he resided that night along with Curtin and Edward Everett.

Gettysburg was overwhelmed with visitors that evening, and accommodations were in short supply. Estimates vary, but it is believed that between 12,000 and 20,000 people attended the ceremony the next day. Many had likely not come to Gettysburg to listen to speeches, but rather to see where the great battle had occurred. It is very possible that a large number had lost a loved one during the fighting. A reporter listened to many of their stories and wrote down two as typical of what he had heard:

> I have a son who fell in the first day's fight and I have come to take back his body, for his mother's heart is breaking and she will not be satisfied until it is brought home to her.... My brother was killed in the charge of the Pennsylvania Reserves on the enemy when they were driven from Little Round Top, but we don't know where his remains are.[12]

All leaders must recognize the importance of "stakeholders"—those who have a clear "stake" in the success of the organization. We defined leadership at the onset as "deciding what had to be done and getting others to want to do it." If that is the case, then the "others" mentioned in the definition are stakeholders. Frequently engaging with stakeholders and getting their buy-in for new projects, strategies, or the general direction of the organization are essential for the leader of any organization.

Stakeholders provide leaders four things that are fundamental to success: (1) they supply essential expertise and intelligence on the organization's operating environment; (2) they can reduce and uncover potential risks that can be mitigated, thus dramatically increasing the possibility of success; (3) their buy-in is imperative for the success of any effort, and the absence of their support may bring about failure; and (4) they contribute to "acceptance," which is essential, particularly if the leader is seeking change in the organization's structure, mission, or vision. Resolving or preventing conflict among the stakeholders and achieving consensus is critical for any effort.

One reason for President Lincoln's attendance was that everyone in the town on the evening of November 18, 1863, was a stakeholder, whether they were a senior politician or simply a voter. As a very astute politician, Lincoln fully understood the "three rules of politics": (1) get elected; (2) get reelected; and (3) don't ever forget rules one and two. Obviously, one motivation for his participation was to gather support among his principal stakeholders—Republican politicians and voters—in order to secure his party's nomination for the presidency and get reelected in the fall of 1864. He knew that all the state governors, senators, and many members of Congress would be in attendance, as well as other important Republican party leaders. The event was a classic opportunity for fence-mending with crucial supporters and gathering political intelligence. John Hay, Lincoln's able assistant, noted the importance of this subject in his diary. On the way back to Washington, Hay further wondered about "the intimate, jovial relations that exist between men that hate and despise each other as cordially as do these Pennsylvania politicians."[13]

Lincoln had reasons to be concerned that he would be rejected for a second term by his party as well as the electorate—his ultimate stakeholders. There were no public opinion polls in the United States in the 1860s that could provide an indication of how a candidate might do. Analysis of an upcoming political campaign depended largely on other elections, especially congressional or state races. The congressional elections of 1862 were widely viewed as a referendum on the president's conduct of the war and his Emancipation Proclamation. The results were a disaster for the Republican Party. Five of the key states Lincoln had carried in 1860—New York, Pennsylvania, Ohio, Indiana, and Illinois—had gone against him and sent Democratic majorities to Congress.[14]

In fact, many in the Republican Party leadership believed Lincoln should not be nominated for a second term, and there is reason to believe that the president doubted it himself. No president since Andrew Jackson in 1832 had been reelected. None had even been nominated for a second term since 1840. Why should Lincoln, who had not brought the war to a successful conclusion, be different? In many ways the dedication of the Gettysburg cemetery was both the beginning of the 1864 presidential campaign and a meeting of Lincoln's principal stakeholders.

Providing strategic vision. Leaders must describe a vision for their organization and communicate it effectively. It is fundamental. Vision is a mental image of what the future world ought to be like and is important for several reasons. First, it provides an organization both direction and focus, which is essential when a leader is promoting change. Second, vision inspires members of the team, as well as encouraging both greater synergy and strategic alignment. Third, it describes a context for decision-making, resource allocation, and overall organizational development. Finally, vision is the basis for strategic thinking, planning, and programming. As it says in the Bible, "*Without vision the people perish….*" (Proverbs 29:18).

On May 25, 1961, President John F. Kennedy provided a vision for America in a joint session of Congress of "landing a man on the moon and returning him safely to the Earth." A year later he reiterated his vision in remarks at Rice University at what he described as "a moment of change and challenge":

> We choose to go to the moon in this decade and do the other things, not because they are easy, but because they are hard, because that goal will serve to organize and measure the best of our energies and skills, because that challenge is one that we are willing to accept, one we are unwilling to postpone, and one which we intend to win....[15]

The speeches delivered by Lincoln in 1863 and Kennedy nearly one hundred years later were organized consistent with the essential characteristics of a vision. All leaders should reflect upon these points as they ponder their organization's future. Both addresses were clear, communicable to others, and comprehensive. Furthermore, they were transformational for the nation and compelling to the population.

Four months after the battle, on the morning of November 19, 1863, Abraham Lincoln left David Wills's home in the center of Gettysburg for the dedication of the new national cemetery for the Union dead. His mind had been greatly relieved by the receipt of a telegram indicating that his son's health had improved significantly.

Everett spoke for over two hours and, remarkably, had memorized every word of his speech. It was reported that the crowd was largely spellbound. Lincoln then mounted the stage to address the crowd that numbered several thousand. His speech lasted only slightly more than two minutes and contained only 272 words. Still in those few words Lincoln communicated a new vision for the nation. The war had begun with a vision to preserve the Union, and he reminded the audience that this remained essential. But the revised vision for the nation now included a "new birth of freedom." It is interesting that when he concluded his remarks with this phrase he did not call for a "birth of freedom." This indicated Lincoln's belief that this vision was always the nation's destiny.

Lincoln's Gettysburg Address is a revised strategic vision of where he believed the nation must go. It argued that "freedom and liberty" were both the starting point and the destination of the nation. Iconic events throughout the nation's history have served to link the Mayflower Compact, Declaration of Independence, the Gettysburg

Address, and Martin Luther King's "I Have a Dream Speech." In each case these leaders moved the nation toward a vision described in the Constitution as an effort to form not a perfect BUT a "*more* perfect Union." As with the Battle of Gettysburg, in each case enormous change and transformation were underway.

Effective communications. Communications is the exchange and flow of information and ideas. It is more than simply words. All leaders realize that it is difficult if not impossible for them to be successful absent the ability to communicate effectively. There are several lessons in communications that can be taken from a close examination of Lincoln's dedication speech. For example, Lincoln used first-person plural pronouns like "we" and "our" frequently throughout his two-minute address. There is research that suggests leaders or those with a higher status within an organization should use fewer "I-words."[16] Over time this will serve to enhance status, position, and confidence from those with whom they are communicating, which will help make the leader's message more compelling and credible.

How successful communications have been is often measured in the immediate response. If that were solely the case, then Lincoln's Gettysburg Address may not have attained the status of perhaps one of the greatest speeches in the English language. John Hay, Lincoln's assistant, described the event in terms that are less than flattering to the president.

> *Mr. Everett spoke as he always does, perfectly; and the President, in a firm, free way, with more grace than is his wont, said his half-dozen lines of consecration, and the music wailed, and we went home though crowded and cheering streets. And all the particulars are in the daily papers.*[17]

Reactions to the speech were at best mixed. The *Harrisburg Patriot & Union* newspaper was perhaps the closest media outlet to Gettysburg, and its coverage of the president's remarks was less than complimentary. It devoted only a single paragraph to the Gettysburg Address. "We pass over the silly remarks of the President. For the credit of the nation we are willing that the veil of oblivion shall be dropped over them, and that they shall no more be repeated or thought of."[18] The editorial board did reconsider this action and printed a retraction in November 2013 on the 150th anniversary of the speech.[19] Edward Everett, however, sent a message to Lincoln in the aftermath complimenting the president on his efforts. "I should be glad if I could flatter myself that I came as near to the central idea of the occasion, in two hours, as you did in two minutes." Lincoln wrote back underscoring his apparent belief that the speech had not been well received, "I am pleased to know that, in your judgement, the little I did say was not entirely a failure."[20]

The speech is brief—only 272 words—and consists of three paragraphs. The first paragraph describes "where the organization has been," the second portrays "where the organization is now," and the final paragraph expresses "where it is going." Any leader can use this outline to organize their thinking and communicate with their team.

The iconic opening of the speech *"Fourscore and seven years ago"* describes "where the organization has been." It signals to the audience that a story is coming, and using an anecdote is an effective way for any leader to be more persuasive. This is not surprising as Lincoln frequently used stories as a means to illustrate his arguments. His narrative at the onset takes the listener back eighty-seven years, not to the signing of the Constitution in 1787, but to the signing of the Declaration of Independence in 1776. This is important as the Constitution accepted slavery as a compromise in order to get Southern states to support ratification. Both the Declaration and Lincoln's speech begin with the proposition that "all men are created equal."

The second part of the speech begins, "*We are met on a battlefield of this great war.*" That is where the organization is now. In this section, he reminds the audience that the vision had been solely to preserve the Union, "*testing whether that nation, or any nation so conceived, and so dedicated, can long endure.*" It further provides him a point that everyone will totally agree on. Both he and the listeners have all come to this battlefield for the same purpose *"to dedicate a portion of it as the final resting place for those who have given their lives that the nation might live."* If a leader is trying to achieve consensus on something big, it is often best to begin by acknowledging where agreement already exists.

He then concluded his remarks by describing where the organization is going: *"a new birth of freedom."* It may not be an overstatement to say that when the ceremony began on that day in November the purpose of the war was to preserve the Union. That is what Lincoln had argued in his first inaugural address delivered on March 4, 1861. With respect to slavery he had very explicitly stated, "I have no purpose, directly or indirectly, to interfere with the institution of slavery in the States where it exists." He further reaffirmed the legality of such controversial laws as the Fugitive Slave Act. As people departed the cemetery at its conclusion, however, the purpose for the war was still to preserve the Union, but it was now also to end slavery.

Trying to move *any* organization in a new and different direction can be perilous for any leader, and that was certainly true for Mr. Lincoln. He knew that a large portion of the North had rejected his Emancipation Proclamation. In fact, some so-called Copperhead Democrats had urged Union officers to resign and soldiers to desert when it was announced. In this moment in Gettysburg, Lincoln showed significant moral courage when he announced his intention to move the nation toward "a new birth of freedom." It would hardly help him as he sought a second term as president.

Time and timing. As previously discussed, one thing that leaders do that no one else gets to do in any organization is to *decide*. Furthermore, they *also decide when they are going to decide*. Leaders manage the crucial resource of time for their organization. That's why the *timing* of important decisions is always a critical question. So why did Lincoln decide to deliver this revised vision at that moment?

A study of entrepreneurial effort suggest that ultimate success depends on four variables: the timing of the new effort's announcement; the quality of the product, process, or vision; the resources available to invest; and the excellence of the team assembled. The analysis concluded that "timing" was by far the most important variable. Clearly, Lincoln's remarks were iconic, but the timing of his speech had an enormous bearing on its overall success.

Lincoln chose this moment for the speech for many reasons. First, militarily the Union army had achieved a victory not only at Gettysburg but also at Vicksburg, Mississippi. This latter success meant the Yankees now controlled the entire Mississippi River, which had been a strategic objective since the beginning of the war. Second, as suggested, Lincoln also knew that all Union governors would be present in

Gettysburg for the ceremony and politically this would be important. Third, Lincoln must have believed that the nation as a whole was now ready to accept a revised vision that embraced ending slavery as a goal of the war. He could not have made this part of his vision during the first inaugural address in 1861 in the aftermath of a very close election. The nation was not ready. Fundamentally, all leaders must "lead," and this requires them to provide direction for their organization. But they must avoid getting too far out in front of the organization's members in terms of what is acceptable. To do so may jeopardize the effort from the very onset.

Finally, contemporary leaders know that they may need to deal with the press in order to communicate broadly or in response to both successes and setbacks. Lincoln realized this as well and had cultivated the press since his early days in politics. He had even put a large portion of the blame for his party's losses during the 1862 elections on Republican newspapers that he believed had vilified and disparaged his administration. He knew every major Northern newspaper would cover the Gettysburg ceremony. If he was going to convey a new vision to the nation, this was the perfect moment to do so, as his message would be quickly communicated to the entire nation.

Newspapers were the "media outlet" of the times. It is estimated that there were 200 newspapers in the United States in 1801. This had grown to roughly 1,200 by 1835 and to over 3,000 by 1861.[21] In addition, over 700 periodicals were in circulation in the United States by the end of the war. According to one estimate the total annual circulation of all newspapers had doubled between 1828 and 1840 from 68 million to 140 million copies.[22] The advent of the telegraph and the creation of the Associated Press (AP) in New York in 1846 further allowed every part of the country to receive the same information at the same moment. This multiplied the impact of a speech or event many times over. The AP would subsequently cooperate with Reuters, which allowed news to be rapidly transmitted abroad.

Most of these newspapers were highly partisan, and editors such as Horace Greeley and Thurlow Weed were powerful political figures. Lincoln ensured that newspaper reporters loyal to the Republican Party were provided transportation on his train to Gettysburg. They were deemed so important that places had been reserved for them on the actual speakers' platform.[23]

President Lincoln finished his remarks, and there was a moment of silence. This may have been because the audience was surprised at the speech's brevity. As the president returned to his seat they began to applaud, and he may have interpreted this as disapproval. He is reported to have turned to his friend Ward Lamon and remarked, "Lamon, that speech won't scour! It is a flat failure, and the people are disappointed."[24]

Following the president's speech, a choir sang a dirge specifically selected for the occasion. The ceremony concluded with a benediction delivered by the Reverend Henry L. Baugher, president of Gettysburg College, and the crowd dispersed. As previously mentioned, the burying of the Union dead resumed and was not concluded until the spring of 1864.

Burials at the Soldiers' National Cemetery in Gettysburg also continued into the twentieth century. Surrounding the original semicircular Civil War–era burial plot are the graves of US military personnel who participated in military conflicts through the Vietnam War, after which further burials were ended due to lack of available space. There are just over 6,000 individual burials in the cemetery today. Every November 19 is Remembrance Day in the town with parades and a march to the site of Lincoln's address. As part of the celebration, a leading figure annually delivers the Gettysburg Address. The Civil War had left Gettysburg, but what happened there would never be forgotten.

"With Malice Toward None..."

The war continued for seventeen more months, and there is no definitive answer to the question "how many soldiers died during the American Civil War?" It was widely accepted for many years that approximately 620,000 perished on both sides from combat, accidents, starvation, and disease. Recent studies, however, suggest that the number may have been as high as 850,000.[1] As a result, nearly half of American war dead throughout our nation's history occurred during the Civil War.

The impact on the country was indescribable. The population of the United States in 1860 was about 31 million, which meant that roughly one out of ten white males who were of military age at that time died because of the Civil War. Gettysburg was almost exactly the midpoint of the suffering. Only half of all who died did so prior to July 4, 1863.

Lincoln realized in the aftermath of the battle that large sacrifices were yet to come. On his way to Gettysburg to deliver his speech he encountered a man who told him his only son had been killed in the fighting. Lincoln sought to console him in his grief but went on to say:

> [B]ut when I think of the sacrifices of life yet to be offered and the hearts and homes yet to be made desolate before this dreadful war, so wickedly forced upon us, is over, my heart is like lead within me, and I feel at times, like hiding in deep darkness.[2]

There was little fighting in the east for the remainder of 1863. In early 1864 Ulysses S. Grant was appointed a lieutenant general and placed in command of all federal armies. In the late spring the bloody and inconclusive Battles of the Wilderness, Spotsylvania Court House, and Cold Harbor were fought in Virginia prior to the onset of the prolonged Siege of Petersburg and Richmond. In the western theater General Sherman made slow progress toward Atlanta. In July 1864 Confederate General Jubal Early led a small army north into Maryland and Pennsylvania. His troops reached the very "gates" of Washington.

Morale in the North plummeted as the war seemed to have no end, and the public blamed Lincoln. He despaired at his reelection prospects, and several senior Republican leaders told him that it was "an impossibility." On August 23, 1864, he wrote the following memorandum to his cabinet:

> *This morning, as for some days past, it seems exceedingly probable that this Administration will not be re-elected. Then it will be my duty to so co-operate with the President elect, as to save the Union between the election and inauguration; as he will have secured his election on such ground that he cannot possibly save it afterwards.*[3]

Curiously, Lincoln then folded the memo and sealed it, so that the text could not be read. He took it to a cabinet meeting and instructed them to sign the outside, sight unseen, to verify its authenticity. Historians refer to this as the "Blind Memorandum." The president had now pledged his administration to accept the verdict of the people in the November election and help save the Union.[4]

But the president's fortunes rebounded. The Democratic Party nominated former general George B. McClellan for president. Their convention saddled McClellan with a peace platform that declared the war a failure and urged immediate efforts to bring hostilities to an end. In early September 1864 General Sherman achieved a crucial Union victory with the capture of Atlanta. This was followed by additional major Union successes that resulted in federal control of the critical Shenandoah Valley in Virginia.

By 9:00 p.m. on election day, November 8, 1864, Lincoln knew that victory was his. He had won the popular vote by over 400,000 votes and dominated McClellan in the Electoral College 212–21. McClellan carried only three states: his home state of New Jersey and two "border states," Kentucky and Delaware. Remarkably, Lincoln's land-slide included the majority of Union soldiers even though his opponent was a former general who had been popular when in command of the Army of the Potomac. Of the 150,633 soldiers' votes that were counted, Lincoln won nearly 117,000.

The Republican election victory also resulted in a three-quarters antislavery majority in Congress, which was powerful enough to ensure the abolition of slavery by constitutional amendment. The Senate had voted to do so in April 1864, and the House of Representatives followed with the passage of the Thirteenth Amendment on January 31, 1865. It was ratified by the required number of states by December 1865. Lincoln saw this as public acceptance in many ways of the vision he had articulated. "It is the voice of the people now," he said, "for the first time, heard upon the question."[5]

On March 4, 1865, President Lincoln, under heavy guard, walked out onto the platform at the Capitol to deliver his second inaugural address. It is reported that Frederick Douglass and John Wilkes Booth

The assembled crowd at President Lincoln's Second Inauguration, March 4, 1865.

were among the onlookers. Douglass had escaped from slavery in 1838 and become a national leader of the abolitionist movement in New York and Massachusetts. He had gained widespread fame as a writer and orator, and periodically had been a critic of Lincoln. Booth was a famous American actor and would assassinate Lincoln roughly six weeks later.

The day was gray and blustery, but as Lincoln rose to deliver his remarks a blazing sun broke through the haze and flooded the entire scene. He later commented, "Did you notice the sunburst? It made my heart jump!"[6] One can only imagine the scene as thousands had gathered. Most of the audience had likely suffered personally from the ravages of the war. They had lost a father, son, brother, uncle, or close friend, but each person knew at that moment that the Union was winning the war. At that moment, the president could have decided to argue for employing harsh measures against the "traitors" who had not only deserted the nation but also fought to destroy their country and brought about the war. Many, if not most, in the crowd would have likely endorsed that sentiment.

But Lincoln chose not to do that, and in his succinct speech—only 703 words—the president, as the leader of the nation, reaffirmed the vision for the nation that he had described four years previously: to preserve the Union. The speech is clearly an attempt at reconciliation. The pronouns recurring through it are "we," "both," and "all." "All thoughts were anxiously directed to an impending civil war. All dreaded it, all sought to avert it…. Both parties deprecated war."

After describing the gloom that surrounded his first inaugural, the president presented his central argument: the war had been fought to resolve the great national "interest" of slavery that he said all knew was, somehow, its cause. As a result, the speech serves as a revelation of Lincoln's struggle to see that ultimately the purpose of the war was "America's unfinished business." Over time he had reluctantly concluded that the war's ultimate purpose was twofold—preserve the Union and bring about an end to slavery. The first inaugural address, Emancipation Proclamation, Gettysburg Address, and second inaugural address were all linked in the development of that expanded vision. John Hay, his able assistant, later described in a lecture he delivered in 1871 that:

The solemnity which you see in the Gettysburg address and the Second Inaugural is but a shadow of the momentous spiritual contests which he fought out alone with his own questioning soul.[7]

Lincoln completed his second inaugural address with the following memorable sentence:

With malice toward none; with charity for all; with firmness in the right, as God gives us to see the right, let us strive on to finish the work we are in; to bind up the nation's wounds; to care for him who shall have borne the battle, and for his widow, and his orphan— to do all which may achieve and cherish a just, and lasting peace, among ourselves, and with all nations.

He urged compassion for soldiers and their families on both sides as the best way to achieve his vision and what he firmly believed should be the nation's goal.

That evening there was an inaugural reception at the White House, and Frederick Douglass attempted to attend. He wanted to congratulate the president on both his speech and reelection but was refused admittance by the police. The president learned of this and directed that Douglass be allowed to join the festivities. Lincoln subsequently asked the famous former slave his opinion of the address, and Douglass described it as a "sacred effort." The president is reported to have simply replied, "I am glad you liked it."[8]

In late March General Grant invited the Lincolns to his headquarters in City Point (now Hopewell), Virginia, along the James River, which was only a few miles from the front. The president immediately accepted and arrived on March 24, 1865, accompanied by his wife and son Tad. He stayed nearly two weeks. On March 27 and 28, Lincoln held meetings with his senior military leadership—Generals Ulysses S. Grant and William Tecumseh Sherman as well as Admiral David Dixon Porter—aboard the *River Queen* to discuss the end of the war. As described in his second inaugural address, Lincoln was convinced the war's aftermath should not be characterized by revenge or "harsh measures." The president told his military leaders that the victors should be firm but also generous and compassionate.

Let them once surrender and reach their homes, they won't take up arms again. Let them all go, officers and all. I want submission and no more bloodshed. Let them have their horses to plow with, and if you like, their guns to shoot crows with. I want no one punished. Treat them liberally all round. We want those people to return to their allegiance to the Union and submit to the laws. Again I say, give them the most liberal and honorable terms.[9]

Both Grant and Sherman followed the president's instructions in terms they agreed upon in accepting the surrenders of General Robert E. Lee on April 9 as well as General Joseph Johnston on April 26.

Lincoln insisted on visiting Richmond, the Confederacy's capital, prior to returning to Washington. The Army of Northern Virginia had evacuated the city on April 2, and Union forces occupied it the following day. The president and his son arrived in Richmond with a small Marine guard and walked the streets of the city that had been largely destroyed during the siege and a fire that had engulfed it.

Charles Carleton Coffin, a war correspondent, recounted that crowds of freed slaves greeted the president enthusiastically as "their Saviour, their Moses, who had brought them through the Red Sea and the desert to the promised land…." Lincoln ascended the steps of the Confederate "White House" and sat in Jefferson Davis's chair. Coffin described the scene as follows:

There was no sign of exultation, no elation of spirit, but, on the contrary, a look of unutterable weariness, as if his spirit, energy and animating force were wholly exhausted.[10]

The nation rejoiced when the news reached Washington that Robert E. Lee had surrendered the Army of Northern Virginia to Grant at Appomattox Court House, Virginia, on Palm Sunday—April 9, 1865. Five hundred cannons boomed a massive salute throughout the capital, shattering windows across from the White House in Lafayette Square. The celebrations continued for the next several days with bonfires, parties, torchlight parades, and other festivities.

On the evening of April 11, a large crowd gathered on the White House lawn, and Lincoln appeared in an upstairs window to address them. It was the last public speech he ever delivered. He began his remarks by noting that they were assembled "not in sorrow, but in gladness of heart." It appeared, he said, that "the surrender of the principal insurgent army, give hope of a righteous and speedy peace whose joyous expression cannot be restrained."

The crowd may have expected a brief speech that simply celebrated the impending end to the war, but the president instead described the challenge of reconstruction, which he argued was "fraught with great difficulty." Lincoln apparently decided the timing was right to expand further on his vision for the nation. He urged that the right of suffrage be conferred on former slaves who were "very intelligent, and on those who serve our cause as soldiers."

It is reported that John Wilkes Booth was present at this gathering and was also accompanied by two of his fellow conspirators, David Herold and former Confederate soldier Lewis Powell (who had assumed the alias Lewis Payne after deserting in January 1865). In the aftermath of Lincoln's remarks Booth exclaimed, "That means nigger citizenship! That is the last speech he will ever make!" He urged Powell to shoot the president immediately, but when he refused Booth proclaimed, "Now, by God, I'll put him through."[11] Three days later John Wilkes Booth delivered on his threat. On the evening of April 14, 1865, Booth shot Lincoln as the president, accompanied by his wife and two guests, watched a play at Ford's Theatre.

Throughout this book leadership has been defined as "deciding what has to be done and getting others to want to do." Lincoln's efforts as president brought full meaning to this definition. He had decided what had to be done, communicated his vision to the nation, and established two critical tasks: preserving the Union and later ending slavery. Throughout four long years of war he had continued to convince the nation to follow that path. The first task had largely been accomplished by the evening of April 14. Lincoln had been successful as a leader.

The impact of Lincoln's sudden death, however, further underscores the critical importance of the "leader" for any organization or even a nation that needs to be transformed. Preserving the Union had transformed the nation. In the aftermath of his presidency it would no longer be the "United States *are*" but rather "the United States *is*."

Sadly, the second part of Lincoln's vision, "a new birth of freedom," was a harder task. It meant ending slavery and living up to the nation's goal that "all men are created equal." This was not accomplished by April 1865 or even with the final ratification of the Thirteenth Amendment to the Constitution. Unfortunately, American leaders who followed him were either unable or unwilling to embrace his vision and continue the effort to convince the nation to move toward greater social justice.[12]

Lincoln did not immediately die after being shot and was carried from the theatre across the street to a private home owned by the Petersen family. Secretary of War Edwin Stanton was immediately summoned and stayed by the president's bedside throughout the long night. At 7:22 a.m., Friday, April 15, 1865, Abraham Lincoln was pronounced dead. It was Good Friday. Stanton's concise tribute to Lincoln and his leadership still echoes from the past—"Now he belongs to the ages."

Dramatis Personae

It frequently happens in historical studies that the lives of the characters in the story stop when the story ends. In the case of this book on leadership with historical background, we wish to continue the lives of the characters to see what became of them. How did the leadership they were exposed to during the American Civil War in general and the battle at Gettysburg in particular affect the remainder of their lives?

Although none were present at Gettysburg, five American Civil War veterans went on to become president of the United States: Ulysses S. Grant (eighteenth), Rutherford B. Hayes (nineteenth), James A. Garfield (twentieth), Benjamin Harrison (twenty-third), and William McKinley (twenty-fifth). All were born in Ohio, and all were of the Republican Party. All but Grant had served in the US Congress, and Grant was the only West Point graduate.[1] So what became of our Gettysburg leaders? We present them by chapter.[2]

Chapter 1

Robert Edward Lee (1807–1870)

Following the Confederate defeat at Gettysburg, Lee's letter of resignation as commander of the Army of Northern Virginia was refused by Confederate President Jefferson Davis. Lee remained in command until the end of the war, twenty-two months after Gettysburg. In January 1865, Davis named Lee general-in-chief of all Confederate armies in the field, but Lee was too busy contending with Union attacks in Virginia to pay more than scant attention to the other theaters of action.

Finally, Lee surrendered his army at Appomattox Court House, Virginia, on April 12, 1865. By that time, the army had been reduced to an estimated 28,000 men due to casualties and high desertion rates as soldiers left the ranks for their homes and families. Although the surrender of Lee's army was not the largest nor the last surrender of Confederate forces at the end of the war, it remains the most symbolic. Confederate general Joe Johnston surrendered 80,000 men two weeks later to Union general William T. Sherman near Durham Station, North Carolina. The last fighting between sizable bodies of men in the war—500 Union versus 300 Confederate—took place at Palmito Ranch, Texas, two months after the Appomattox Court House surrender.[3]

During the course of the war Lee and his wife lost the family home and estate in Arlington, Virginia, the plantation grounds becoming Arlington National Cemetery for burial of US war dead. Soon after the end of the war, Lee was named president of Washington College, a colonial-era college named for the nation's first president. Although he retook the required oath of allegiance to the United States at the end of the war, Lee's US citizenship was denied him until finally restored posthumously by an act of Congress in 1975. In poor health since before the end of the war, Lee passed away in October 1870, apparently from heart disease. After his death Washington College was renamed in his honor and is now known as Washington and Lee University. Lee is buried there beneath the chapel, his horse Traveler buried nearby.

George Gordon Meade (1815–1872)

Although President Lincoln was very disappointed with the Confederate army's successful escape and retreat back to Virginia, he retained George Meade as commander of the Army of the Potomac until the end of the war. In March 1864 Lincoln brought General Ulysses Grant east as general-in-chief of all the Union armies. Grant chose to co-locate his headquarters in the field with Meade's headquarters, an arrangement that seemed to work well for both men. Possessed with a sizable temper, Meade had come into conflict with many newspaper men covering the war who agreed among themselves not to mention Meade in future correspondence except in reference to setbacks.

Another challenge for Meade in the spring of 1864 was his being called before the onerous Joint Congressional Committee on Conduct of the War, a supposed bipartisan group of congressmen and senators who took it upon themselves to publicly critique the conduct of the war by the military leadership. In this forum Meade was taken to task for the Confederate army's successful escape after Gettysburg. The proceedings went on for several weeks. Chief among the accusers were former Army of the Potomac corps commander Daniel Sickles and chief of staff Daniel Butterfield. In the end, the committee did criticize Meade, just as the president did in the letter he never sent. The committee finally published its report in May 1865, after the end of the war and Lincoln's death.

It was all too little, too late to get Meade relieved of command if that was the committee's objective. At war's end Meade mustered out of volunteer service and rejoined the Regular Army in the rank of major general performing reconstruction duties in the Southern states and serving as commander of the Division of the Atlantic then headquartered in Philadelphia, Pennsylvania. Until his death in 1872 he worked at defending his reputation, which had been clouded by the Joint Committee hearings and poor publicity. George Meade is buried in Laurel Hills Cemetery in Philadelphia. The US Army's Fort Meade in Maryland is named for him.

Chapter 2

John Buford (1826–1863)

Having been relieved of his position on McPherson's Ridge by General John Reynolds and the infantry on the first day of the battle, John Buford and his cavalry division stayed on scene the remainder of that day and the coming night protecting the flanks of the army. The next day they received orders to fall back twenty-five miles southeast to Westminster, Maryland, to guard the army's supply base and to rest and refit. As one of Buford's troopers allegedly put it, they were sent back because in the days leading the army to Gettysburg and fighting on the first day, the soldiers and their horses had existed five days on two-days' rations.

Thus, Buford and his cavalry division did not see further action in the three-day battle. They were, however, very active in pursuing Lee's army back to the Potomac River crossings. Subsequently, in the fall of the year while campaigning in Virginia, Buford came down with typhoid fever. As horse cavalrymen often spoke of it, "He had been ridden hard and put away wet too many times." John Buford was forced into a leave of absence from the field on November 20, 1863, and he entered a military hospital in Washington, DC. President Lincoln and other dignitaries visited him there on his death bed. The president ordered he be promoted to major general of volunteers, and the commission was presented to him prior to his passing on December 16, 1863. Buford had two funerals. The first took place in Washington, where eight general officers served as honorary pallbearers. The second took place at West Point, his alma mater. He is buried in the cemetery there next to another Gettysburg hero, lieutenant of artillery and Medal of Honor awardee Alonzo Cushing, whose artillery battery successfully withstood Pickett's Charge at Gettysburg. In 1888 the Buford Memorial Association was formed by his friends and former comrades. They erected a statue of him on July 1, 1895, along the Chambersburg Turnpike on what was the McPherson farm.

Chapter 3
Ambrose Powell Hill (1825–1865)

The inconsistent leadership exhibited at Gettysburg by Confederate Third Corps Commander A. P. Hill continued for the remainder of the war. His chronic health problems were probably the reason for his frequent lapses in performance. He had been a bold and brave leader in the Mexican War, and prior to Gettysburg, he had performed heroically in rescuing the army at Antietam-Sharpsburg. When he was a major general and division commander, Lee thought of him as the best at that rank and position in the army. But having been advanced to a higher level of expectation and his medical issues becoming more persistent, he became less instead of more effective. On April 2, 1865, A. P. Hill was killed in action during the Third Battle of Petersburg, Virginia, seven days before Lee's surrender at Appomattox Court House. He is buried in Richmond. Both Stonewall Jackson and Lee called for Hill and his division from their death beds. Perhaps it was the old Hill they were calling for. The US Army's Fort A. P. Hill in Virginia is named for him.

Henry Heth (1825–1899)

A. P. Hill could not have graduated last in the West Point class of 1847 because classmate and future subordinate commander Henry Heth had the spot all to himself. Henry—the only senior Confederate officer General Lee referred to by his given name—spent fourteen years on routine frontier duty in the Regular Army prior to resigning his commission to enter Confederate service in 1861. It was division commander Heth's troops who opened the fight on July 1 against Brigadier General Buford's cavalry and then the infantry General Reynolds subsequently brought onto the field. Wounded in action that day, Henry was incapacitated and out of action during his division's attack on the third day with Pickett's men.

Henry Heth survived Gettysburg and continued to provide effective leadership as a division commander the remaining twenty-two months of hard fighting. He surrendered with Lee and the rest of the Army of Northern Virginia at Appomattox Court House on April 9. After the war, he was engaged in the insurance business in Richmond. He died in Washington, DC, in September 1899, and is buried with his Confederate comrades in Hollywood Cemetery in Richmond, Virginia.

Lucius Fairchild (1831–1896)

We include Colonel Lucius Fairchild on our list for postwar follow-up because he stands as an excellent example of the majority of civilians-turned-soldiers in providing leadership to the mobilized armies on both sides. Within five days of the Confederates opening the rebellion with the firing on Fort Sumter, South Carolina, Fairchild, the elected clerk of the Dane County circuit court in the state of Wisconsin, recognized his duty to country and enlisted into the 1st Wisconsin Volunteer Infantry. Fairchild was immediately elected by the troops as a captain and company commander. Fairchild's leadership resulted in his promotion and assignment as lieutenant colonel and deputy commander of the 2nd Wisconsin Regiment. On September 1, 1862, Colonel Fairchild assumed command of the regiment that he led at Gettysburg.

On July 1 at Gettysburg, Fairchild was at the head of the 2nd Wisconsin regiment on the eastern edge of Herbst Woods on McPherson's Ridge, encouraged by General Reynolds to advance through the woods to "drive those fellows from the trees." A Confederate volley of rifle or cannon fire shattered Fairchild's left arm. Briefly captured by the enemy, he escaped, though badly wounded, and found his way back into friendly lines on Cemetery Hill, where the remnants of his left arm were cut away.

Fairchild saw no more active service. Even though promoted to brigadier general of volunteers in mid-October 1863, he resigned from active service the following month. He had done his share. Elected governor of Wisconsin in 1866, he served until 1872, his empty coat sleeve was a symbol to the voters of his dedication and sacrifice. Following several federal political appointments, he unsuccessfully ran for US Senator in 1885. At the time of his death in Madison, Wisconsin, in May 1896, he held the title of commander in chief of the Military Order of the Loyal Legion of the United States, a Union veterans' organization. Fairchild is buried in Forest Hill Cemetery in Madison, Wisconsin.

Jonathan Letterman (1824–1872)

Having initiated reform in the organization, process, and procedures of the army's system of medical care, surgeon Letterman still felt discouraged that the chain of command did not allow his recommendations and ideas to be all they could be. He resigned from the army in December 1864, having served as a military surgeon since 1849. Letterman and his wife, Mary, went west to San Francisco, California, where, after a failed business venture, he served as the city coroner from 1867 until his death in 1872 at forty-seven years of age. Jonathan and Mary are buried in Arlington National Cemetery. In 1911, the military hospital at the Presidio of San Francisco was named Letterman Army Hospital in his honor.

Chapter 4

Richard Stoddert Ewell (1817–1872)

"Old Bald Head" remained in command of the Second Corps after Gettysburg into the spring of 1864, when ill health forced him into temporary retirement from active field duty. He finished the war in charge of the futile defense of the city of Richmond, Virginia—the Confederate capital. He was captured at Sayler's Creek three days before the surrender at Appomattox Court House. After a brief incarceration in Fort Warren, Massachusetts, he spent the remainder of his life as a gentleman farmer near Spring Hill, Tennessee, where he died in January 1872. He is buried in the Old City Cemetery in Nashville, Tennessee.

Oliver Otis Howard (1830–1909)

West Point graduate and abolitionist O. O. Howard commanded the XI Corps of the Union Army of the Potomac at Gettysburg. Two months after Gettysburg, the XI and XII Corps were transferred to General Sherman's forces in the western theater of operations. In the spring of 1864, the two corps were consolidated into one corps. Howard was given command of the IV corps, which he led during the Atlanta Campaign. Sherman then placed Howard in command of the Army of the Tennessee, which formed Sherman's right wing in the Savannah and Carolinas Campaigns at the end of the war.

After the war, Howard pursued two of his passions: abolitionism and education. In May 1865 President Andrew Johnson appointed Howard the first commissioner of the Freedman's Bureau, which was established to aid the resettlement of former black slaves. He also founded Howard University in Washington, DC, and served as its first president from 1869 to 1874.

Returning to active field service with the US Army, Brigadier General Howard spent several years campaigning against rebellious Native American tribes, including the Apache, led by Chief Cochise, and the Nez Perce, led by Chief Joseph. Returning east, Howard served as superintendent at West Point from 1881–1882. In 1893 he was awarded the Medal of Honor for heroism in the American Civil War Battle of Seven Pines, where he was severely wounded and lost an arm. Major

General Howard retired from the army in 1894 and settled in Burlington, Vermont, where he died October 1909.

Carl Schurz (1829–1906)

Born near Cologne, Germany, Carl Schurz made his way to America as a refugee from the abortive European uprisings of 1848. His leadership of the German immigrant community in the American midwestern states made him a valuable asset to the newly formed Republican Party. He served as division commander and acting XI Corps commander at Gettysburg. When the XI Corps was transferred to the western theater of operations in September 1863, he went with it. Schurz took time out from field duty in 1864 to campaign among the German immigrant communities in the upper midwestern states on behalf of President Lincoln.

Schurz returned to field duty with the army following the national elections in the fall of 1864. His greater contributions to the country occurred after the war. In 1868 he became the first German American to be elected to the US Senate, representing the state of Missouri. During his six years as a senator his principal interest was Civil Service Reform, becoming the first senator to offer a bill on the issue to the US Congress. From 1877 to 1881 he served as secretary of the interior and worked for government reforms on behalf of the Native American peoples.

In between and during government appointments, Schurz served as founder and editor of several newspapers and magazines. Toward the end of his life he was regarded as an elder statesman and consultant on virtually every political and social question of national importance. Paralleling her husband's life, Carl's wife, Margarethe, worked for the good of the public by championing the idea of early childhood education and was instrumental in establishing the kindergarten system in the United States.

Carl Schurz died in New York City at the age of seventy-seven. He is buried in Sleepy Hollow, New York, just north of New York City. Many secondary schools in the United States and in Germany are named in his honor. Both authors of this book remember well from our military service during the Cold War two US Army garrisons in Germany named in honor of Schurz.

Francis Channing Barlow (1834–1896)

On the first day of the battle, XI Corps division commander Francis Barlow disregarded his orders and moved his infantry division's defensive line forward of its assigned position north of the town. This movement opened the right end of the line to envelopment by attacking Confederates. With his men forced to retreat to Cemetery Hill, the wounded Barlow was left for dead on the field. But he lived and was cared for by the enemy and by his wife, who was allowed to come behind enemy lines to do so. Barlow was subsequently exchanged back into Union hands, and he briefly rejoined the army the following spring and was in the field at intervals until war's end.

After the war, Harvard graduate and attorney Francis Barlow returned to New York City, resumed his law practice, entered politics, and became a founding member of the American Bar Association. He was twice elected state secretary of New York, and he served as a US Marshal. In 1871 he was elected New York state attorney general and initiated the investigation and prosecution of the "Tweed ring" of criminal activity in New York City. He was still practicing law in New York City at his death in January 1896 at sixty-two years of age.

Chapter 5

James Longstreet (1821–1904)

R. E. Lee's "old war horse" was still by his side at the Appomattox surrender. The following day Longstreet and prewar buddy Ulysses Grant, the senior Northern general, spent the afternoon playing cards, drinking whiskey, and talking about what lay ahead for each of them and the country. In 1868 Grant won election as the eighteenth president of the United States. Much to the consternation of his fellow Southerners Longstreet, who had settled in New Orleans, Louisiana, supported his friend Grant and the Republican Party in the national election and postwar reconstruction activities in the South. That same year Longstreet's US citizenship was restored, and Grant appointed him senior US Customs official in the Port of New Orleans. His acceptance of a patronage job in the federal government and his support of the Republican Party did not sit well with white Southerners.

In 1873 the governor of Louisiana gave Longstreet command of the state militia and Metropolitan Police Force of the City of New Orleans, which at that time served as the state capital. In mid-September 1874, these military and paramilitary forces representing the Republican Party became embroiled in a violent confrontation with a Democrat-led organization known as the Crescent City White League. The clash resulted in thirty-eight killed and seventy-nine wounded on both sides. In directing the actions of partially black military and paramilitary troops against an organization composed mostly of white Confederate veterans, Longstreet was viewed as being a strong Radical Republican, and he became a pariah throughout the South.[4]

In 1877 he converted to Catholicism, a very unwise move in the minds of post–Civil War Southerners. In 1880 he accepted yet another Republican Party patronage-appointed position as US ambassador to the Ottoman Empire, a position he actually occupied for less than a year. He then served the government as the senior US marshal in the state of Georgia from 1881–1884 and US commissioner of railroads 1897–1904.

In 1889 Longstreet's wife, Louise, passed away at the age of sixty-two after a brief illness. She and James had been married forty years, and she had borne ten children, only five of whom lived to adulthood. They first met in 1844 at Jefferson Barracks, Missouri, home of the US Army's Fourth Infantry Regiment. James was a newly arrived second lieutenant, and Louise was the regimental commander's daughter. From her childhood she had witnessed the sacrifices required of a soldier's wife, and when her time came, after Longstreet's safe return from the war with Mexico, she chose a soldier to be her husband.

Longstreet was devastated by Louise's death. He consoled himself in the coming years by writing his memoirs. That work was complicated by the fact that a house fire earlier in 1889 had destroyed all his personal correspondence and records. His book, *From Manassas to Appomattox*, was published in 1896. It was his expectation that completion of this five-year project would clear his name and make things right again with his former comrades and the Southern people.

He was wrong. His book and some of his other writings in *Century Magazine* made things worse. The passing of time had displaced some facts, but the worst grievance for his critics was that in *From Manassas to Appomattox* he criticized General Lee, particularly for the Gettysburg defeat. Although the book was a good account of his four years serving the Confederacy, his detractors used its pages to make James Longstreet one of the principal scapegoats for the Confederate defeat at Gettysburg and the war.

After eight years as a widower, seventy-six-year-old James Longstreet married thirty-four-year-old Helen Dortch. Born three months before the Battle of Gettysburg was fought, Helen proved to be a remarkable woman in her own right over the years. A newspaper reporter, owner, editor, and publisher, she was well placed to work at correcting her husband's personal reputation and improving his image. During the Second World War, she worked as a "Rosie the Riveter" aircraft construction worker in an aircraft plant in Atlanta, Georgia. Helen died in May 1969 at ninety-nine years of age.

Like so many other old soldiers in his later years James Longstreet had "retired to the farm," in this case at Gainesville, Georgia. He died an old soldier's death in January 1904. His right arm was withered and useless from Civil War wounds, his body was racked with rheumatism, he was so deaf in his later years he had to use an ear horn, and he had a cancer in his right eye—but it was pneumonia that killed him. He is buried in Alta Vista Cemetery in Gainesville, Georgia. Over the years after his passing, the diligence of his wife, Helen, and the work of twentieth-century historians have restored James Longstreet's reputation as an excellent soldier-leader in the American Civil War and civil leader in the latter half of the nineteenth century. In 1998 an equestrian statue of Longstreet and his favored horse, Hero, was installed and dedicated on the Gettysburg Battlefield by the Sons of Confederate Veterans.

Daniel Edgar Sickles (1819–1914)

We introduced you to the Union III Corps commander in Chapter 1. He survived the amputation of his right leg but saw no further service on the battlefields of the war. From 1865 to 1867 he served in the rank of major general as commander of the Department of South Carolina, the Department of the South, and the Second Military District, where he supervised reconstruction policies and the resettlement of former black slaves.

Appointed US ambassador to Spain by President Grant in May 1869, he served the nation nearly five years in that capacity. During his tenure he managed to mangle US foreign policy with Spain, mainly over the question of annexation of the island of Cuba, which was at that time a Spanish possession. Additionally, he had a notorious and very public love affair in Paris with the deposed Spanish queen, Isabella II.

Upon his return home he became very active in veterans' affairs. In 1886 the New York state legislature established the New York Monuments Commission for the placement of battlefield memorials on the battlefields of Gettysburg, Chattanooga, and Antietam. Sickles was appointed honorary chairman, a position he held for the next twenty-six years, until he was dismissed over a missing $27,000 from the coffers of the organization. The allegations against him were convincing, but the missing funds were never recovered. Nonetheless, during his tenure the commission funded the placement of 123 monuments and memorials to New York regiments and leaders on the Gettysburg Battlefield.

Dan Sickles served a two-year term in the US House of Representatives representing New York State's Eleventh Congressional District from March 1893 to March 1895. It was during that time he wrote the legislation and drew a boundary map that, when approved by Congress and signed by President Cleveland in February 1895, created Gettysburg National Military Park.

Having lived a lavish lifestyle, Daniel Sickles died in New York City on May 3, 1914, with $500 to his credit.[5] Although the subject of great controversy over what happened during the battle, his legacy was his leader's vision for what we today have as Gettysburg National Military Park.

Chapter 6

Gouverneur Kemble Warren (1830–1882)

The New York Monuments Commission funded the placement of a statue of Chief Engineer Brigadier General Warren on the summit of

Little Round Top to signify his role in occupation of that piece of key terrain by Union forces on the second day of the battle.

With the Gettysburg Battle over, Warren was given temporary command of the Army of the Potomac's II Corps in place of the wounded Winfield Scott Hancock. From late March 1864 to April 1, 1865, he commanded the V Corps. However, at the Battle of Five Forks in the last days of the war, Warren fell afoul of his superior, Major General Philip Sheridan, who, for more personal than professional reasons, relieved Warren of command.

Most military professionals who have studied this case have found that Sheridan's relief of Warren was unwarranted. In any event, Warren's military career and reputation were severely damaged by the incident. Warren continued in the Regular Army in his permanent grade of lieutenant colonel of engineers, during which time among his many accomplishments, he served as superintendent for the building of the railroad bridge over the Mississippi River at Rock Island, Illinois.

A court of inquiry later exonerated Warren while condemning Sheridan for the manner of Warren's relief from command. However, by the time the court's findings were made known, Warren had died at his home in Newport, Rhode Island, in August 1882. Deeply embittered by the injustice, Warren left instructions that he not be buried in military uniform.

Strong Vincent (1837–1863)

We told the story of the Pennsylvania attorney-turned-soldier in Chapter 6. Setting aside his original orders, Vincent led his 1,400-man brigade to the south side of Little Round Top just before Confederates attacked the hill. In the fighting between Vincent's men and the Alabamians and Texans of Hood's Confederate division, Vincent was mortally wounded. Vincent received a promotion to brigadier general on his deathbed, but he likely never knew of it before succumbing to his wounds on July 7. His remains rest at Erie Cemetery, Erie, Pennsylvania. In 1930 Strong Vincent High School in Erie was named in his honor. In 2017 the school was reclassified as Strong Vincent Middle School.

Joshua Lawrence Chamberlain (1828–1914)

We discussed some of the wartime exploits of the college professor-turned-soldier in Chapter 7. By war's end Chamberlain had been wounded in action six times, having participated in twenty-four combat engagements ranging from small skirmishes to the larger battles of the war, to include Fredericksburg, Chancellorsville, and Gettysburg. After the war he declined a commission in the Regular Army, preferring to return to civilian life.

In his long life after Gettysburg and the Civil War, Chamberlain continued to serve the public good. He was governor of Maine from 1866 to 1870 and then served the next thirteen years as president of Bowdoin College. He also became a prolific writer of important and still-useful studies of the military campaigns in which he participated. Like so many senior leaders from this and other wars, Chamberlain became a champion of and spokesman for the common soldier, and was very involved in veteran activities. His description of Gettysburg as the "vision place of souls" at the 1889 dedication of the 20th Maine Volunteer Infantry Regiment memorial has become iconic. Michael Shaara's 1974 novel *The Killer Angels* and the 1993 TNT-produced movie *Gettysburg*, based on Shaara's novel, made virtual cult figures of Chamberlain and his men.

Joshua Lawrence Chamberlain died in Portland, Maine, on February 24, 1914. According to his newspaper obituary, the effects of his war wounds, particularly the severe wound he received at Petersburg, Virginia, in June 1864 ultimately killed him fifty years later. He is buried in Pine Grove Cemetery, Brunswick, Maine.

William Calvin Oates (1833–1910)

Alabama attorney-turned-soldier William C. Oates commanded the 15th Alabama Infantry Regiment at Gettysburg. He and his men were the principal adversaries of Joshua Chamberlain and the men of the 20th Maine. After Gettysburg Oates continued in command of the 15th and later the 48th Alabama Regiments. He was seriously wounded in the defense of Petersburg, Virginia, in late 1864 suffering the amputation of his right arm. He remained with the Confederate army on limited duty for the remainder of the war.

At war's end Oates resumed his law practice in Henry County, Alabama, and also entered the political arena. He represented Alabama in the US House of Representatives from 1881 to 1894. Like his Gettysburg opponent, Chamberlain, Oates also served as governor of his native state, in this case in the years 1894–1896. In 1898 President William McKinley commissioned Oates as a brigadier general of US Army volunteers during the Spanish-American War. Four other former senior Confederate officers were commissioned by McKinley as major generals of US Army volunteers during that war.

With the war over, Oates again returned home to Alabama, his law practice, and real estate speculation. In 1905 his memoirs of the American Civil War were published with the solemn title *The War Between the Union and the Confederacy and Its Lost Opportunities*. William Calvin Oates died September 9, 1910, at seventy-five years of age. He is buried in Oakwood Cemetery, Montgomery, Alabama.

Chapter 9

James Ewell Brown "Jeb" Stuart (1833–1864)

"Jeb" Stuart remained the senior commander of Confederate cavalry in the eastern theater of operations well into 1864. During General Grant's drive on Richmond in the spring of 1864, Stuart's men halted Union General Sheridan's cavalry at Yellow Tavern on the outskirts of Richmond. It was there Stuart, the bold cavalier, was mortally wounded in combat on May 11, 1864. He died the next day in Richmond and is buried there in the Hollywood Cemetery. Like his close friend Stonewall Jackson and his commander R. E. Lee, Stuart had become a legend in his own time, and their legends still linger on Civil War battlefields to this day.

Chapter 10

George Edward Pickett (1825–1875)

In the withdrawal from Gettysburg, Pickett and the remnants of his division were relegated to guarding Union prisoners on the retreat to the Potomac River crossings. In compliance with the regulations of the time, Pickett, as did the other commanders, filed an after-action report of what happened with his division in the Gettysburg Campaign. His report was apparently so embittered that General Lee asked Pickett to revise and resubmit it. Pickett never complied.

The fortunes of Pickett and his men did not improve much in the coming months. After seeing limited duty in North Carolina while attempting to rebuild the division, he and his men acted as a mobile reserve during the latter part of 1864 in the defense of Richmond and Petersburg, Virginia. Defeated at the Battle of Five Forks on April 1, 1865, with his command once again decimated by enemy action, Pickett was finally relieved of command by General Lee, but he surrendered with the rest of the army at Appomattox Court House.

After the war, Pickett and his wife, Corbell, and children settled in Richmond. He had difficulty finding a profession in which he was comfortable. Unlike a few other former Confederate officers who took the opportunity, Pickett twice refused offers from the khedive of Egypt to help impart a modern Western influence on his armies as mercenary instructors and trainers. Instead he secured steady work as a general agent for the Washington Life Insurance Company. While the job provided adequate income for his family and him, he found it awkward for a former major general to try to sell a product that his impoverished customers could not afford and in most cases did not want.

In March 1870 before General Lee's death, Pickett and his close friend, Virginia partisan ranger John Singleton Mosby, had an awkward chance meeting with the old Confederate commander. When Pickett brought up the subject of Gettysburg, the tenor of the meeting turned cold, formal, and embarrassing to both parties. As they parted ways, Pickett, referring to Lee, is alleged to have said to Mosby, "He had my division massacred at Gettysburg." Mosby is alleged to have replied, "It made you immortal."[6]

In June 1872, George Pickett served as chief marshal at ceremonies honoring the reinternment in Richmond's Hollywood Cemetery of the first group of almost 3,000 Confederates who had fallen at Gettysburg. George Edward Pickett died of heart failure in a hospital in Norfolk, Virginia, on July 30, 1875. In his twilight hours he turned his head toward his wife's uncle, who had served with him during the war, and whispered, "Well, Colonel, the enemy is too strong for me again… my ammunition is all out."[7]

James Lawson Kemper (1823–1895)

Virginia attorney and politician James Kemper was the only one of Pickett's three subordinate brigade commanders to survive the attack of July 3. Initially wounded and captured by the enemy during the attack, he was exchanged back to the Confederate army in September 1863. While the nature of his wounds made him unfit for continued active service in the field, he proved to be a capable commander of the reserve forces of Virginia, holding the rank of major general. He finally surrendered and was paroled a month after the Appomattox surrender. After the war he resumed his legal and political careers, serving as governor of Virginia from 1874 to 1877. He died and was buried in Orange County, Virginia, in April 1895.

Bibliography

Civil War

Alexander, Edward Porter. *Fighting for the Confederacy: The Personal Recollections of General Edward Porter Alexander.* Gary W. Gallagher ed. Chapel Hill: University of North Carolina Press, 1989.

Boritt, Gabor. *The Gettysburg Gospel.* New York: Simon & Schuster, 2006.

Brown, Kent Mastertson. *Retreat from Gettysburg—Lee, Logistics & the Pennsylvania Campaign.* Chapel Hill: University of North Carolina Press, 2005.

Busey, John W. and David G. Martin. *Regimental Strengths and Losses at Gettysburg,* 4th ed. Hightstown, NJ: Longstreet House, 2005.

Chamberlain, Joshua Lawrence. *The Passing of the Armies.* New York: G. P. Putnam's Sons, 1915.

Coddington, Edwin B. *The Gettysburg Campaign—A Study in Command.* New York: Charles Scribner's Sons, 1968.

DiNardo, R. L., and Albert A. Nofi, *James Longstreet—The Man, the Soldier, the Controversy.* Conshohocken, PA: Combined Publishing, 1998.

Fishel, E. C. *The Secret War for the Union.* Boston: Houghton Mifflin, 1996.

Freeman, Douglas Southall. *R.E. Lee: A Biography,* 4 vols. New York: Charles Scribners and Sons, 1933.

Gwynne, S. C. *Hymns of the Republic—The Story of the Final Year of the American Civil War.* New York: Simon & Schuster, 2019.

Haskell, Frank A. *The Battle of Gettysburg.* Wisconsin Historical Commission, 1910.

Hess, Earl J. *Civil War Infantry Tactics.* Baton Rouge: Louisiana State University Press, 2015.

Hessler, James A. *Sickles at Gettysburg.* El Dorado Hills, CA: Savas Beattie, 2009.

Hessler, James A., and Wayne E. Motts. *Pickett's Charge at Gettysburg—A Guide to the Most Famous Attack in American History.* El Dorado Hills, CA: Savas Beatie, 2015.

Kreidberg, Marvin A., and Merton G. Henry. *History of Military Mobilization in the United States Army, 1775-1945*. Washington, D.C.: U.S. Department of the Army, 1955.

Long, E.B. and Barbara Long. *The Civil War Day by Day—An Almanac 1861-1865*. Garden City, NJ: Doubleday and Company, 1971.

Longacre, Edward G. *The Cavalry at Gettysburg*. Lincoln: University of Nebraska Press, 1993.

Longstreet, James. *From Manassas to Appomattox*. Philadelphia: J.B. Lippincott, 1896, De Capo Press republication, 1992.

"Lee's Right Wing at Gettysburg." *Battles and Leaders of the Civil War*, 3 vol. Secaucus, NJ: Castle, a division of Book Sales, Inc. undated.

McPherson, James M. *Tried by War—Abraham Lincoln as Commander-in-Chief*. New York: Penguin Group, 2008.

Reardon, Carol. *Pickett's Charge in History and Memory*. Chapel Hill: University of North Carolina Press, 1997.

Reardon, Carol, and Tom Vossler. *A Field Guide to Gettysburg—Experiencing the Battlefield through Its History, Places, and People*, 2nd ed. Chapel Hill: University of North Carolina Press, 2017.

Reus, Edmund J. Jr. *A Generation on the March: The Union Army at Gettysburg*. Gettysburg, PA: Thomas Publications, 1996.

Sifakis, Stewart. *Who Was Who in the Civil War*. New York: Facts on File Publications, 1988.

Stewart, George R. *Pickett's Charge: A Microhistory of the Final Attack at Gettysburg, July 3, 1863*. Boston: Houghton Mifflin, 1959.

Trulock, Alice Rains. *In the Hands of Providence: Joshua L. Chamberlain & the American Civil War*. Chapel Hill, NC: University of North Carolina Press, 1992.

Tucker, Glenn. *High Tide at Gettysburg*. Dayton, OH: Morningside Bookshop, 1958.

U.S. Department of War. *The War of the Rebellion: A Compilation of the Official Records of the Union and Confederate Armies*. 128 vols. and index. Washington: 1880-1901.

Warner, Ezra J. *Generals in Blue: The Lives of the Union Commanders*. Baton Rouge: Louisiana State University Press, 2002. *Generals in Gray: The Lives of the Confederate Commanders*. Baton Rouge: Louisiana State University Press, 2006.

Wert, Jeffery D. *James Longstreet: The Confederacy's Most Controversial Soldier*. New York: Simon and Schuster, 1993.

Wills, Garry. *Lincoln at Gettysburg*. New York: Simon & Schuster, 1992. *A Glorious Army*. New York: Simon and Schuster, 2011.

Wilson, Douglas L. *Lincoln's Sword*. New York: Alfred A. Knopf, 2006.

Wittenberg, Eric J., and J. David Petruzzi. *Plenty of Blame to Go Around—Jeb Stuart's Controversial Ride to Gettysburg*. El Dorado Hills, CA: Savas Beatie, 2011.

Business Leadership

Blanchard, Kenneth, and Spencer Johnson. *The One Minute Manager*. New York: William Morrow, 1982.

Brooks, David. *The Road to Character*. New York: Random House, 2015.

Collins, Jim. *Good to Great*. New York: HarperCollins, 2001. Contains a good discussion of how to determine success for an organization.

Gladwell, Malcolm F. *Blink—The Power of Thinking without Thinking*. New York: Little, Brown, 2007.

Goleman, Daniel. *Emotional Intelligence*. New York: Bantam Books, 1915.

Johnson, Brad. *The Elements of Mentoring*. New York: St. Martin's Press, 2004.

Kolditz, Thomas A. *In Extremis Leadership*. New York: John Wiley & Sons, 2007. An interesting examination of leading during a crisis.

Lehrer, Jonah. *How We Decide*. New York: Houghton Mifflin Harcourt, 2009.

Lencioni, Patrick. *Five Dysfunctions of a Team*. San Francisco: Jossey-Bass, 2002.

Maxwell, Christopher. *Lead Like a Guide*. Denver, CO: Praeger, 2016. A fascinating examination of leadership "style."

Morgan, Angie, Courtney Lynch, and Sean Lynch. *Spark—How to Lead Yourself and Others to Greater Success*. New York: Houghton Mifflin Harcourt, 2017. Describes the power of decentralization in organizations.

Sinek, Simon. *Start with Why—How Great Leaders Inspire Everyone to Take Action*. London: Penguin Books, 2009.

Useem, Michael. *The Leadership Moment*. New York: Three Rivers Press, 1998.

———. *Leading Up—How to Lead Your Boss So You Both Win*. New York: Random House, 2001.

General Leadership

Brown, Daniel James. *The Boys in the Boat*. New York: Viking Press, 2013.

Coram, Robert. *Boyd: The Fighter Pilot Who Changed the Art of War*. New York: Back Bay Books, 2002.

Lord, Walter. *Day of Infamy*. New York: Henry Holt, 1957. Covers the attack on Pearl Harbor and the USS Nevada.

Stockdale, James Bond. *Thoughts of a Philosophical Fighter Pilot*. Stanford, CA: Hoover Institute Press, 1995.

Acknowledgments

Battle Tested! is intended to be a book that uses the story of the officers and men on both sides that fought the Battle of Gettysburg to examine concepts and principles of leadership that both authors believe are enduring. Any book is made possible by the efforts of many people beyond the author(s), and that is especially true with this one. It was, in many ways, a "team" effort.

We began working on this idea over ten years ago when Jeff asked Tom to assist him in developing and delivering a leadership seminar on the Gettysburg battlefield. In the intervening years we have been honored to host leaders from all over the United States and several foreign countries for this developmental experience. We have used the stories of those who fought and, in some cases, died during the battle to develop not only attendees' individual leadership skills but also their organization's ability to deal with a rapidly changing world. Both of us have been gratified to receive significant feedback that these seminars have helped participants better lead corporations, government agencies, nonprofits, education associations, school districts, military units, universities, and so on. The discussions that we have had with them over the years have not only stimulated our thinking in many, many ways, but also encouraged us to now write this book.

We are both indebted to the staff of Diamond6 Leadership & Strategy, LLC who have assisted us in the planning/execution of these efforts and the production of the book. Phillip McCausland served as our initial editor for the book proposal and each draft chapter along the way. His critical insights, professional editing, and diligence were essential to the final product. Holly Tiley, Bri Buffington, and Tanya

Acknowledgments

McCausland are the backbone of Diamond6 Leadership. Their hard work, workshop planning/execution, and encouragement were indispensable during this journey. Research assistants Ben Fleming and Will Smith conducted timely and rapid research that was invaluable.

Many of Jeff and Tom's friends and colleagues at both Dickinson College (where Jeff is a professor) and the Army War College (where they both served on the faculty) were extremely beneficial. We would like to particularly acknowledge Dr. Matt Pinsker, Pohanka Chair in American Civil War History at Dickinson College. Matt provided critical advice and assistance with his vast knowledge of Abraham Lincoln and the American Civil War. Lieutenant General (retired) Walt Ulmer was the initial holder of the Bradley Chair of Strategic Leadership for both the War College and Dickinson. He has been a mentor for Jeff for many years and provided invaluable advice from his vast knowledge of leadership. Tom remembers with advantages General Ulmer's astute leadership of the III (Armored) Corp at Fort Hood, Texas during the Cold War years of the early 1980s.

Esmond Harmsworth was our literary agent in this process, and we learned a great deal from him about publishing a book! His encouragement and enthusiasm for this project sustained us for over two years in the search for a publisher. We would also like to thank the Post Hill Press team—Heather King, Managing Editor; Meredith Didier, Associate Publicist; and Debby Englander, Consulting Editor. They have been a pleasure to work with and learn from.

Finally, we both want to thank again our two spouses—Barbara and Marianne. This book would have never happened without their love and support. It is dedicated to them, and if any credit derives from it, those honors are largely theirs. Lastly, the American soldiers, non-commissioned officers, and fellow commissioned officers that we served with during our careers in combat and peacetime were not only an inspiration to us, but in the end—they taught us leadership.

Endnotes

Introduction

1 Peter Lyon, *Eisenhower: Portrait of the Hero*, (Boston/Toronto: Little Brown and Company, 1974) p. 217.

2 Marvin A. Kreidberg and Merton G. Henry, *History of Military Mobilization in the United States Army, 1775-1945* (Washington, DC: US Department of the Army, 1955; reprint, US Army Center of Military History, 1984), 88.

3 Kreidberg and Henry, 92–93.

4 Kreidberg and Henry, 108.

5 E. B. Long and Barbara Long, *The Civil War Day by Day—An Almanac 1861-1865* (Garden City, NY: Doubleday & Company, 1971), 706–707.

6 Long and Long, 704.

7 US War Department, *Revised Regulations for the Army of the United States, 1861* (Washington, DC: US War Department; reprint Dover Publications, 2013), 519.

8 John W. Busey and David G. Martin, *Regimental Strengths and Losses at Gettysburg*, 4th ed. (Hightstown, NJ: Longstreet House, 2005), 245.

9 Busey and Martin, 346.

Chapter 1

1 US War Department, *War of the Rebellion: A Compilation of the Official Records of the Union and Confederate Armies*. 128 vols. (Washington, DC: Government Printing Office, 1880–1901), part 2, 27:305. (Hereinafter referred to as *Official Records*.)

2 Douglas Southall Freeman, *R. E. Lee—A Biography*, 4 vols. (New York: Charles Scribner's Sons, 1933), 3:19.

3 Freeman.

4 *Official Records*, part 2, 27: 305, 313.

5 James M. McPherson, *The Illustrated Battle Cry of Freedom: The Civil War Era* (Oxford, UK: Oxford University Press, 2003), 560.

6 Edwin B. Coddington, *The Gettysburg Campaign—A Study in Command* (New York: Charles Scribner's Sons, 1968), 8.

7 Busey and Martin, *Regimental Strengths and Losses*, 5.

8 John C. Waugh, *The Class of 1846—From West Point to Appomattox* (New York: Ballantine Books, 1994), 288–293.

9   Waugh, 378–380.

10 Coddington, *Gettysburg Campaign*, 209.

11 Ezra J. Warner, *Generals in Blue—The Lives of the Union Commanders* (Baton Rouge: Louisiana State University Press, 2002), 315–316.

12 Busey and Martin, *Regimental Strengths and Losses*, 345.

13 Warner, *Generals in Blue*, 203–204.

14 Warner, 446–447.

Chapter 2

1   Eric J. Wittenberg, *John Buford at Gettysburg—A History and Walking Tour* (El Dorado Hills, CA: Savas Beatie, 2014), 16.

2   Warner, *Generals in Blue*, 165–166.

3   Warner, 123–124.

Chapter 3

1   *Official Records*, part 3, 27:416–417.

2   Warner, *Generals in Blue*, 396–397.

3   Busey and Martin, *Regimental Strengths and Losses*, 125, 131, 129.

4   *Official Records*, part 3, 27: 419–420.

5   Civil War Cycling, "Famous Quotations from the Battle of Gettysburg," May 1, 2017, https://www.civilwarcycling.com/index/gettysburg-quotations/.

6   For alternative accounts of Reynolds's death, see Carol Reardon and Tom Vossler, *A Field Guide to Gettysburg—Experiencing the Battlefield through Its History, Places, and People*, 2nd ed. (Chapel Hill: University of North Carolina Press, 2017), 53–54.

7   Coddington, *Gettysburg Campaign*, 277.

8   Michael Useem, *The Leadership Moment* (New York: Three Rivers Press, 1998), 65–93. See also Edgar M. Cortright, *Apollo Expeditions to the Moon (Washington, DC: NASA Scientific and Technical Information Office, 2019), p. 247.

9   Useem, 68–69.

10 Useem, 79.

11 Earl J. Hess, *Civil War Infantry Tactics* (Baton Rouge: Louisiana State University Press, 2015), 27–28.

Chapter 4

1   Busey and Martin, *Regimental Strengths and Losses*, 289, 302.

2   Glenn Tucker, *High Tide at Gettysburg* (Dayton, OH: Morningside Bookshop, 1958; Bobbs-Merrill reprint, 1983), 181. See also Douglas Southall Freeman, *Lee's Lieutenants*, vol. 3 (New York: Charles Scribner's Sons, 1944), 97.

3   *Official Records*, part 2, 27:445.

4   Coddington, *Gettysburg Campaign*, 318.

5   Justus Scheibert, *Seven Months in the Rebel States* (Tuscaloosa: University of Alabama Press, 1958), 14. See also Jeffrey D. Wert, *A Glorious Army* (New York: Simon & Schuster, 2011), 256; and Tom Carhart, *Lost Triumph: Lee's Real Plan at Gettysburg—and Why It Failed* (New York: G. P. Putnam's Sons), 183.

6   G. F. R. Henderson, *Stonewall Jackson and the American Civil War* (New York: Da Capo Press, 1988), 36, 601–602, 614.

7   Henderson, 193, 150.
8   Freeman, *R. E. Lee*,1.
9   A. T. Kearney Corporation and Kelley School of Business, *The Key to Superior Long-Term Financial Performance Is Managing Succession* (Indianapolis: Indiana University, 2011).
10 Kearney.
11 General Stanley McChrystal, *Team of Teams—New Rules of Engagement for a Complex World* (New York: Penguin Publishing Group, 2015), 78.
12 Coddington, *Gettysburg Campaign*, 318–319.
13 Letter from former Confederate Major General Isaac Ridgeway Trimble to Colonel J. B. Bachelder dated February 8, 1883, in *The Bachelder Papers—Gettysburg in Their Own Words*, vol. 2 (Dayton, OH: Morningside House, 1994), 930–931.

Chapter 5

1   Jeffery D. Wert, *James Longstreet—The Confederacy's Most Controversial Soldier* (New York: Simon & Schuster, 1993), 28, 31.
2   William Garrett Piston, "Petticoats, Promotions and Military Assignments—Favoritism and the Antebellum Career of James Longstreet," in *James Longstreet—The Man, the Soldier, the Controversy*, ed. R. L. DiNardo and Albert A. Nofi (Conshohocken, PA: Combined Publishing, 1998), 54.
3   *Civil War Generals from West Point*, found at http://sunsite.utk.edu/civil-war/wpclasses.html.
4   Ezra J. Warner, *Generals in Gray—Lives of the Confederate Commanders* (Baton Rouge: Louisiana State University Press, 1959), 192–193.
5   James Longstreet, *From Manassas to Appomattox* (Philadelphia, PA: J. B. Lippincott, 1896; unabridged republication by Da Capo Press, 1992), 358.
6   Tucker, *High Tide at Gettysburg*, 187.
7   Adam Bryant, "On a Busy Road, a Company Needs Guiderails," *New York Times*, October 12, 2012, E2.
8   Daniel James Brown, *The Boys in the Boat* (New York: Viking Press, 2013), 23.

Chapter 6

1   *Official Records*, part 1, 27:115–116.
2   Malcolm Gladwell, *Blink* (New York: Little, Brown, 2005).
3   Malcolm Gladwell, *The Tipping Point* (New York: Little, Brown, 2000).

Chapter 7

1   Edmund J. Reus Jr., *A Generation on the March—The Union Army at Gettysburg* (Gettysburg, PA: Thomas Publications, 1996), 47, 63, 121. All engaged strength numbers are taken from John W. Busey and David G. Martin, *Regimental Strengths and Losses at Gettysburg*, 4th edition (Highstown, NJ: Longstreet House, 2005), 62.
2   John J. Pullen, *The Twentieth Maine—A Volunteer Regiment of the Civil War* (Dayton, OH: Morningside House, 1991), 13.
3   Warner, *Generals in Blue*, 5, 6.
4   Alice Rains Trulock, *In the Hands of Providence—Joshua L. Chamberlain & the American Civil War* (Chapel Hill: The University of North Carolina Press), 39.

5   Trulock, 7.
6   *Official Records*, Vol. 27, ptl, 623.
7   Coddington, *Gettysburg Campaign*, 336, 392. See also Matt Spruill, *Summer Thunder—A Battlefield Guide to the Artillery at Gettysburg* (Knoxville: University of Tennessee Press, 2010), 281.
8   Daniel Goleman, *Emotional Intelligence* (New York: Bantam Books, 1995), 43–44.
9   Thomas A. Desjardin, *Stand Firm Ye Boys from Maine* (Gettysburg, PA: Thomas Publications, 1995), 17.
10 *Official Records*, Vol. 27, pt. , 623.
11 Joshua Lawrence Chamberlain, *The Passing of the Armies* (New York: G. P. Putnam's Sons, 1915), 195.

Chapter 8

1   Quoted in Harry W. Pfanz, *Gettysburg—The Second Day* (Chapel Hill: University of North Carolina Press, 1987), 425.
2   Wert, *General James Longstreet*, 72.
3   *Official Records*, part 1, 27: 72.
4   Participants included Meade, his chief of staff, Brigadier General Daniel Butterfield; his chief engineer, Brigadier General Gouverneur K. Warren; acting I Corps commander, Major General John Newton; II Corps commander, Major General Winfield Scott Hancock; acting III Corps commander, Brigadier General David Birney; V Corps commander, Major General George Sykes; VI Corps commander, Major General John Sedgwick; XI Corps commander, Major General O. O. Howard; XII Corps commander, Major General Henry Slocum; Major General Alpheus Williams of the XII Corps; and division commander Brigadier General John Gibbon of the II Corps. *Official Records*, part 1, 27: 73.
5   John Gibbon, "The Council of War on the Second Day," in *Battles and Leaders of the Civil War,* eds. Robert Underwood Johnson and Clarence Clough Buel (Secaucus, NJ: Castle, a division of Book Sales, Inc., undated), 313.
6   *Official Records*, part 1, 27:73.
7   Gibbon, "Council of War."
8   Coddington, *Gettysburg Campaign,* 444.
9   Tucker, *High Tide at Gettysburg*, 318.
10 Stephen W. Sears, *Gettysburg* (Boston, MA: Houghton Mifflin, 2003), 346.
11 Sears, 348.
12 Freeman, *R .E. Lee*, vol. 3, 105.
13 Glenn Tucker, *Lee and Longstreet at Gettysburg* (Dayton, OH: Morningside House, 1982), 241.
14 William Deresiewicz, "Solitude and Leadership" (lecture delivered at the United States Military Academy at West Point, March 1, 2010). See also Raymond M. Kethledge and Michael S. Erwin, "It's Lonely at the Top—or It Should Be," *Wall Street Journal*, June 19, 2017.
15 Stephen Budiansky, "America's Unknown Intelligence Czar," *American Heritage* vol. 55, October 5, 2004, 55–63.

Chapter 9

1 Edward G. Longacre, *The Cavalry at Gettysburg* (Lincoln: University of Nebraska Press, 1993), 23.

2 Warner, *Generals in Gray*, 296–297.

3 Robert I. Girardi, *The Civil War Generals: Comrades, Peers, Rivals—In Their Own Words* (Minneapolis, MN: Zenith Press, 2013), 254.

4 Jeffrey Wert, *A Glorious Army* (New York: Simon & Schuster, 2011), 220.

5 Longacre, *Cavalry at Gettysburg*, 148–149.

6 *Official Records*, part 2, 27:692.

7 *Official Records*, Vol. 27, pt.2, 694.

8 *Official Records*. Vol. 27, pt. 2, 694

9 *Official Records*, Vol. 27, pt. 2 696.

10 Quoted in Eric J. Wittenberg and J. David Petruzzi, *Plenty of Blame to Go Around— Jeb Stuart's Controversial Ride to Gettysburg* (El Dorado Hills, CA: Savas Beatie, 2006 and 2011), 157.

11 Official Records, Vol. 27, pt. 2, 321.

12 Captain Robert E. Lee, *The Recollections and Letters of General Robert E. Lee* (Secaucus, NJ: Blue and Gray Press, 1988), 125.

13 Suzanne de Janasz and Maury Peiperl, "CEOs Need Mentors Too," *Harvard Business Review,* April 2015. See also Rick Woolworth, "Great Mentors Focus on the Whole Person, Not Just Their Career," *Harvard Business Review,* August 9, 2019.

14 *Official Records*, part 3, 27:913.

15 Craig M. Hales, MD; Margaret D. Carroll, MSPH; Cheryl D. Fryar, MSPH, and Cynthia Ogden, PhD, "Prevalence of Obesity Among Adults and Youth: United States 2015–2016," Center for Disease Control and Prevention, *National Center for Health Statistics Brief No. 288,* October 2017.

16 Milja Milenkovic, "42 Worrying Workplace Stress Statistics," American Institute of Stress, September 23, 2019.

17 Dr. Farrell Cahill, "Optimize the Returns of Your Wellness Investment," Medisys Health Network, 2019, https://blog.medisys.ca/roi-of-wellness.

Chapter 10

1 *Official Records*, part 2, 27:320.

2 Wert, *General James Longstreet*, 283.

3 Shelby Foote, *Stars in Their Courses—The Gettysburg Campaign* (New York: The Modern Library, 1994), 260.

4 Don Fehrenbacher and Virginia Fehrenbacher, *Recollected Words of Abraham Lincoln* (Stanford, CA: Stanford University Press, 1996), 426.

5 Tim Rives, "Just What Did Ike Say When He Launched the D-Day Invasion 70 Years Ago?," *Prologue* (Spring 2014): 36–43.

6 James Stockdale, *Thoughts of a Philosophical Fighter Pilot* (Stanford, CA: Hoover Institution, 1995), 36–43, 190, 241. See also James C. Collins, *Good to Great* (London: Random House Business, 2001), 85.

7 David Streitfeld, "Behind Success, Amazon Finds Room for Risk," *New York Times,* June 17, 2017, 1 and 21.

Endnotes

8 Streitfield.

9 James Longstreet, "Lee's Right Wing at Gettysburg," *Battles and Leaders of the Civil War*, vol. 3 (Secaucus, NJ: Castle, a division of Book Sales, Inc., undated), 343.

10 James A Hessler and Wayne E. Motts, *Pickett's Charge at Gettysburg—A Guide to the Most Famous Attack in American History* (El Dorado Hills, CA: Savas Beatie, 2015), 66.

11 Warner, *Generals in Gray*, 239.

12 Warner, 169–170.

13 Warner, 11–12.

14 Warner, 99.

15 Tucker, *High Tide at Gettysburg*, 334.

16 Hessler and Motts, *Pickett's Charge at Gettysburg*, 40.

17 George R. Stewart, *Pickett's Charge—A Microhistory of the Final Attack at Gettysburg, July 3, 1863* (Boston: Houghton Mifflin, 1959), 96.

18 Foote, *Stars in Their Courses*, 228.

19 American Psychological Association, "Change at Work Linked to Employee Stress, Distrust, and Intent to Quit, New Survey Finds," May 24, 2017.

20 The Conference Board, "Poll: Job Satisfaction Climbs to Highest Level in Over Two Decades," Cision PR Newswire, August 29, 2019.

21 Stewart, *Pickett's Charge—A Microhistory*, 175.

22 Warner, *Generals in Blue*, 202–204.

23 Warner, 223–224.

24 Warner, 171.

25 Jonathon Horn, *The Man Who Would Not Be Washington* (New York: Scribner Publishing, 2015), 197.

26 *Official Records*, part 1, 27:706.

27 Edward Porter Alexander, *Fighting for the Confederacy—The Personal Recollections of General Edward Porter Alexander*, ed. Gary W. Gallagher (Chapel Hill: University of North Carolina Press, 1989), 258.

28 Longstreet, *From Manassas to Appomattox*, 392.

29 Longstreet.

30 Tucker, *High Tide at Gettysburg*, 356.

31 Tucker, 357 and 361.

32 *Official Records*, part 2, 27:386.

33 Tucker, *High Tide at Gettysburg*, 329.

34 Frank A. Haskell, *The Battle of Gettysburg* (Wisconsin History Commission, 1910), 97–98.

35 Johnathan Asbury, *Churchill's War in Words—His Finest Quotes, 1939-1945* (London: Trustees of the Imperial War Museum, 2018), 126.

Chapter 11

1 Foote, *Stars in Their Course*, pp. 242–243.

2 Hessler and Motts, *Pickett's Charge at Gettysburg*, 255–256.

3 Hessler and Motts, 147.

4 Hessler and Motts, 256.

5   Stewart, *Pickett's Charge—A Microhistory,* 248.

6   Wert, *A Glorious Army,* 278.

7   *Official Records,* part 1, 27:78.

8   Tucker, *High Tide at Gettysburg,* 384–385.

9   Coddington, *Gettysburg Campaign,* 565.

10 Coddington, 570.

11 Doris Kearns Goodwin, *Team of Rivals* (New York: Simon & Schuster, 2005), 536.

12 Robert Slater, *The Wal-Mart Decade* (New York: Portfolio Publishing, 2004).

13 Lee Iacocca and William Novak, *Iacocca—An Autobiography* (New York: Bantam Books, 1984).

14 Edward J. Stackpole, *They Met at Gettysburg* (Harrisburg, PA: Stackpole Press, 1956), 316.

15 Stackpole, 318–319.

16 Allen C. Guelzo, *Gettysburg—The Last Invasion* (New York: Alfred A. Knopf, 2013), 448.

17 Goodwin, *Team of Rivals,* 537.

18 Bruce Catton, *Never Call Retreat* (New York: Doubleday, 1965), 214–216. See also James M. McPherson, *Tried by War* (New York: Penguin Press, 2008), 187.

19 Sheena Frenkel and Kevin Roose, "Zuckerberg, Facing Facebook's Worst Crisis Yet, Pledges Better Privacy," *New York Times,* March 21, 2018. See also Maya Kosoff, "Mark Zuckerberg Refuses Responsibility for Facebook's Latest, Greatest Scandal," *Vanity Fair,* November 15, 2018.

20 Horn, *Man Who Would Not Be Washington,* 200.

21 Wert, *A Glorious Army,* 283.

Chapter 12

1   Hessler and Motts, *Pickett's Charge at Gettysburg,* 254.

2   Reardon and Vossler, *Field Guide to Gettysburg,* 53.

3   Reardon and Vossler, 246.

4   Adams County Historical Society, *Farms at Gettysburg,* compiled by Timothy H. Smith (Gettysburg: Thomas Publications), 33.

5   James M. Cole and Rev. Roy E. Frampton, *Lincoln and the Human Interest Stories of the Gettysburg National Cemetery* (Hanover, PA: Sheridan Press, 1995), 8.

6   "Report of Samuel R. Weaver, Superintendent of Exhuming the Bodies, March 19, 1864," in John Mitchell Vanderslice, *Gettysburg, A History of the Gettysburg Battle-Field Memorial Association, with an Account of the Battle* (original copyright 1896 by John M. Vanderslice; Nabu Public Domain Reprints, undated), 175–176.

7   Garry Wills, *Lincoln at Gettysburg* (New York: Simon & Schuster, 1992), 24.

8   Wills, 25.

9   Michael Burlingame, *Abraham Lincoln: A Life,* vol. 2 (Baltimore, MD: Johns Hopkins University Press, 2013), 569.

10 Joshua Zeitz, *Lincoln's Boys: John Hay, John Nicolay, and the War for Lincoln's Image* (New York: Viking, 2014), 141.

11 Erick Schenck Miens, ed., *Lincoln Day by Day, A Chronology 1809–1865, Volume III 1861–1865* (Washington: Lincoln Sesquicentennial Commission, 1960), 220.

12 Bruce Catton, *Never Call Retreat* (New York: Doubleday Broadway Publishing Group, 1965), 283.

13 Michael Burlingame and John R. Turner Ettlinger, eds., *Inside Lincoln's White House: The Complete Civil War Diary of John Hay* (Carbondale: Southern Illinois University Press, 1999), 122.

14 S. C. Gwynne, *Hymns of the Republic* (New York: Scribner Publishing, 2019), 153.

15 President John F. Kennedy, Address at Rice University on the Nation's Space Effort, Houston, Texas, September 12, 1962, https://www.jfklibrary.org/learn/about-jfk/historic-speeches/address-at-rice-university-on-the-nations-space-effort.

16 James W. Pennebaker, *The Secret Life of Pronouns: What Our Words Say About Us* (New York: Bloomsbury Publishing, 2011).

17 John Hay, *Letters of John Hay,* vol. 1, 1908, 125.

18 "Retraction for Our 1863 Editorial Calling Gettysburg Address 'Silly Remarks': Editorial." *Patriot-News*, November 14, 2013, https://www.pennlive.com/opinion/2013/11/a_patriot-news_editorial_retraction_the_gettysburg_address.html.

19 *Patriot-News.*

20 Paul Revere Frothingham, *Edward Everett, Orator and Statesman* (Boston: Houghton Mifflin, 1925), 454–455. See also Miens, *Lincoln Day by Day,* 222.

21 Frank Luther Mott, *American Journalism: A History of Newspapers in the United States through 250 Years, 1690–1940* (New York: Macmillan, 1941), 216.

22 Dan Schiller, *Objectivity and the News: The Public and the Rise of Commercial Journalism* (Philadelphia: University of Pennsylvania Press, 1981), 12.

23 Gabor Boritt, *The Gettysburg Gospel* (New York: Simon & Schuster, 2006), 57.

24 Goodwin, *Team of Rivals,* 586.

Epilogue

1 J. David Hacker, "Recounting the Dead," *New York Times*, September 20, 2011, https://opinionator.blogs.nytimes.com/2011/09/20/recounting-the-dead/#more-105317.

2 E. W. Andrews, Union army officer as recorded in *Reminiscences of Abraham Lincoln by Distinguished Men of His Time,* ed. Allen Thorndike Rice (New York: Harper & Brothers Publishers, 1885), 297.

3 Erin Allen, "Abraham Lincoln's 'Blind Memorandum,'" Library of Congress Blog, 2014, https://blogs.loc.gov/loc/2014/08/abraham-lincolns-blind-memorandum/.

4 Allen.

5 Gwynne, *Hymns of the Republic,* 209.

6 Jay Winik, *April 1865—The Month That Saved America* (New York: HarperCollins, 2001), 31.

7 Brown University Library, *The Life and Works of John Hay, 1838–1905* (Providence, Rhode Island: Brown University, 1961), 12.

8 Stanley Appelbaum, ed., *Abraham Lincoln Great Speeches* (Mineola, NY: Dover Publications, 1991), 106.

9 Lieutenant General William T. Sherman, "Letter to the Honorable I. N. Arnold," November 28, 1872; Vice Admiral David Porter, "Account of the Interview with Mr. Lincoln"; https://cwcrossroads.wordpress.com/2015/03/27/the-river-queen-conference-march-27-28-1865/.

10 Charles Carleton Coffin, war correspondent, as recorded in *Reminiscences of Abraham Lincoln by Distinguished Men of His Time,* 187.

11 Michael W. Kauffman, *American Brutus: John Wilkes Booth and the Lincoln Conspiracies* (New York: Random House, 2004), 210. See also Goodwin, *Team of Rivals,* 728.

12 Adam Gopnik, "The Takeback," *New Yorker,* April 8, 2019, 76–82. See also Henry Louis Gates, *Stony Road: Reconstruction, White Supremacy, and the Rise of Jim Crow* (New York: Penguin Press, 2019).

Dramatis Personae

1 W. Dennis Keating, "Presidents Who Were Civil War Veterans," *Essential Civil War Curriculum,* https://www.essentialcivilwarcurriculum.com/presidents-who-were -civil-war-veterans.html.

2 Unless otherwise noted, biographical information is taken from one of three sources under entries for each individual: Ezra J. Warner, *Generals in Blue—Lives of the Union Commanders* (Baton Rouge: Louisiana State University Press, 1964). Ezra J. Warner, *Generals in Gray—Lives of the Confederate Commanders* (Baton Rouge: Louisiana State University Press, 1959). Stewart Sifakis, *Who Was Who in the Civil War* (New York: Facts on File Publications, 1988).

3 E. B. Long and Barbara Long, *The Civil War Day by Day,* 682 and 688.

4 Wert, *General James Longstreet,* 416.

5 James A. Hessler, *Sickles at Gettysburg* (El Dorado Hills, CA: Savas Beatie, 2009), 387.

6 Edward G. Longacre, *Pickett—Leader of the Charge* (Shippensburg, PA: White Mane Publishing Company, 1995), 179.

7 Longacre, 180.

Index

Note: A page number in italics refers to a figure, illustration, map, or photograph.

A

Abbott Laboratories, business success and clear succession plan, 71

Adams County, Pennsylvania, 175

Adams, John (US president), quote on integrity of future presidents, xiii

Adaptation, definition of, 37

Alabama
Heth's and Pender's soldiers from, 145
regiments at Seminary Ridge from, 155
standardized test cheating in public schools in, 106–107

Alexander, Edward Porter (Confederate)
Confederate Lieutenant Colonel, 140, 141
organized cannon line on Cemetery Ridge, 153–154

Alignment, definition and metaphor of rowing, 78–80

"All men are created equal," Declaration of Independence and Gettysburg Address, 186

"America's unfinished business," Lincoln and, 193

American Bar Association, founding of, 206

American Institute of Stress, 133

American Revolution, British offered freedom but slaves fought with Continental Army, 3

Ames, Adelbert (Union)
brigadier general of XI Corps, 99, 130
Colonel of 20th Maine, 98
fought at Chancellorsville and Fredericksburg, 98
fought in First Bull Run and Virginia Peninsula Campaign, 98
fought in Seven Days Campaign, 130
mentored Chamberlain, 130

Anaconda Plan, 6, 7

Anderson, Richard H. (Confederate), fought at Gettysburg, 75

Antietam Creek, Sharpsburg and Battle of, 6, 19, 22, 201

AP. *See* Associated Press

Apache, Native American tribe, 204

Appomattox Court House, surrender of Lee to Grant at, 107, 195, 199

Archer, James (Confederate), Brigadier General, 46

Aristotle, on leadership, 48

Arlington National Cemetery, 199

Armistead, Lewis Addison (Confederate)
Brigadier General, *143*
Cemetery Ridge and death of, 157, 159
expelled from West Point, 142
friend of future Union General Hancock, 142
Lieutenant in US-Mexican War, 142, 144
stationed in Los Angeles, 151
troop movement by, at Gettysburg, *145*

Army of Northern Virginia (Confederate)
burial of dead at Gettysburg not done by, 176–177
casualties after Gettysburg on July 4, xv
defensive line at Williamsport and Falling Waters, 165
leaves Richmond, 195
Lee as commander of, 198
Lee set new organizational structure for, 14
Meade's missed opportunity to destroy, 165
number of men and animals in, 13–14
percentage of professional soldiers in, xviii
reassembled at Hagerstown, 164
retreat stopped by impassable Potomac River, 164–165
saved from destruction at Antietam by Hill, 17
Stuart's reconnaissance around Union Army, 19
successful, cohesive organization of, 147
trapped in Vicksburg, 7

Index

Index

Hill fought in, 17
in Virginia, 98
Meade commanded brigade in, 21
Stuart fought in, 19
Pennsylvania
Cumberland Valley in, 26
Lee's plan to invade, 12
soldiers at Cemetery Ridge from, 150
Personal power, definition of, 91
Petersburg, siege of, 191
Peterson home, after assassination Lincoln
taken to, 197
Petraeus, David, 68–69
Pettigrew, J. Johnston (Confederate)
brigade commander, 146
commanded division at Gettysburg, 159
Confederate position on Seminary Ridge
and, 155
troop movement at Gettysburg by, *145*
Peyton, Charles (Confederate), Major in
Garnett's brigade, 155
Pickett, George Edward (Confederate)
at Seminary Ridge, 154–155
Division commander, 141, *141*
fought in US war with Mexico, 142
graduated last in West Point 1846 class,
141
his I Corps arrives for reinforcement on
second day, 115
his division at Cemetery Ridge, 136
his division on Emanuel Pitzer farm, 141
his division and position on Seminary
Ridge of, 144
his officers said, "Home, boys, home," 148
Lee consoled, 173
Lieutenant in US-Mexican War, 144
Major General, 135
military career, postwar life, and death
of, 213
relieved of command by Lee, 213
Pickett's Charge
Alonzo Cushing and, 201
at Gettysburg, *145*
casualties in fields of, 176
Pettigrew and Trimble divisions in, 159
Pipe Creek, Meade told Reynolds to defend,
24
Piston, William Garrett (biographer of
Longstreet), 75
Pitzer, Emanuel, Gettysburg farm
Hill's headquarters at, 162

Pickett's division on, 141
Plan of succession
corporate boards need to have, 71–72
military has established, 70–71
Planning, what it does for organization, 82
Plato, study of leadership did not begin with,
xiii
Pleasonton, Alfred (Union)
commander of Cavalry Corps, 29
General, 124
Major General, 18–19
surprise attack on Stuart at Brandy
Station, 124
Plum Run, *89, 97*
Pocock, George (University of Washington
rowing team), 80–81
Pol, leadership without ethics in, xiii, 32
Politics, three rules of, 182
Polybius, study of leadership and history
by, xiv
Porter, David Dixon (Union), meeting with
Grant and Sherman, and, 194
Positional power, definition of, 91
Potomac River, *164*
flooded crossing sites on, 164–165
retreating Confederate Army crossed, 168
Powell, Colin (former Secretary of State), 152
Powell, Lewis, conspirator with Booth, 196
Presidio, military hospital at, 203
Process metrics, definition of, 167–168
Pullen, John (Maine historian), 97

R

Rappahannock River, Confederate and Union
armies on opposite sides of, 8, 10, 18
Republican Party
did not want to nominate Lincoln for
second term, 183
promise to prohibit western expansion of
slavery, 4
Responsibility, 170–171
leader's personal, versus an organization's,
173
Revenge, Lincoln says victors of war not to
take , 194–195
Reynolds, John Fulton (Union)
acted on subordinate Buford's suggestion,
34, 36
arrived at Buford's position on
McPherson's Ridge, 45
birth and education of, 43

Index